I Love My Work...But, I Hate My Job

I Love My Work...But, I Hate My Job

✦

How to Survive Crisis & the Abuse of Power in the Workplace

Richard Werre

iUniverse, Inc.
New York Lincoln Shanghai

I Love My Work...But, I Hate My Job
How to Survive Crisis & the Abuse of Power in the Workplace

iUniverse, Inc.

For information address:
iUniverse, Inc.
2021 Pine Lake Road, Suite 100
Lincoln, NE 68512
www.iuniverse.com

Disclaimer

You will encounter many examples of oppression and incompetence in the workplace throughout the pages of this book. Some readers may believe they recognize themselves (or someone else) in various examples portrayed. Actually, they will only be identifying with those patterns common to oppressive behavior and incompetence. Care has been taken in every example to change all identifying details. Accounts of behavior and circumstances have been blended, and locales have been changed. It will be impossible for the reader to determine the identity of any specific individual, regardless of how familiar the circumstances may seem, or how much the behavior may resemble the behavior of anyone you may know or have ever known. Any similarities to such people either living or dead, is purely coincidental.

ISBN: 0-595-32914-4

Dedication

To every person who wishes to improve the quality of experiences in the workplace, thank you for taking time to read this book. It is my hope that in some manner you will gain strength and knowledge from the thoughts and ideas contained on these pages. If you have somehow endured injustice due to incompetence, or due to the abuse of power in the workplace, I hope you will receive information to assist you on your journey, and to allow you to help those you encounter along the way.

Contents

Acknowledgments

Very few of us achieve meaningful things on our own. In fact, it would not be possible to acknowledge everyone from whom I have received ideas for this book. However, I will thank some who have had a profound and lasting influence on my life, and on this work.

My wife, June, whose patience, strength, companionship, and love have sustained me in moments of achievement, and in times of defeat.

Kelly, Bobbie, Chris, and of course…Haley and Paige!

J. Nicolas Schutz who first introduced me the beauty of language and the power of words.

Olov Gardebring, my mentor, colleague, and friend.

All of whom, in the truest sense, have taught me how to…and how not to treat people.

Introduction

A Message for the Silent Majority

This is a book written for people. Hard-working, everyday people who are not so dramatically oppressed that they attract media attention. It does not reflect the behaviors of the notoriously corrupt, with offensiveness so great that the bounty hunters seek them out. No, this book has been written for folks like you and me. Those of us who continue to do what is right. It is a book written for those who work among their colleagues without complaint or demand for special consideration. It is a book designed to recognize and assist the common person whose experiences of oppression and injustice in the workplace go largely unnoticed. Or, when those experiences are acknowledged, the posture frequently presented by oppressive officials is, "What do they have to be upset about, they have jobs, don't they?"

Yet, the impact of oppression and corruption upon those who are unheard and unrecognized causes no less trauma than that experienced by the victims of the more brazenly callous and powerful. They fear no less to be imprisoned by an oppressive workplace culture. They hurt no less than those victims who reach the headlines of today's media. They are the silent majority. Their stories, their needs, and their sense of outrage are no less profound than those of whom we have heard so much. They are the everyday workers, colleagues, and employees, and it is time they are considered. It is to that end that this work is dedicated.

"I Love My Work...But, I Hate My Job" is based on the belief that, if we become more thoughtful, and if we use our intelligence and sound judgment, we will be better prepared to overcome the reality of today's work environments that are troubled. We will then become more effective in responding to workplace oppression and incompetence...even if the behavior of the corrupt among us changes little or not at all!

As we become more aware of the feelings and concerns of our fellow workers, it becomes increasingly clear that very few employees are truly happy and fulfilled

1

as they perform their assigned duties and responsibilities. So many of them just seem to cope with their work-related circumstances. The majority, settling for average, mundane positions of employment have resigned themselves to their limited employment options. Many of these workers present an outward display of productivity, while at the same time their work has come to lack meaning. These are the employees who don't often acknowledge their concerns and frustrations. Instead, they continue to perform their work in a responsible manner, even though they feel anger and resentment due to the oppression and incompetence of officials in the troubled workplace.

Resignation to oppression and incompetence without viable choice has become a way of life for far too many workers. When the rights of unhealthy (bad) and unproductive employees have greater validation then those who are healthy, it is a sign that we have entered the realm of a disintegrating workplace culture. When the rights of corrupt officials take president over the rights of their innocent victims, the scale of justice has lost its balance in the work environment.

Who is it that will speak for the loyal, hard-working employees who must endure the unfair practices of oppressive workplace officials and their equally insensitive work associates? Perhaps we must learn to do it ourselves through rising above circumstance, despite the obstacles that may block our paths. William James, philosopher and psychologist, once observed that the discovery of our age has been that we, by changing the inner aspects of our thinking, can change the outer aspects of our lives. This statement suggests that we can become effective in countering the patterns of oppression and incompetence that exist in the troubled work environments of today.

Trends in the Oppressive Workplace

Successful public and private sector organizations need dynamic and innovative employees who are encouraged to serve the needs of the community, and to meet the demands of a competitive market. However, in oppressive organizations the ideas of creative and innovative workers are almost always resented by officials who feel threatened by change or by the potentials of subordinates. All too often, oppressive officials do not support, nor do they encourage creative and innovative thinking. Employees who work in troubled organizations often feel discounted by the response of oppressive supervisors because their ideas are rejected and discarded.

In oppressive work environments, the callous and incompetent postures of workplace officials are frequently displayed despite the legitimate concerns of employees. The chief executive officer claims to have an open-door policy. But, the official then distorts that policy by undermining the legitimate efforts of sincere supervisors and employees. The official who requires teamwork from her staff does so only as a means of maintaining control and power. The leader of a department who demands cooperation insists upon doing things only his way.

Opportunities to form strong and healthy alliances are almost always restricted in a workplace that is troubled. This is particularly true when otherwise effective employees have been required to work in an environment that promotes resentment and discontent. Instead of enjoying the rewards of being colleagues, they devote themselves to opposing each other. Troubled workers then magnify their problems out of proportion. They become wrapped up in their difficulties and absorbed in how they feel about their colleagues and the troubling workplace circumstances that they must endure.

Employees should be treated with respect. Leaders should be dynamic and caring role models who set an example of professionalism and fairness. With thoughtful and fair-minded leadership, employees are then motivated to follow that positive example. The effective leader stimulates workplace performance through searching out and encouraging the creative and innovative ideas of employees. But, too often in today's oppressive work environments, those opportunities are missed.

Employees who have been targeted by callous officials almost always feel a nagging sense of isolation and despondency within the oppressive work environment. This is true, even with workers who have devoted their lives to their jobs, most often with a primary motivation not just to be good employees, but with the wish to make a meaningful contribution. These men and women deserve something better than what they will receive if positive change is not somehow forthcoming. The problem, of course, has its roots in the structure of the troubled workplace. All too often, the fact that has gone unnoticed or has been ignored is that basic survival has become the main foundation of employment. When we look at the deepest core of these circumstances, we become profoundly aware of how right Dr. Albert Schweitzer was when he said, "We are all so much together, and yet we are all slowly dying of loneliness."

Men and women in the workplace often have innovative ideas, and the skills and talent necessary to create a positive and productive work environment. They also wish to have an opportunity to work in an atmosphere of cooperation and fairness. But, in a work environment in which the striving is for power and control, there is little to inspire creative thought, camaraderie, or freedom of expression. As such, employees are placed, or they place themselves, in positions in which they believe there is no way out. Sadly, some employees just beginning their careers exist solely on the knowledge that they will someday have an opportunity for retirement. These conditions continue indefinitely because the central problems are never truly resolved due to the abuse of power. The oppression is experienced over and over again, and the problems remain unresolved.

If you find yourself in a job where you feel mistreated, and unable to face your work with enthusiasm and confidence, you may be a member of the silent majority. If you are frustrated by your workplace circumstances and unwilling to continue to accept the abuse of power, these pages offer alternatives. If you become open to new concepts and different beliefs, you will discover how to respond more effectively to the incompetence and oppression of the workplace.

How do I know these ideas are important to workers? Well, among other evidence that I will explore throughout this book, when I give talks on patterns in the workplace, the audience listens. However, they do not only listen. Most of them start to nod. No, it's not what you just thought. They are not nodding off to sleep. I assure you of that! They are nodding in agreement as they realize that so many of their experiences with ineffective and oppressive supervision are much like mine, and like those I have counseled over the years.

As you read the pages of this book you will realize that I have said very little about the truly creative and dynamic leaders in the workplace of today. The reason is simple. Creative and dynamic leaders speak for themselves. They speak through their positive behavior and performance. They speak through their sense of fairness, and through their willingness to do the right thing. And, most of all they speak through the fundamental decency that they display toward all that they encounter.

The initial pages of this book will focus primarily on negative aspects of the workplace. I am convinced that those postures and patterns must first be exposed, before we can truly understand the dilemma of the oppressive workplace of today, and before the power and potential of solutions suggested later can be fully appreciated. I do not expect anyone to accept at face value, the ideas and concepts that I present in this book. My only wish is that they will be thoughtfully considered. If they are then recognized to be of value, I encourage you to retain them, and to use them in any manner that you believe will assist you in bringing increased levels of quality to your life, and to your experiences in the workplace. With those thoughts in mind, I encourage you to remember the words of James Baldwin as you explore the ideas contained in this work...

"Not everything that is faced can be changed, but nothing can be changed until it is faced."

1

DYNAMICS OF TROUBLED ORGANIZATIONS

Patterns in the Troubled Workplace

When we look beneath the surface patterns of the troubled workplace, we discover the true feelings and postures of the silent majority. We see more clearly, the views and perspectives of employees who have been threatened and mistreated by those who abuse power through oppression and incompetence. These discoveries reveal the patterns of chronic dissatisfaction that actually exist. They explain why productive and loyal employees feel compelled to leave the jobs they might otherwise continue to appreciate and enjoy. Productive and loyal employees do not leave because of the type or amount of work they must complete. In fact, workload issues are rarely the cause for their departure. What is it then? It is not the work. It is the postures of ineffective and abusive administrators, managers, and supervisors that cause them to leave.

I want to emphasize, as I introduce you to the dynamics of troubled organizations and the oppressive postures of officials, I am not talking about the sincere, genuine and conscientious leaders in the workplace today. No, it is the officials who function out of greed and selfishness, lustful of power, and callously indifferent to those who must endure their abuse that I wish to expose. Whether they will admit to their ineptness and postures of oppression is doubtful. But, as they are exposed to the thoughts contained in this book, they will know who they are, and so will we.

The Most Frequent Reasons that Employees Leave the Troubled Workplace

- Employees lack job satisfaction. They don't feel valued by the officials of the organization, nor are the skills and talents of employees recognized or challenged. Supervisors promote stagnation and discourage new ideas or fresh viewpoints. When supervisors provide a response to the efforts of employees, their remarks are most often critical and negative.

- The facility tolerates, and frequently encourages contaminants among the staff who look good on the surface. But, those individuals are devious and undermining in the interest of achieving power and control over their colleagues. A distant and misinformed administration then impulsively over (or under) reacts to the troubling events of the organization.

- Workers are subjected to unrealistic deadlines and meaningless work. Supervisors create an atmosphere of conflicting job demands, and uncertainty about responsibilities, procedures, and expectations. They take their own interests and concerns too seriously, but then fail to consider the legitimate suggestions or concerns of subordinates.

- A common situation involves being caught between two (or more) officials with opposing demands. Employees then have more than one supervisor with each demanding that top priority be given to different work assignments or projects. Workers are then placed in positions in which they cannot succeed regardless of how hard they try. They can only please one official by upsetting or offending the other.

- Officials demand rigid conformity from employees. They repeatedly emphasize the belief that there is only one right way to do things, and that their way is that *"right way."* They promote the "status quo" because the effectiveness of subordinates often threatens them. Staff opinions are ignored and changes are implemented without explanation. The overall climate is one of smugness and self-righteous complacency.

- The organization sanctions mid-management staff and line supervisors who, during challenge or crisis, misrepresent the situation to administrative officials. Misleading beliefs and expectations created by oppressive and incompetent officials create an environment in which employees are unable to work together effectively.

- Management is made up of officials who use a process of scapegoating to misplace responsibility for errors, problems and inefficiency. They often identify a given employee to use as a target for their hostility…and to blame when things go wrong.

Dynamics of Dysfunctional Work Environments

Employees experience oppressive conditions and hear troubling rumors on a frequent basis in dysfunctional work environments. Those circumstances then cause patterns of chronic anxiety and frustration. Tension is often in the air. The organization is a difficult, humorless, and frustrating place to work. This creates a "snowballing" effect among employees to the point where they become "stressed out." They develop false impressions of their own capabilities, and of the motives of their associates. The work performance of oppressed employees is then diminished instead of being permitted to evolve in a thoughtful and potentially progressive manner.

It is relatively rare that employees who work in today's dysfunctional work environments are able to reach their true potential. Too often, these workers are forced to accept what oppressive and incompetent officials have told them without being provided an opportunity to prove anything for themselves. And, too often, these oppressed, but potentially creative workers find it necessary to follow the controlling postures and unrealistic rhetoric of self-proclaimed experts. They are required to endure these circumstances without having a chance to determine whether the postures and messages those "experts" present actually reflect the realities of what is important in the workplace of today.

Employees who work for oppressive workplace officials do not work for them because they appreciate the approaches and postures of their supervisors. No, they work because they have to work. And, it is not just taxes, the economy, or a wish for the finer things in life that bring this about. The majority of employees who stay under the tyranny of oppressive officials do so because they believe that they have no choice. And indeed, that may be true. After all, they have spouses, families and other loved ones to consider. They long for opportunities to grow in their careers and they wish to make a meaningful contribution. Most of all, they wish to maintain their dignity as persons. But, those goals become evermore difficult to reach when attempting to survive the storms created by oppression and incompetence.

Many struggles would be eliminated if oppressed employees would have an opportunity to assert their rights as individuals in the workplace. They would be stronger and more effective if they were not required to allow their potential and creativity to be marred by conformity. Oppressed employees would be more productive and dynamic if they were not required to comply with the oppressive and unrealistic standards of those who abuse power.

If productive change and the effective use of authority are to evolve in the troubled workplace, a "crisis for change" must occur. Crisis, although difficult to experience, can create an opportunity for positive development in our personal and professional lives. Could there be a better time to move in the direction of positive and meaningful change then now? The question remains, however, will a positive course be taken? All too often, sincere and dedicated employees spend valuable, irreplaceable years trying to survive dysfunctional work environments. Far too many employees have found it necessary to endure authority figures who have been weak and ineffective, or who have been rigid, overpowering, demanding, and unyielding. Neither of these positions provides what is needed from those in charge. What is needed is positive leadership based on fairness, stability, consistency, and opportunities for mutual respect among colleagues at all levels of the organization.

Rights in the Troubled Workplace

We hear a great deal about rights in our world…the right to liberty, the right to property, human rights, and the right to "due process" under the law. But, there is another level of rights, more fundamental, yet as significant as those we voice at a more global level. Those are the right to form our own opinions, the right to express those opinions whether wise or foolish, and to do what we believe to be right.

Along with these basic rights, we also have responsibility to respect the rights of colleagues and not to interfere with the choices they make, as long as they do not infringe on our rights or the rights of others. All too often in today's troubled workplace, oppressive officials forget these very concepts. They become zealots who see themselves as "champions" of the common good, but without true interest and concern for the needs of others. They seek quite deliberately to meet their own self-serving purposes through the acquisition and abuse of power. We see examples in all realms of the troubled work environment.

The hidden costs of a work environment that denies and violates the fundamental rights of conscientious employees may be greater than is generally suspected. There is of course, the impaired quality of conditions in the oppressive workplace itself. When unhappy workers attempt to be productive in this state of stressful and frustrating interaction, they also absorb messages that will negatively shape their future as employees. In such an environment, the potentially constructive spirit of the troubled facility and its employees may be diminished for succeeding generations. If the young people of today have a cynical view of employment, it is important to remember that too many of them have parents who have struggled with patterns of oppression and incompetence in the workplace. As such, employees may convey the message to those who are just beginning their careers that employment in today's workplace has much to be desired.

The Question of Employee Equity

From a philosophical and operational perspective, there is a concept that is almost always overlooked or disregarded by oppressive officials. That concept is employee equity. Most healthy employees spend more time and energy on the job than they do with their spouses, friends, and families. While at work, they invest their talents, their creative energy, and their emotional stamina in carrying out daily work assignments. These patterns evolve well beyond what the average, "salary-oriented" employee contributes. In fact, the qualities and commitments displayed are the very ingredients that distinguish the truly creative and dynamic leaders from those who cause discontent and turmoil in the work environment. They also separate those employees who are dedicated to quality and service, from those who simply do what they need to do to collect their paychecks, avoid additional responsibility, and stay out of trouble.

When creative and dynamic employees are mistreated, ignored, or threatened by oppressive supervisors, they are doubly jeopardized. They are not only placed at risk of losing an opportunity to make a living. They are also placed at risk of losing the equity of their investment. Perhaps, loss of equity is the most important and painful to experience. Employees who truly love their work and wish to make a meaningful contribution are also those who establish deep loyalties if given a fair chance and appropriate recognition for their efforts. When hopes, dreams, plans, and efforts are disregarded or distorted by callous and power-oriented officials, the creative and dynamic employee's sense of fairness and justice becomes a two-edged sword. What is for healthy and dedicated employees, their finest characteristic also causes them to feel hurt and betrayed when they are treated unfairly. In those circumstances, everyone is the loser.

Certainly from the standpoint of the employer, that is the case. The reason is simple. Should the oppressive official continue down the troublesome path, the creative and dynamic employee will eventually shutdown. Or, the employee will leave to seek employment elsewhere. While the changes and transitions involved will be temporarily painful for former employees, almost always, they will survive and do even better in a future environment. But, the oppressive regime, whether aware of it or not, will experience a far greater loss. As creative and dynamic employees leave an organization, they take with them their talents, experiences, and potentials. And, it is unlikely those qualities will be replaced by those chosen to fill the positions…or, if they are, at what price?

Now, I am well aware of the principles of employment that suggest that the employee who leaves the workplace has no real complaint. The posture presented is that the job applicant was hired to do a job. The employee was then paid an agreed upon salary. So, what's the problem? The employee really has no right to expect consideration beyond that point. Of course in one sense, that posture is valid…if the employer only wants workers who function at a mediocre level at best. But, when extraordinary effort with the goal of excellence is the standard, then the only fair exchange must involve much more. The exchange must not only involve an exchange of services for financial compensation, but, an *inherent right* of the employee to have choices, and to some degree, ownership in the productive and creative effort. This is particularly true when truly excellent employees must work among those who are doing just enough to get by.

Our Untapped Potential

Today's work environments have undergone dramatic change and wide-scale restructuring during the past decade. Along with movements toward downsizing of the American workforce, opportunities for meaningful employment have become limited for increasing numbers of employees. We also have more skills, talent, and technical resources than any previous generation of workers. Most of us have not begun to tap our own potential for effectiveness and productivity in the workplace. We are functioning way below capacity. And, we will continue as long as we are looking for someone else to understand and take care of us. How poorly (or how well) we handle our lives is determined by our attitude. And, our attitude will determine whether we will be part of the problem or part of the solution. It is somehow an eloquent, and yet sadly reassuring testament for those of us who are enduring the changing flavor of the work environment to realize that nobody gets through this life without some struggle and anxiety.

When I worked at the North Dakota State Penitentiary, I had the privilege to serve under the guidance of Warden Winston Satran, a truly effective and inspiring leader. After serving more than fourteen years at the facility, with several of those years as the chief executive officer, Winston announced his resignation to assume the helm of a facility that provides services for troubled youth. In saying goodbye to the Penitentiary staff, Winston talked about many positive accomplishments that had evolved under his leadership. The departing warden spoke eloquently of the difficult times as well. Among Winston's comments were examples of life threatening circumstances he encountered in attempting to deal with inmate residents who were under the influence of mood altering substances, psychotic, or just very dangerous. Winston said, "You know, there were many times that I just wanted to run away and let somebody else try to deal with the problem. But then, I always remembered…the broken nose I might get will heal, but the knowledge that I have behaved like a coward will never heal." I think all to often we forget that when we choose the easy course in life, and fail to follow the course of true integrity, decency, and courage.

Almost all workers, if sufficiently motivated, trained, and given the opportunity, have the capacity to exceed present performance. Unfortunately, employees in oppressive organizations are rarely permitted the opportunity to tap this capability. This occurs because the talents, knowledge, and skills of subordinates are not fully exercised by their incompetent and oppressive supervisors. As a result, these oppressed employees experience evolving patterns of stagnation and discontent. The employee who is capable of performing loyally and well is entitled to more. Supervisors, managers, and administrators who do not accept this obligation fail in their responsibility to the organization and to the employees whose career fate they hold in their hands. And, they limit their own growth as well. It takes exceptional leaders to create opportunities for growth and achievement.

2

THE "STEWARDS" OF THE WORKPLACE

Profiles of Oppression & Incompetence in the Workplace

The German philosopher, Goethe, once observed, *"There is no more horrible sight than ignorance in action."* I can think of no better summation for the behavior of an oppressive or incompetent workplace official. These supervisors, managers, and administrators tear at the very fiber of the workforce, and at the individual employees who must endure their abuse and ineffectiveness. Optimism cannot exist without the dimension of justice. Yet, employees who work in oppressive work environments frequently experience injustice. If oppressive supervisors remain in control, their oppressive postures and the circumstances they create remain unchallenged. If incompetence and oppression are allowed to continue, optimism is gradually destroyed and replaced by fear, resentment, and uncertainty.

When supervisory oppression and incompetence exist in the workplace, there is almost always a discrepancy between the chief executive officer's description of how the organization is functioning, and the perceptions of the employees who must endure the daily excesses and abuse of power. Oppressive and incompetent supervisors often fail to present an accurate picture of the workplace circumstance to administrative levels. In these circumstances, the attempts of sincere employees to counter the abusive and troublesome patterns are curtailed. As a result, the abuse and incompetence may then continue year after year, as these unscrupulous officials continue to run roughshod over the needs and feelings of their workers.

As employees work under oppressive circumstances, they become torn between the need to be accepted by the offending official, while at the same time, they are compelled to protect their own integrity through postures of resistance and the wish to retaliate. This dilemma is related to a primitive characteristic that, throughout history has been fundamental to human nature. That characteristic is known as the *"fight"* or *"flight"* response. Whenever an individual's life or sense of well being is threatened, the human response is to either fight the person who has caused the abuse, or to flee from the pain caused by such action. The victim who has been repeatedly traumatized by such behavior becomes entwined, causing the individual to emotionally move back and forth between the two poles.

Oppressive and incompetent supervisors are almost always intensely preoccupied with the wish to gain status, recognition, and control. But, they may already have reached the limits of their skills and potential. And, they compensate for this dilemma by controlling and criticizing those that they see to be effective around them. When they are then challenged by upper management due to their ineffectiveness, these supervisors most often blame the effective employees for their own failures and excessive patterns. When employees accept the blame, they accept the oppressive and incompetent postures as well, because the acceptance of blame removes responsibility from where it rightfully belongs.

Responsibility also rests with administrators who have been too distant to be aware of what has been occurring, or too much in reliance on those they have chosen to manage on the front lines. Classic examples are ineffective administrators and managers who report themselves to be proud of their "hands-off" management styles. These officials have clearly misinterpreted the message of Theodore Roosevelt who suggested that being a good leader really isn't that difficult. He suggested, all you really need to do is pick good people for the task, tell them where you want them to go with it, and then have the "good sense" to stay out of their way while they go there. Of course, in the context of what I have been saying, what is most often overlooked is the selection of truly "good" men and women to assume the role of leadership in the first place. Then of course, sufficient monitoring must be provided to assure that the "end justifies the means" used by those who have been designated to carry out the mission.

The "Snitch Society"

With the power of their offices, oppressive and incompetent administrators have incredible latitude to destroy the morale of valuable employees. This emerges in particular, when these troublesome and controlling officials create a "Snitch Society." As "snitches" are established, oppressive and incompetent officials encourage the flow of information. The information provided is typically distorted, vindictive, or limited at best.

A few months ago, a new state official was hired to assume an administrative position as the leader of a branch of a parent agency in Nebraska. After an initial period with the new official at the helm, the newcomer became painfully aware of the oppressive and incompetent postures of the established chief executive officer. As such, she began to explore alternatives for resolving a variety of blunders and oppressive practices that had been established before her arrival. Upon seeing the obvious and superior skills of the newly established junior official, the CEO became extremely threatened. He then, began a desperate quest to get rid of the more talented administrator.

During the first phase of the CEO's plan, he gave the new official extensive latitude to use her own discretion in handling administrative problems brought about by the CEO's oppression and incompetence. Then, as the new official began to implement her plan of action, the CEO also began to solicit feedback on the new official's activities. Since the positive changes required more productive activity on the part of many of the CEO's snitches, they were quite willing to "offer the goods" the CEO needed. Once complaints began to flow, substantiated or not, (and, none of them were), the CEO made it known that he had an "open-door" policy for anyone who wished to talk with him. And, of course, the disgruntled employees had a field day. Then, with a sufficient amount of distorted information gathered, the inquisition began, and the productive and conscientious official found it necessary to abandon her position.

How the Process Evolves

Candidates for the snitch society are typically selected, or they emerge from the ranks of the most ineffective or unethical employees in the organization. These individuals are often selected based on the official's undisclosed view that they are gullible fools. Certainly they are seen as gullible enough to align themselves with the treachery of the official. Once the system for "snitchery" is in place, an employee or lower level supervisor will soon be targeted for extinction. Most often, this is an effective employee who is believed to be a threat to an oppressive official in power. Another possibility is that the targeted worker may be secretly admired, but resented by members of the snitch society. The resentment is most often due to the positive characteristics the targeted individual displays in carrying out daily assignments in the workplace.

With the individual identified for extinction, the oppressive official forms a rigid and negative opinion about the merits of the capable and effective line supervisor or employee who has been targeted. The targeted individual is then confronted without warning about any distorted allegations that surface through input from the snitch society in place. When the accused worker attempts to provide accurate information related to the false allegations, the unscrupulous and controlling administrator emphatically denies, rationalizes, distorts, and otherwise justifies the notions and decisions established through corrupt maneuvering and motivations. Then, no matter what the targeted supervisor or effective employee does to provide a factual or positive response, the corrupt official, and members of the snitch society, undermine all attempts to bring forth the truth about what has been occurring.

As the "snitch saga" continues, the oppressive official occasionally tells the targeted worker that he or she will be supported, "all-the-way." Then, that posture is abruptly changed. When the targeted individual's guard is down, the worker is abruptly accused about some trivial matter, and without the slightest foundation. The effective supervisor or employee is then left hanging with the issue without guidance, follow-up, or any other consideration. Later, the effective worker is again called to the corrupt official's office. Without warning or an opportunity to offer a factual response, the effective employee is told that complaints have been received from other staff implying that he or she is too rigid, controlling or otherwise disruptive to colleagues.

As a target of the snitch society, the effective supervisor or employee is rarely permitted to know the source of the accusations. The oppressive official will simply say that the snitches are too afraid of the effective worker's response. Therefore, they have asked that their names be kept confidential due to fear of retaliation. This posture on the part of oppressive officials and their snitches is never based on valid or genuine concern. It is simply another means of intimidation and control that denies targeted workers the right to face their accusers, and to move in the direction of fairness and justice. On those rare occasions when the accusers and the accused are brought together, the entire event is orchestrated. The targeted individual is collectively attacked without true opportunity to present the truth or the facts that might bring about a positive and just resolution to the matter for everyone who is involved.

In response to snitch society complaints, a promising young supervisor was called to an oppressive official's office and asked, "Why don't you provide your staff with more coffee breaks? You're just too rigid. Let your staff have some fun." When the conscientious supervisor attempted to explain that members of her staff were already taking coffee breaks according to policy, the oppressive official responded with anger saying, "I really don't care. Just keep them happy. We can't afford to lose the valuable people you have in your department."

Two months before the challenge for not allowing more coffee breaks, the same official had abruptly displayed anger and frustration with the supervisor, expressing his view that her staff really shouldn't be allowed to have coffee breaks at all. During the previous encounter that had also been orchestrated by his snitches, the oppressive official demanded that the coffee breaks be significantly curtailed. The official remained adamant in his posture, despite the effective supervisor's attempt to explain that the coffee breaks, taken properly, were a morale booster that promoted a more efficient flow of work. However, the supervisor's attempt to stand up for her staff during that encounter was unsuccessful. The official in fact, demanded that the breaks be drastically restricted to the point where most of the employees found it to be unrealistic to try to take them.

The circumstances created by the oppressive official and his snitches were required to continue until complaints were presented by the now, disgruntled employees. In responding to those complaints, the oppressive official expressed agreement with the staff, saying that their supervisor was wrong in not allowing them to have the longer breaks. The oppressive official's actions not only undermined the young supervisor's authority and credibility with her staff, they also provided an opportunity for one highly manipulative member of the snitch society to begin a campaign of "divide and conquer." These tactics were continued until irreparable damage had occurred to the effective supervisor's relationship with her staff.

How the Final Blow is Administered

In the most oppressive circumstances of the snitch society, the oppressive administrator deliberately overwhelms the targeted supervisor or employee with a barrage of stressful events. When it is believed that the process has been successfully implemented, just to be sure, the oppressive official calls the targeted individual into the office. Then, the official quite unexpectedly compliments the individual on a minor accomplishment. If the victim becomes overwhelmed with emotion and begins to sob uncontrollably...the oppressive mission has been accomplished! Another member of the snitch society has been initiated into the clan! If no such emotion surfaces, the persecution continues until the targeted individual either submits or leaves.

From the point of submission on, if the targeted supervisor or worker does not leave the organization within a year, the oppressive official can relax. The targeted individual will be a mediocre employee for life. The victimized employee will never be a threat to the oppressive official's abuse of power again. A minor annoyance perhaps, but not a threat. The oppressive official will always have an unhappy and subdued employee around to criticize if one is needed...and the employee will put up with it! In fact, the now subdued individual might even contribute to the disruptive and unethical standards created by the oppressive official, by joining the snitch society as other worthwhile employees are targeted for extinction.

Who's Next?

In particularly dysfunctional organizations, oppressive officials frequently create a climate in which there is a need to always have someone to target as a scapegoat, and to constantly badger and harass. For example, Irene, a sincere and conscientious clerical worker accepted a position to work in a public sector agency under the general supervision of Alexis, an extremely deceitful and manipulative office manager. The manager initially presented a cordial and supportive posture toward Irene as she developed in her role, and as she carried-out her assigned duties and responsibilities in an effective manner.

At the same time, the manager focused her hostility and contempt on the activities of Marnie. Marnie, who was also an effective and conscientious employee, was constantly badgered and harassed by Alexis. This occurred despite the fact that the quality and quantity of Marnie's work was far superior to the work of all of the manager's cronies. The cronies in fact, frequently spent several hours a week socializing and visiting with each other about their personal lives and activities, and about the latest office gossip. That gossip frequently focused on Marnie in a rather spiteful and malicious manner. Not once were any of them challenged by Alexis about their unprofessional behavior.

On the other hand, Alexis constantly monitored Marnie's activities. She actively offered criticism during those rare occasions when Marnie received a brief personal telephone call. Alexis even complained if Marnie occasionally spent as little as three minutes longer on break than was authorized by agency policy. During those confrontations, the manager would severely chastise Marnie until she was reduced to tears.

Alexis often carried-out her reprimands in the presence of Marnie's co-workers. The co-workers then found great pleasure in discussing the episodes at length. The manager also regularly talked about Marnie with her co-workers, expressing negative comments about the quality of her work and making derogatory remarks about Marnie and her efforts. Alexis even encouraged the co-workers to prevent Marnie from receiving work-related information. She also encouraged Marnie's co-workers to avoid her during work-related functions, and to exclude her from social activities.

Eventually, Marnie became so depressed and frustrated that she found it necessary to offer her resignation. Within two months of Marnie's departure, Irene became the focus of the manager's wrath, and the whole cycle was repeated until Irene too, found it necessary to abandon her position. But, the story doesn't end there. Within a month after Irene's departure, a new target had been identified in the form of Helen, who is now the focus of the manager's hostility, and a target for her unprofessional behavior and postures.

"It's All a Priority"

A variation on the "Who's Next" approach involves the insensitive and unrealistic response that oppressive and inept supervisors offer to concerns expressed by hard-working employees when their workload requirements have become overwhelming. The typical scene involves a conscientious employee who has come to the official to receive guidance on what priorities to establish to meet the unrealistic deadlines that have been assigned to the extreme amount of work to be completed. When the question is presented by the employee, the insensitive official abruptly responds with, "Well, it all a priority, and you are just going to have to get it all done."

Adding "insult to injury," once the unscrupulous official is aware of the dilemma being experienced by the overwhelmed employee, the official will then follow-up on the discussion by forwarding a series of memos or e-mail messages inquiring about the status of the projects. This is done even though the official is fully aware that the deadlines are unrealistic. The official is aware that, no matter how hard the employee may try to meet the unrealistic demands, the work simply cannot be completed within the time allotted. The insensitive official is also aware that if he or she wished to do so, alternatives and appropriate levels of priority could easily have been assigned as initially requested by the conscientious employee. This pattern is continued until sincere employees are eventually forced to turn in their resignations in defeat.

Postures of Oppression & Incompetence

In dysfunctional organizations, oppressive and incompetent supervisors are promoted to their positions by equally oppressive and incompetent senior officials. They are selected because they have been identified as "good workers." The truth is that the newly established supervisor has simply been clever enough to align with the oppressive policies and postures of the senior officials. These individuals leave little or no room for their subordinates to contribute to the decision-making process. In the extreme, these managers and supervisors expect subordinates to follow orders without ever challenging them or questioning their unrealistic demands. And, of course, the cardinal rule of oppressive supervision and management is always applied. That rule is…"Never, under any conditions, consider the possibility that you might be wrong."

"Let's You & Them Fight"

This is supervision or management by "divide and conquer" in that the corrupt official or supervisor plays one staff member against the other to see what will happen. Rivalries are created under the guise of testing to see who is most effective or deserving of recognition.

Jack T. Ripper, a corporate official in New York, just delights in playing his employees against each other. Jack will typically target two or three of his most promising employees. He then, offers them all the same opportunities for responsibility and achievement. But, he does it individually without letting the staff members know that they have all been offered the very same position, project or opportunity within the structure of the organization. Once private commitments are individually made, Jack T. cautions each person with, "Let's keep this on the 'Q.T.' for now. I haven't briefed the CEO on this yet, so we don't want to let it leak out prematurely, do we?"

Despite that word of caution, Jack encourages the employees to proceed with the assignment in a "discreet" manner, implying that each employee will have both the authority to act, and his full support as they take the action they believe to be required to accomplish the task at hand. Then, Jack just sits back and watches the action. From that point on, Jack actively avoids meeting with the targeted employees collectively. He is never honest with them about the game he is playing. If they come to him (individually, of course) with a complaint or request for support when opposing posture's surface, Jack quite actively offers verbal support and encouragement. Jack tells the employee, "You know, I told you were in charge, and I am behind you all the way on this." He then sends them on their way with the encouragement, "Now, go forth and slay dragons!"

Bear in mind now, old Jack T. plays his game quite deliberately, under the guise of "survival of the fittest," and "let the better (most sadistic like himself) person win!" Jack's philosophy, in fact, is quite simple. That philosophy, "If you are clever enough, and if you have enough demoralized employees on your staff, you will have an excuse for any and all of the failures you have caused...and a readily available scapegoat at any given time." If his employees momentarily succeed, Jack can brag about how good he is and take the credit for it. Of course, those opportunities will be rare unless he fabricates them, which he does without hesitation. Most often, the work his employees perform will be mediocre at best. But rest assured, Jack T. will be fine.

When things go wrong, and when Jack is then challenged due to his deceptive approaches, he simply points out what he claims to be the shortcomings of his demoralized staff. He then blames them for the problems he created through his own oppressive and incompetent postures. With each opportunity, Jack makes the statement "Just look at how well I've handled this, even with the incompetent staff I am forced to put up with." Then, Jack adds, with just the right touch of melancholy "And, after all I have done to keep them on the right track!" That just might set the stage for another unearned raise for old Jack T.

Now, how does Jack T. get away with such blatant abuse of power and callous disregard for the needs and feelings of the employees who look to him for leadership and guidance? The answer to that question is also quite simple. Because Jack T. is such an imposing individual, it is extremely difficult for anyone, including upper management, to successfully challenge him. During those rare occasions when he is questioned more persistently about his deceptive and unprincipled tactics, Jack assumes an extreme posture of defensiveness, actively denying any level of wrongdoing. He then claims that there has apparently been some sort of misunderstanding on the part of those who have been deceived and victimized. Should those manipulations fail, Jack T. then adopts the posture of an extremely aggressive defense attorney. Upon assuming that role, Jack actively, and in rapid-fire fashion, engages in an intense "cross examination" of anyone who dares to challenge him. Jack's approach is so intense and so overwhelming that the challenger, and the upper level managers become threatened to the point where they feel compelled to back down.

"My Door is Always Open"

Some oppressive administrators and managers wear their "open-door" policies like a "badge of righteousness," claiming that it is a reflection of their deep concern for the employees who work under their command. In reality however, when oppressive and incompetent officials make this claim, it is actually an indication of their excessive need to control and to contain the activities of the workplace. The result is that the open-door approach being used undermines the authority of line supervisors, thereby creating feelings of resentment and frustration. The approach sends messages to troublesome employees indicating that anytime they feel dissatisfied with the decisions of their immediate supervisors, they can simply appeal to management and get off the hook.

Because of these dynamics, it is vital that respect for chain of command structure is exercised at all levels of workplace responsibility and authority. Respect, both up and down the chain of command is the foundation of the workplace. From respect for chain of command comes the possibility of clear lines of accountability, postures of responsibility and authority, and patterns of effective communication. Therefore, never violate the chain of command of your organization, no matter what position you hold...or how much power you have! When chain of command is violated, effective leadership is lost. Employees then display limited initiative, become tentative in decision-making, and potential and productivity are diminished.

Some months ago, Shane was hired to serve as a line supervisor under the guidance of Marie, a well-established and effective manager. The two officials were assigned to supervise and manage workers providing direct services for the mentally disadvantaged at a facility in Tennessee. Being a highly aggressive and manipulative individual, Shane quickly sized-up the operational patterns of the facility. Discovering that his female counterpart had a position that permitted her to work the day shift, Shane very actively engaged in a campaign to discredit the established manager. His primary goal was to gain access to Marie's more desirable shift.

Upon learning that the facility's administrator was a somewhat gullible individual, and one who took pride in his "open-door policy," Shane quickly took advantage of the situation. With a series of highly deceptive and manipulative maneuvers, Shane made repeated visits to the administrator's office with a progress report on his "accomplishments." With gradually increasing intensity, Shane also made a series of distorted accusations about Marie. He falsely claimed that Marie was unwilling to consider his ideas for operational processes that appeared to be of a cost-saving nature, and of potential benefit to the clients of the facility. What Shane did not report, however, was that Marie had already implemented more effective approaches than the new employee was proposing. Shane also failed to inform the administrator that Marie had already provided him with a clear explanation of why his proposals were unsound. During those discussions, Marie had provided factual evidence that Shane's proposals would be potentially more costly and less effective than the procedures already in place.

Unfortunately, Shane was quite convincing in his presentations to the somewhat detached, yet controlling administrator. As such, the administrator accepted Shane's position and complaints at face value, assuring the deceptive junior official that the matter would be "taken-care-of." The administrator then actively chastised Marie for what he described as her "pettiness and jealousy" toward Shane's "new and innovative ideas." He also accused her of not being willing to work with Shane as a "team player." The fact is that none of the information presented by Shane was accurate or valid. Yet, due to his acceptance of Shane's deceptive and manipulative reports during "open-door" visits, the administrator refused to consider Marie's posture. As a result of the administrator's impulsiveness and failure to investigate the circumstances more fully, Marie's creditability was significantly damaged for several months until the truth of Shane's dishonesty was finally revealed.

"Knee-Jerk Supervision"

Stan is the director of an occupational health unit in a major urban hospital in Texas. Although competition is extremely vigorous in the occupational health field, Stan has never really developed a marketing plan to assure a continuing flow of business. Instead, he relies on a "word-of-mouth" approach to attaining new accounts. Now, in the early evolution of Stan's program, the approach was quite successful. However, with expanding competition, the flow of opportunity has dramatically dwindled. But, Stan's approach has not changed. As such, Stan discovers on frequent occasion that his competition has "beaten him to the draw."

Each time Stan misses an opportunity, he panics. In that state, he assembles his staff to convey the bad news. Stan then offers expressions of doom and gloom by stating, "If we don't get with it, I may have to let some staff members go." What is so troubling about Stan's approach is that it is simply not necessary. Clearly, Stan has resources available to establish ongoing progress for his department. If he established a more active and thoughtful approach to marketing his program, Stan could also create opportunities for upward mobility for his staff. Yet, Stan overlooks those opportunities, time and again. When his feelings of panic subside, Stan promotes business as usual. Of course, everyone on the staff knows, the next episode of panic and crisis is just around the corner.

In essence then, knee-jerk supervision involves a pattern of overreaction when things go wrong...followed by lack of attention as future crises evolve. This leads to an ongoing crisis in the workplace, and continuing feelings of frustration and anxiety among staff.

"Supervision by Memo"

Supervision by memo involves the use of written directives to control or manipulate staff members without making personal contact. For example, Wayne, the administrator of a public sector facility in Minnesota decided to do a blanket restructuring of staff schedules. Being aware that his decision would receive major opposition from staff throughout the facility, Wayne decided to announce his decision with a memo. The memo established the new shift-scheduling pattern without explaining why the change was even being considered or believed to be necessary. Once written and signed, the official cautioned his secretary to not discuss the contents of the memo with anyone. He then directed her to hold the memo until Friday afternoon at 4:15 p.m. with instructions to do a general distribution to all employees at that time. Wayne then left for a two-week vacation at 4:00 p.m. that day. The official's hope was that by the time of his return, the controversy would have settled down among most employees, leaving only minor scrimmages with the most vocal employees to contend with.

However, the scheme didn't quite work out that way. Upon reading the memo, the entire staff became agitated. A committee was formed to present the matter to the facility's board of directors. Two key officials turned in their resignations in protest. Several employees submitted highly critical, yet perceptive memos, explaining how the new scheduling was causing major and unnecessary hardship for employees and their families. Another group of employees submitted letters offering alternative proposals, which having more merit than the plan established by the official, could have prevented the flurry of resentment and disruption that had spread throughout the facility.

This is a classic example of the abuse of power and how **not to** manage or treat people. It is also a lesson on the importance of providing a "forum for communication" that provides an opportunity for staff input into the functioning and operations of the workplace.

Supervision Through "Rose-Colored Glasses"

In this approach, supervisors interpret everything in the best possible light, despite the legitimate concerns expressed by staff to the contrary. The position causes resentment and frustration among employees who are aware of what is really going on. These officials focus only on the positive elements of the organization's activities. They assume the posture, "No news is good news, and all news received to date has been good." There is then lack of viable focus, and the troubled and troubling circumstances of workers are ignored with feelings of insecurity and discontent left to escalate to their destructive conclusions.

Officials who supervise through "rose-colored glasses" also send the message, "Don't create ripples." They do that by avoiding conflict or confrontation with strong, but troublesome and inappropriate subordinates. They also take that posture to avoid the attention and challenges of higher-level officials when problems surface. These incompetent supervisors look the other way to the power plays of subordinates and the problems that those individuals create. As a result, chaos and oppression reign supreme, with the more power-oriented being free to run "roughshod" over the feelings and postures of associates. Misleading messages are then sent to ineffective employees suggesting that they are doing well. Since the situation does not improve, effective employees leave and poor employees stay. When new positions are filled, the replacements are unlikely to be as effective.

Sheldon is the branch manager for a firm that processes insurance claims in a community in an urban area of Montana. In recent months, major disruption among staff has occurred due to significant job inequities. Within the operational structure created by Sheldon, one group of employees is required to carry significantly overburdened workloads. The group must also meet rigid processing deadlines. An adjacent group's workload requirements are characterized by abundant amounts of free time. The adjacent group in fact, makes it common practice to routinely arrive for work several minutes after the designated starting time. They then gather in the facility's cafeteria for a leisurely breakfast involving forty-five minutes to an hour and one-half of small talk and socialization during company time. Near the end of their "work" day, members of this group are often seen leaving the facility one-half hour to forty-five minutes earlier than official policy mandates.

Despite the expressions of concern presented by the overworked employees related to their circumstances, Sheldon provides no meaningful response. He also proceeds without apparent concern about a recent central office memorandum announcing the possibility of layoffs if production and efficiency do not improve. Sheldon simply "stays the course" with apparent detachment and reverie. To central office administrative officials, Sheldon reports work activities as proceeding at full capacity with "no apparent problems noted."

To overworked employees requesting relief, Sheldon responds with false claims that although "everyone is somewhat challenged right now, the situation is only temporary, and workloads will soon be lighter for everyone." And all the while, Sheldon actively offers praise to members of the "breakfast club" for their "extraordinarily positive attitude" in light of workload demands. In fact, it is not at all unusual for Sheldon to be seen joining the group for their leisurely morning interlude that continues without challenge.

"Direction on High"

In this model, oppressive and incompetent supervisors hide behind the power structure of administrative officials. The message conveyed with each controversial or difficult issue, "I can't help it, this is what the CEO wants." Almost always, the chief executive officer is not even aware of the issues that are brewing. This in turn, creates a sense of frustration and resentment among staff, who adapt through postures of inefficiency. Or, they go underground and end their employment at the earliest opportunity.

Lucinda and Wade, two mid-level managers were assigned by the chief executive officer of a manufacturing firm to revise the company's policy and procedures manual. The two officials, being highly controlling and power-oriented, systematically revamped the manual from cover to cover based on their own personal perceptions and preferences. Lucinda and Wade proceeded without consultation with colleagues, and without consideration for the impact that many of their personal preferences would have on the morale and effectiveness of those assigned to carryout the operational processes of the company.

When drafts of the new policy and procedures manual were issued to the staff for review, the two officials were confronted with a blizzard of challenges and complaints. In response to the legitimate concerns presented by employees at all levels of the facility, Lucinda and Wade repeatedly offered the claim that the manual was only a reflection of the CEO's mandates and requirements. When the chief executive officer learned of the discontent surrounding the manual's revision, the two officials responded with the claim that the manual reflected the "solid thinking of the majority of staff," and that, "it is simply impossible to produce a document of this type without offending someone."

"Who's in Charge Here?"

Some highly controlling and incompetent workplace officials approach their roles from a position of lust for power and control. At the same time, these officials crave the recognition and praise that they receive from the most troublesome or outspoken employees of the facility. They actively support the employees who complain most often about work requirements, or about the activities of the conscientious workers who are trying to do the right thing. These oppressive officials frequently place themselves in positions in which they control every aspect of the decision-making process. Yet, they actively cater to the whims and expectations of the otherwise troublesome employees who respond to the official's power-oriented and controlling demands. As a result, who is actually in charge comes into serious question in the daily operation and functioning of the organization.

Trevor, a highly controlling and yet, inadequate mid-level manager of a production facility rules his employees with an "iron hand." Trevor insists that every significant decision or change in procedure be presented for his review and approval prior to implementation. Should he anticipate that a suggestion for improvement will not be acceptable to the more vocal and troublesome employees of the facility, Trevor abruptly rejects the proposal. Regardless of merit or potential, the official adamantly refuses to permit the process to evolve. When conscientious staff members present their legitimate concerns related to the behavior and attitude of members of the work force that go along with Trevor's demands, he supports the ineffective and troublesome individuals to the extreme.

When challenged about his patterns of favoritism and unrealistic support of troublesome workers, Trevor actively defends his postures. His typical response, "We really don't want to upset the production department because, after all, they are the 'bread and butter' of the company. Without them we would all really be in trouble around here." As a result, the problems of the company, of which there are many, remain essentially unresolved. The bright and perceptive employees of the facility who try to do the right thing clearly recognize that Trevor, although officially granted authority within the company, is not really in charge.

"Supervision by Duress"

Some oppressive and incompetent supervisors address any significant challenge to their authority or decisions with the response, "Well, if you don't like it, you don't have to work here." The message conveyed is that employees have no real value to the supervisor or to the organization. Employees who must endure this type of supervisory posture suffer from feelings of low self-esteem and collective loss of morale.

Roland, a shift supervisor for a parts manufacturing firm in Detroit is a highly power-oriented and controlling individual. He routinely approaches his employees with the attitude and posture, "It's my way or the highway." Whenever his employees come to him with work-related concerns, legitimate or not, Roland quite aggressively responds with "Well, if you don't like it, you don't have to work here. We were looking for an employee when we hired you, and there are plenty more where you came from. You know, employees like you are a 'dime-a-dozen'." Occasionally Roland even responds by singing the song, *"Got along without you before I met you…Gonna get along without you now!"*

"Supervision by Plagiarism"

In this approach, supervisors steal the ideas of staff, and then take credit for them. This type of supervisor is a "glory monger" who feeds his or her hunger through the theft of the talents and abilities of those who hold subordinate positions. What these oppressive and incompetent officials have never learned is that when the crew looks good, everybody including the leader, looks good. The supervisor oriented to plagiarism does so at every opportunity, thereby creating strong feelings of resentment among those who have been cheated out of their rightful recognition.

Most of these officials also pursue their lust for recognition and power by placing themselves in positions that expose them to first-hand information within the organization. They then accept responsibility to send that information down the chain of command in a timely manner. However, as the information is conveyed, only superficial segments are provided to subordinates. Information conveyed is enough for employees to carry out their assignments in a manner sufficient to make the supervisor "look good." That way, the "me big...you small" type of individual is assured a position of power and recognition in the eyes of the administration. But, the employees doing the work are left feeling frustrated and resentful.

Ed is a mid-level manager who works for a technology company in Maine. He frequently stops by to visit with employees and supervisors throughout the facility. Ed starts most of his conversations by saying, "I just wanted to 'touch base' to see how things are going." He then rather subtly shifts the conversation to ask his victims about the latest projects that they are working on. Ed is particularly inquisitive about, "What's on the horizon." As soon as he has enough information to deceptively reveal a new design or approach, Ed bids his farewell to the victimized colleague. He then aggressively documents the ideas shared by the targeted individual, frequently backdating the material. Ed then submits the information to the CEO as his own.

While the conscientious employee that Ed has just victimized is engrossed in making sure that all factors are considered and properly tested prior to publication, Ed without hesitation, and in a highly unscrupulous way, has assumed the glory for himself. When occasionally challenged by victimized colleagues, Ed presents himself as the epitome of self-righteous innocence. At the same time, he actively presents the falsely documented (backdated) evidence in support of his posture.

"Blue-Collar Capers"

Surviving oppression and incompetence in some oppressive blue-collar environments can be particularly difficult to endure. This is largely due to the insensitivity and crudeness of line supervisors who are not properly monitored or held accountable due to the detached postures of the higher-levels of management. These circumstances permit sadistic and incompetent supervisors to feel free to ridicule their employees, and to present their "macho" images to their equally sadistic and incompetent peers. Although a multitude of examples could be provided, I will offer only three.

- The insensitive supervisor who worked in a county maintenance shop on the east cost. The supervisor often found it to be humorous to light the spray from a pressurized can of ether and then chase employees around the shop as though he was attempting to set them on fire. He found it humorous that is…until the day that a can exploded. The former supervisor is now spending time in rehabilitation learning to use his new artificial limb.

- The sadistic supervisor who worked the night shift in a manufacturing plant in the Midwest. He thought it would be funny to fashion a hanging noose and suspend it from a pipe near the ceiling while he was alone in the shop. In making the noose the supervisor made sure that it would not tighten and cause death. He then waited until he knew that a particularly vulnerable employee would arrive. Upon hearing the employee approach the building, the supervisor placed the noose around his neck and then pretended to be dead as the employee entered the shop. When the employee came upon the scene, he experienced extreme levels of anxiety and panic. Although prior to the incident, the employee had thoroughly enjoyed his work, the trauma experienced as a result of the sadistic supervisor's actions was so intense that he was no longer able to maintain his employment.

- The shift supervisor who worked at an energy generating facility in the southwest. This character thought of himself as being extremely macho and a true "ladies man." As female employees were changing into their street clothes in the women's locker room, our "hero" found great pleasure in jumping out from a darkened corner of the room totally nude. In talking with his buddies later, the supervisor acknowledged that he did it just to see their reactions as the women ran from the room. The women, however, reported only feelings of anger and disgust.

Cover Your Anatomy Gimmicks

When oppressive and incompetent private sector officials begin to recognize that they have been exposed due to their inappropriate methods and postures, they become actively defensive, threatened, and increasingly deceptive. If they believe that they may soon be challenged by administrative officials, or by their board of directors, fascinating patterns of manipulative maneuvering begin to emerge. These patterns also emerge in dysfunctional public sector agencies as officials become aware that they are in trouble due to their oppressive or incompetent methods. The patterns occur in particular, when public sector officials fear that they are about to be held accountable to a governor, the President, representatives of a state legislative assembly, or the Congress.

Using state government as an example, a state employee may become disillusioned and frustrated with the troublesome postures of the state officials who have been designated to properly manage the operation of a state agency or department. In desperation, the employee contacts the governor, or a member of the legislative assembly to present the concerns. The governor or legislator in turn, contacts the executive director of the troubled agency or department to ask, "What's going on here?" The executive director then agrees to investigate the matter. This is actually a ploy to permit the executive director to stall for time. The ploy will permit the detached official to discuss what has been happening with the oppressive or incompetent junior official involved. It also permits the inept executive director to stall long enough to formulate a response to the governor or legislative representative.

After closing out the conversation with the governor or legislative representative, the executive director then contacts the manager involved with the troublesome circumstances to ask, "What's going on here?" And of course, the manager goes to the immediate supervisor of the employee who has issued the complaint to ask, "What's going on here?" The supervisor then becomes highly threatened and defensive, deceptively providing the excuse, "Aw, he (or she) is just a disgruntled employee who is trying to cause trouble." The executive director then calls the governor or legislative representative with the message, "The situation involves a troublesome employee, but we're on top of the problem. It looks like we'll have it resolved in a couple of weeks. There is no need to be concerned." The governor or the legislative representative then responds with, "Well I certainly hope that's the case. We don't need to have any negative publicity so close to the election. Just to be sure you get this taken care of, I'll be monitoring the situation."

Of course, in dysfunctional and oppressive public sector organizations, the ultimate concern is that the matter might come to the attention of the media who will then reveal the information to the public at large. Oppressive and incompetent public sector officials attempt to avoid that development like the plague. To avoid the possibility of public exposure, and to contain the situation, the executive director typically schedules a series of "closed-door" meetings. Those invited to attend the meetings are then asked to focus on the question, "What are we going to do to get this situation under control?"

The oppressive or incompetent management team then goes into a "brain storming" mode. The result of the brainstorming blizzard is that one or more of three possible "solutions" is agreed upon. In making their decision, the management team is fully aware that what is to be arranged will not bring about meaningful or positive change. None-the-less, one of the "solutions," a combination of two, or perhaps even all three will typically be implemented. The primary purpose of the action to be taken is to provide a means of "covering the anatomy" of the oppressive and incompetent officials. The three "solutions" that have been considered are employee "time charting," conducting an "employee satisfaction" survey, or arranging for an "evaluation" by outside consultants.

Time Charting

Oppressive and incompetent officials often retaliate against employees who have filed grievances against them by requiring the complaining employee to carry out a time study of each and every action that the employee engages in throughout the day. The typical requirement is that the employee must record in fifteen-minute segments, every single activity to account for his or her time. The approach is designed to create a subtle and indirect threat to the employee saying without actually using the words, "Okay buster, if you think you can control or intimidate us you are badly mistaken. You can complain all that you want, but we're watching every move that you make. We will treat you like a child who is not trustworthy until you make a mistake. Then, we are going to *'nail'* you!" The goal of this approach is to cause the employee to feel so threatened, degraded, and controlled that he or she will quit. Or, the goal may be to cause the employee to become so threatened that no further effort to bring about justice will be attempted.

"Let's Do a Survey"

The second "solution" that threatened or challenged officials may come up with to cover their anatomy is to conduct an "employee satisfaction" survey. This gimmick is implemented as a means of gaining documented evidence that employees are generally satisfied and comfortable with the "leadership" of the troubled organization. Oppressive and incompetent officials frequently use the employee satisfaction survey as a device to avoid closer scrutiny by those in higher authority. It is also a device that is used to prevent greater accountability on the part of the troublesome officials. In implementing this gimmick, oppressive officials elect to do a survey of the opinions of all staff. The results of the survey are then used as a means of establishing a case on behalf of the oppressive or incompetent officials, and they are used as a basis for their defense.

Employee satisfaction surveys that are conducted in dysfunctional or oppressive organizations are almost always based on postures of manipulation and control. The survey is initiated based on the posture, "We need to do a survey of how the staff sees us just in case this gets worse." If the challenges to their inept and oppressive methods continue, and an investigation is undertaken, the officials will simply provide the results of the survey as evidence that they are essentially doing well in the general management of their agency or organization.

In presenting their "evidence," the oppressive officials also misrepresent the facts as they claim that the complaint of the employee is simply "an isolated exception that is not really justified." The deceptive officials use the survey results to "substantiate" the idea that the majority of employees are "quite content" with the supervisory and management approaches of the officials. Tragically, this gimmick all too often works to distort the truth of how the employees actually feel, and it covers the truth of what is actually occurring. This happens as a result of the clever and extremely manipulative circumstances in which the survey is implemented.

Oppressive and incompetent executive directors typically introduce the plan to conduct an employee satisfaction survey when they are holding an all-staff meeting. At a point during the meeting, the official will make an announcement stating, "We are going to ask all employees to participate in a survey so that we can get a better understanding of how we are doing as your 'leaders.' Now, we want to assure you that we have only your best interest at heart, and we pledge to you that no negative repercussions will occur. We therefore, encourage you to be totally honest and candid in your responses. In fact, to demonstrate our sincerity, there is no need to sign your name to the survey. Your answers will be totally anonymous. However, you will notice that the survey form you receive will have a number in the upper right-hand corner. That number is there only for the purpose of processing the results of the survey. There will be absolutely no way that the number will link you to the survey form that you complete. Participation in the survey is mandatory, and it must be returned to your immediate supervisor or the Human Resource department not later than…"

Now of course, the employees receiving the survey say, "Yea, right! There is no way that I am going to say what I really think!" And so, for the most part, the employees only offer highly superficial responses, saying nothing of their true concerns due to the fear of retaliation that they know is sure to come in one form or another.

Consultants

The third "solution" used by officials in oppressive organizations to address the dissatisfaction or complaints of their employees is to call in outside "experts" with the hope that the consultants will substantiate that the organization is doing well. Or at least, it is believed that retaining the consultants will give an indication that the oppressive or incompetent officials have the "best interest" of their employees at heart. It is hoped that this will be evidenced by the fact that the officials are willing to receive guidance from an outside resource. The belief held by oppressive and incompetent officials is that they will be seen as "concerned" and "compassionate" if they are willing to have their methods investigated and assessed by outside consultants.

Actually, when oppressive and incompetent chief executive officers or upper-management officials begin to detect generalized patterns of unrest among first level supervisors and employees, they are often quite fond of calling in "experts" to assess the functioning of the organization. The motivation to engage these consultants is almost always to gain support for the oppressive or incompetent methods in place. The officials will then be able to use the results of the consultation as a device to regain power and control over their employees. The message conveyed to the employees who have dared to challenge them is, "We are now compelled to continue the course that we have established (or, to implement these changes). After all, this is what the "experts" have recommended, and they certainly know what is the best course for us to take." But of course, when the "experts" offer recommendations that the oppressive and incompetent officials do not like, no changes are implemented at all!

In the vast majority of cases when oppressive and incompetent officials engage in the use of consultants, the recommendations of the consultants are extremely basic and superficial. This is the case even though it is quite common for the consultants to be paid thousands, and sometimes, hundreds of thousands of dollars for the recommendations that they offer. It is almost always the case that an individual or small group of sincere and dedicated employees who actually know what has been going on in a given organization, could have come up with recommendations of equal or greater value by far, if they had only been given the opportunity to do so.

Oppressive and incompetent workplace officials frequently disregard the opinions of the consultants that they have hired. This is true even when they have been provided sound professional recommendations based on the judgment of recognized and respected experts. The unscrupulous officials often disagree with what the consultants suggest, although it would clearly be in their best interests to follow the recommendations offered. To illustrate this point, officials of a public sector organization decided to make arrangements with a consulting firm to assess employee inefficiency and patterns of excessive absenteeism. Although the officials were not willing to acknowledge it, the inefficiency and absenteeism were occurring as a result of diminished morale among workers. Morale at the facility was at an all time low due to the inability of the facility's employees to counter the oppressive and incompetent practices of the management team.

To address the matter, the facility's chief executive officer decided to retain the services of a respected and reputable consulting firm. The CEO then reached an agreement with the firm to conduct an onsite review of the policies, practices, and operational patterns in place. It was agreed that the consultants would conduct the review, and then make recommendations for addressing the problems of the facility. Upon concluding preliminary discussions, Michael, a competent and highly skilled professional consultant, was assigned to conduct the review. He was selected due to his broad range of experience in resolving workplace conflict. Michael was also selected due to the fact that he was a recognized expert on fair employment practices, healthy supervisory-employee relations, and the rights of workers.

As an attempt to demonstrate their "sincerity," the oppressive officials who were to be interviewed were in agreement that they would all offer the same posture to the consultant. They all agreed to claim that their primary wish was to enhance the morale of the employees of the facility. The employees, however, presented quite a different picture as they truthfully described the oppressive and incompetent practices that they were required to endure.

After completing his interviews with staff at all levels of the facility, Michael arranged a meeting to report his findings and to offer recommendations to the CEO and his management team. Michael presented a clear, factual, and forthright picture of the oppressive and incompetent practices of the management team. He offered example after example of ineffective management and supervisory practices. Included in his presentation were illustrations reflecting how those practices were clearly the primary factors leading to the diminished morale of the facility's employees. He also illustrated how ineffective management and supervisory practices were contributing to the patterns of excessive workplace absenteeism. Upon concluding his presentation and recommendations for improvement, Michael summarized his findings with a simple statement of fact. That statement, "And so essentially, you don't have a problem with employee inefficiency or absenteeism at this facility, you have a management problem!"

Upon hearing Michael's closing comment, two or three managers began to whisper to each other. As they then left the meeting, several officials joined them as they nodded in agreement to the remarks of one particularly inept manager. That manager had said, "Well, those 'crackpot' ideas might work where Michael comes from, but it is quite obvious that they won't work here. That guy has no idea about how employees function in this place. If we tried to implement those procedures here, the employees would just think that they could do pretty much as they please."

The chief executive officer then scheduled a follow-up meeting. The meeting was supposedly scheduled to review the consultant's report and recommendations, and to then determine how to implement them. However, the gathering turned out to be primarily an opportunity to make disparaging remarks about Michael and his "crackpot" ideas. In concluding the meeting, the CEO, being an inept and inadequate administrator, gave-in to the postures of the management team as they elected to totally disregard the consultant's recommendations. They chose instead, to implement several additional measures of a largely punitive and oppressive nature.

The Right to Appeal

It is quite common in oppressive organizations to offer employees opportunities to appeal the decisions and postures of oppressive and incompetent workplace officials. The grievances may be reviewed by appointed officials of the organization, or by an internal grievance committee made up of a cross section of employees and officials. Grievances may also be addressed through referral for review by a grievance committee made up of members outside of the immediate structure of the organization or agency. An alternate approach is to refer the employee who has issued the appeal, and the challenged supervisor to an "independent" mediator as a means of addressing the grievance. However, rarely are these grievance or mediation processes of any value. In the vast majority of cases, the decisions and postures of oppressive officials are not reversed in favor of the unjustly treated employee. Even when recommendations for reversal of the oppressive decisions and postures are forthcoming, rarely if ever, are the recommendations or changes implemented.

A fundamental problem with grievance reviews, appeal processes, and mediation by outside resources is that, in the vast majority of cases, no authority has been granted to assure that the recommended changes will be implemented by the oppressive or incompetent officials in power. That then, leaves the mistreated employee with only three options, all of which have significant shortcomings. One option is to accept the oppression and incompetence, and any forms of retaliation that may now be initiated by disgruntled officials. The second option is to seek employment elsewhere. The third option is to seek legal remedy, and that can be a costly process in time, financial resources, and energy. And, adding insult to injury, even if the employee wins the battle the hostile environment remains intact.

Characteristics of Oppressive & Incompetent Supervisors

Contrary to what is suggested by the positions of power that they hold, officials who display oppressive and incompetent postures are not effective leaders in the workplace. They over-control and criticize the work of effective employees while supporting the work of those who are less competent. They then offer the less competent individuals recognition as their inferior work is accepted as exceptional. Officials who develop this type of posture have never learned that when they have a need to take advantage of others to make them feel important, they are not really important. They pursue life on the basis of the "end justifies the means." Over time however, oppressive officials gain only resentment, and not respect from their subordinates, or from themselves for that matter. Oppressive officials often abuse power to escape the awareness that they are empty and shallow.

As I encounter oppressive officials, I often think of an incredible scene from the Steven Spielberg movie, "Schindler's List." In the scene, Oskar Schindler, as portrayed in the film, is attempting to dampen the zeal of Commandant Amon Goeth, the psychopathic Nazi officer who found such pleasure in the cold-blooded murder of innocent men, women, and children. As the commandant described his sense of power, Schindler quite perceptively conveyed to the commandant that what seems to be power, is not necessarily so. No, Schindler suggested, true power is demonstrated by the person who has the power to destroy, but chooses instead, not to exercise that opportunity.

Although not as severely pathological as the psychopathic commandant in Spielberg's movie, some oppressive officials will lie, distort, and cheat without regard for who might be hurt in the process. At times we may look upon such individuals with admiration, as they appear to do so well. Their possessions may reflect the finer things in life. They may appear to have attained the best of what life has to offer. And, that may in fact, in a material sense, be true. However, when we look beneath the surface, what lies below may be something quite different. There, we may see the emptiness that is the inevitable result of a lust for power and recognition achieved through callousness and indifference.

The hallmark of the oppressive supervisor is reflected in the phrase "I want, what I want, when I want it!" During early associations, in particular while attempting to impress authority figures, oppressive officials may be quite clever in presenting themselves as exceptionally capable and self-confident. They love to talk about themselves and their achievements as they harbor unrealistic opinions of their talents and abilities. While inflating their accomplishments, they dwell on fantasies of recognition and power. Beneath the facade of confidence, they often suffer from envy, insecurity, and frustration. Any unfulfilled goals are intolerable, and they must find someone to blame for their own shortcomings and failures. When others challenge them as arrogant and self-centered, they cannot understand why. They then become angry and seek to retaliate.

Bill Faultless

Following a series of major problems caused by incompetence and the abuse of power in a State facility, the State's governor became determined to correct the matter. Unfortunately for him, and for many others, the governor chose to accomplish this mission by relying on the very same oppressive and incompetent officials he had trusted to handle the problems of the facility in the first place. Based on the governor's mandate to "Get this mess cleaned up," the officials arranged a nationwide search to select the finest possible candidate to serve at the helm of the agency. Following several months of interviews and screening, the candidate was selected. However, since the officials doing the selection were almost wholly oriented to postures of power and control, they had blinded themselves to a simple fact. The person the inept and oppressive officials selected, was a mirror-image of themselves.

As Bill Faultless assumed command, he began to make sweeping changes. With blatant disregard, he quickly changed programs existing at the facility to what he described as a movement toward "excellence." Bill's primary message to his staff, "Aren't you lucky I came here. Before I arrived, this place was so screwed up that the only answer is to wipe it all away and start over. Besides, with my experience, I will be introducing you to how it really should have been done anyway!" However, Bill failed to recognize that a great deal of excellent programming had already been established at the facility. The problems of the facility prior to his arrival were not the programs that had been established. The problems were caused by the lack of sound leadership to maintain them professionally. A second mistake Bill made was to ignore the needs, feelings, and investment of the reliable staff members who had salvaged the facility time after time as corrupt or incompetent officials came, made things worse, and were then replaced. Despite expressions of concern by those employees who had displayed competency all along, Bill continued his patterns of reform.

After a few months, and much to the official's surprise, a number of crises began to surface and then escalate, as a result of the poorly thought-out programs that Bill had implemented. When the self-centered and egotistical official saw what was happening, he promptly unleashed a barrage of accusation and blame directed toward his staff. Within weeks, the facility was reduced to chaos. Eventually, Bill was required to offer his resignation in defeat. Staying in character, however, as he was leaving the facility, Bill continued to boast that his mission had been a total success. He claimed as his reason for leaving that he had received a more promising job offer at a facility in another State. Screening done later revealed that Bill in truth, had no place else to go. He in fact, took a position in an unrelated field, and later found work as a minor State official. Whether Bill has been able or willing to contain his passion for pomp and grandiosity remains in question.

Despite the self-assured and capable image that they attempt to convey, oppressive officials want to know how their subordinates and upper level officials think they are doing. At the same time, they have a sense of special entitlement and the conviction that they deserve recognition and praise. When work associates fail to provide the admiration they crave, they become angry and resentful. Oppressive supervisors resent an employee's innovative ideas, and challenges to their way of doing things. They deeply resent an employee's recognition for extraordinary accomplishment that may be conveyed by upper management. These events cause the oppressive individual to react with the need to adopt increasing postures of hostility and control. They then take out their hostile and resentful feelings on the effective employees that serve under their command. These oppressive individuals will even turn against their own colleagues.

Beatrice Beastly

Beatrice Beastley was an extremely power-oriented nurse who was hired to serve as director of nurses at a home for the elderly in Michigan. During hiring interviews, this woman presented herself as one of the most perceptive and conscientious candidates the interview committee had ever encountered. She described extensive levels of professional experience. She presented superb qualifications for the direction of the facility's infirmary unit. The interview team unanimously chose the woman over several other candidates who had done extremely well in the interviews, and who also had impressive credentials and experience. However, Beatrice ranked above them all.

Then, following a brief "honeymoon period," it started. Beatrice became increasingly resistant to the guidance of her designated manager, while ruling her own staff with hostility and contempt. She refused to accept feedback, and when asked to respond more cooperatively, Beatrice viciously attacked the integrity of her manager. Eventually, and in despair, the manager requested assistance from administrative officials. As inquiries were made, Beatrice initially presented herself with a surface image of the utmost surprise that the manager could somehow be dissatisfied with her performance and willingness to be a member of the team. Because of her sadistic ability to manipulate and present herself in the best possible light, the officials initially questioned the perceptions of the manager. However, as circumstances became increasingly out-of-control due to Mrs. Beastly's postures, the officials became aware of the truth. As such, they became determined to do something about it.

As interventions were initiated, Beatrice became openly vicious and hostile, challenging official efforts at every turn with an often repeated, two word phrase, "prove it!" Beatrice repeatedly redirected the focus of administrative directives and management responses by citing passages from official sources and case law, thereby bringing each attempt to resolve matters to an abrupt standstill. Mrs. Beastly quoted federal and state regulations. She expounded upon fair employment practices, whether or not she was presenting them accurately. Regardless, her sole purpose was to maintain power and control and when those postures lost potency, she threatened to seek legal remedy.

It was almost three years later that Mrs. Beastly was finally dealt with in an effective manner. Behind the scenes, Beatrice had been actively involved in the theft and illegal sale of the facility's prescription medication. Upon discovering those activities, officials were finally able to take decisive action leading to Mrs. Beastly's dismissal.

Oppressive supervisors often possess an incredible ability to present themselves as dedicated and conscientious in the work environment. They convey the idea that they have great concern for those around them. However, they react with resentment and anger when employees challenge their unreasonable demands and expectations. Oppressive supervisors will emotionally batter all who attempt to stand up to their inept and abusive postures. They simply lack empathy, or the ability to recognize how others feel. And, they find it difficult to appreciate the distress of someone who is having difficulty, or to recognize someone who has a legitimate concern.

Emma, a sixty-three-year-old conscientious employee wished to remain on the job for one more year. The woman had served loyally and well for more than forty years. But, oppressive officials of the company wished to assign her office to one of their cronies. To approach the matter, the chief executive officer called

Emma into his office. After a brief period of small talk, he suggested that at her age, "It might be nice to consider retirement to enjoy life for a change."

But, Emma, knowing both the quality of her contribution, and her personal circumstances, declined the suggestion saying, "Thank you so much for the offer, but what I really want to do is stay on for another year. Then, I plan to sell my house and move in with my sister so we can be free to travel. Working another year will provide just the right amount of money for us to do that, and I know I can be of service." Without another word, the CEO excused Emma from his office. Then, two days later he sent an assistant to move her desk into a hallway outside of her office because "we just need the space." Without asking Emma's opinion the official added, "Besides, you can be far more efficient here anyway." Emma got the message! Within the week she turned in her resignation, as a hurt and angry woman, and rightly so!

Oppressive and incompetent supervisors often have intense need for reassurance during times of stress. These supervisors fear loss of control and this reinforces their self-doubt and resentment. As a result, they attempt to monitor all of their employee's activities. Some of these officials require frequent accountability with even the most trivial issues. This is demonstrated by oppressive and incompetent officials who require subordinates to submit monthly reports in the form of "goals and objectives." These troublesome and controlling officials create a "trickle-up" system in this regard by demanding that mid-management staff require their subordinates to produce a monthly report of even routine activities. These lists, submitted by employees and supervisors are reviewed by mid-management staff who then develop their own lists and submit them to upper management. Upper-management then generates lists that are submitted to the chief executive officer.

This approach to management and supervision is incredibly time-consuming. Essentially, it is an exercise in futility in that nothing really changes or improves beyond inflating the postures of control, and the sense of importance of officials in the upper-echelons of the organization. The only changes occurring among first-level supervisors and line staff are increasing feelings of resentment based on accurate perceptions that they are not trusted or respected as professionals, and that they are being treated like children.

Oppressive and incompetent officials who require this type of process have either misunderstood or distorted the concept of "management by objectives" that has a valid place in the work environment. The problem is one of extremes involving the purpose and frequency of the reporting process that simply evolves to compliance "by rote." In other words, the reports are submitted as a required exercise, listing only the routine activities of the given position. Creativity, or true dynamic planning and goal-setting occur only inadvertently, if at all!

Extremely oppressive supervisors frequently maintain control over their employees through engaging in power plays and methods of intimidation involving expressions of anger and rage. However, when challenged by those in authority, they will express intense loyalty and devotion. They will then display a surface posture of cooperation toward their own managers for a time. Inside, however, they look upon their leaders with contempt, and secretly believe those in charge to be fools who do not deserve to hold their positions of power and authority.

The "Sadistic" Workplace Official

Sadistic officials are the most disturbed and treacherous individuals in any organization. Supervisors displaying these characteristics poison the workplace through the abuse of power and they use anybody they can. Sadistic officials have little, if any true substance or character, and so they attempt to steal those qualities from the truly effective and dynamic employees with whom they associate. They will often present themselves as extremely dedicated individuals only wishing to do what is best for the organization, their employees, and their colleagues. But, sadistic officials are interested only in themselves. The workplace is looked at from the standpoint of what they can get out of it. They can be extremely deceptive, actively defending the manipulations they present as excuses for their treacherous behavior. Despite the pain and anxiety they cause for others, their manipulative approaches and deceptive postures permit them to come out, "smelling like a rose" time, after time, after time.

Sadists can look unsuspecting administrative officials in the eye and calmly deny whatever it is that they have been challenged about, or they deceptively redirect the issue to falsely accuse others. Should an employee challenge or disagree, the attempt leads to resentment and retaliation. To build their image and sense of power, sadistic supervisors treat their employees like possessions. Their notion of teamwork is to control, not truly to lead. Instead of following thoughtfully established and fair-minded policies, they make up the policies to suit their own self-serving needs and purposes. Indeed, sadistic officials never actually develop an accurate understanding of what teamwork really is. Sadistic supervisors love to play one employee against the other. They find pleasure in being clever and deceptive, and they experience an intense sense of power when they are controlling others by intimidation and humiliation.

Although sadistic officials may be causing severe devastation for employees, administrators closely associated with the sadist may be totally unaware of what is occurring. Because administrative officials may be mislead and deceived for years, attempts to solve the problems caused by sadistic officials may not surface until it is too late. The sadist represents the epitome of the phrase "the end justifies the means." In their extreme form, they will attack anyone who tries to stop them. And, they will too often remain untouchable because their corrupt postures are undetectable to almost everyone but the most perceptive…or to those victims who have felt their sadistic wrath. Their ultimate goal is absolute power and control over whomever they encounter.

Millicent Vile

Millicent Vile is an extremely convincing liar. Despite her pettiness and absolute lust for power, she has maintained, at any given time, a certain number of followers and admirers. While this is true, most of her followers and admirers do not hang around for very long. She either targets them for abuse, or they wise up to her sick deceptiveness and get away from her.

Millicent first displayed her sadistic patterns as a young woman beginning her career in social work. She was assigned to Steve, a genuine and dedicated social worker who was asked to provide Millicent with the supervision and training necessary for her to become effective as a professional counselor in a California social service agency. Programming at the facility was as professional and effective as any in the country as a result of Steve's superb talents and abilities. During the first two years of their association, Millicent was an eager and energetic student. She took advantage of the excellent training Steve was providing for her and about twenty other professional staff. Eventually, Millicent was promoted to a first level supervisory position under Steve's guidance and management.

The Setup

Millicent, being an extremely clever and deceptive sadist, approached Steve one day with a "concern." Millicent mentioned that, whenever Steve participated in the program's weekly staff meetings, members of the staff would redirect their attention to him. Realizing the importance of respect for chain of command structure, and at that point, being unaware of Millicent's treachery, Steve agreed to limit his participation to only occasional management briefings.

Divide & Conquer

Once the coast was clear, Millicent swung into action. With each opportunity, Millicent engaged in cunning, and malicious undermining of Steve's activities. She would misrepresent every directive and suggestion Steve offered her in the private meetings she frequently requested. Millicent actively poisoned staff attitudes with the suggestion, "I don't know what's happening to Steve. He is becoming so unreasonable and difficult to deal with." Millicent even went to the extreme of encouraging members of the staff to use caution in approaching Steve. She in fact, suggested that the staff consider her to be a resource to protect them from any risks that might be presented in attempting to deal with Steve.

About one-half of the staff accepted Millicent's deceptions and manipulations at face value, despite the fact that Steve had never, in any way, mistreated them. He offered all of them superb training, frequent opportunities for professional development, and he provided continuing latitude for upward mobility. Every employee under Steve's leadership during a twelve-year period grew tremendously in professional skills and abilities, increased levels of responsibility in the organization, and regular advances in salary. Staff turnover in Steve's department remained at an all-time low. But, unfortunately for them, Steve, and the organization, several staff also succumbed to Millicent Vile's incredible lack of integrity and powers of persuasion.

The Betrayal

Once Millicent was confident that the scene had been set, she very cleverly bypassed chain of command structure. She approached officials of the organization with sometimes subtle, but more often malicious attacks directed toward Steve's character and postures. Millicent presented one report to Steve, another report to her staff, and yet another report to officials of the facility. Eventually, morale in the department deteriorated to the point where an informal investigation was conducted. With the findings of the investigation being obviously disturbing to officials, they elected to implement a "restructuring" process. The officials assigned Steve to several other areas of responsibility, and gave Millicent complete control over the program's staff.

Unbridled Oppression

With Steve now "out of the way," Millicent began a reign of terror on members of the staff. Within two years of her assumption of complete authority, the twenty-staff program had undergone more than 100 percent turnover. Millicent systematically targeted one staff member after another. She lied about their capabilities to officials of the organization. Being an expert at tactics of "divide and conquer," Millicent maliciously played one member of the staff against another. Then, when objections related to her supervisory style were presented, Millicent scheduled what she defined as a "peer" evaluation. Millicent required any employee who attempted to challenge her to stand before the entire staff. She then required each staff member to discuss the "negative" characteristics of the victim.

However, before the scheduled inquisition, Millicent made sure she coached the staff on the direction she wished the meeting to take. She also made it clear that they better cooperate with her or they would be next. Interestingly, Millicent always remained silent during the inquisitions, commenting only after the "subject" was shattered and in tears. "You know, Louise, I agreed to let the staff hold this meeting because I care so much about you. I believe the staff really said what they did to try to help you."

The Fall

Seeing the destructiveness of Millicent's sadistic maneuvers, most of her staff eventually lost their taste for the proceedings. Conditions within the department became so oppressive that the staff approached the administrator of the facility with a list of charges against Millicent. They declared their intention to quit if decisive action was not taken to remove her from her position of authority. To illustrate the truly sadistic character of Millicent Vile, as attempts to investigate her behavior were undertaken, Millicent presented herself as a superb actress, crying and expressing postures of "anguish." "I just can't understand how the staff could do this to me after all I have done for them." Fortunately, administrative officials refused to accept her sadistic manipulations anymore. However, the story does not end there.

The Double Cross

Following her demotion, Millicent retained the services of an attorney, charging the administration with improper handling of her circumstances and demanding reinstatement. It should be remembered, these are the same officials that accepted her lies against Steve. The officials who protected her time after time while she quite deliberately, and without conscience, lied to them, misrepresented her motives, and displayed blatant disregard for their trust and office. You see, the officials responsible for managing Millicent overlooked a very fundamental principle of human nature. That principle, while it may be true that there is an element of truth in the complaint of a coward, there is also a much larger picture not talked about. For their oversight in this regard…they too have paid a price. They have failed in their responsibilities as stewards of the workplace, and many innocent people have been hurt as a result.

A Message to Oppressive Officials

Designated officials…those in positions of authority, have license to lead! They do not have license to harm. It is important for all of us to realize that workplace officials have the authority to practice their specialties and to hold their particular office. Of course, for that they deserve our respect. However, equally important is to realize that workplace officials do not have the right to run "roughshod" over the feelings and needs of employees. Those who do not understand this have lost sight of the ethics of their profession and the responsibility to inspire productivity, decency, and fairness in the workplace. Whether it is for those they are pledged to serve, or for those they may oppose. No one has the right to abuse power, whether it is in the realm of standing up for our rights as men and women, or to promote our self-aggrandized perspective on our own station in life.

What the smug and complacent oppressors have forgotten is that they are first and foremost, stewards of the workplace. These individuals have also forgotten the adage, "Power tends to corrupt…and absolute power corrupts absolutely." *In other words, ineffective managers have never learned…*when they treat employees like possessions, they promote mediocre employees and work performance. When they play favorites or play staff against each other, they create an environment of resentment and discontent. When oppressive officials establish rigid and self-serving policies, they create a sterile environment and promote the status quo. When they fail to apply to themselves…the policies, principles, and standards that they mandate for others, they present themselves as hypocrites. They then encourage staff to become disillusioned and ineffective. Oppressive officials may then eventually get exactly what they deserve, but at far too great a price to be paid by their innocent victims!

When corrupt officials fail to recognize the contributions of extraordinary staff, they destroy initiative for creativity and innovation. When they support and recognize ineffective employees, while disregarding and belittling the sincere efforts of effective employees, those who are effective eventually shut down in their positive contribution. Or, they leave the first chance that they get! The abuse of power by those in authority imperils solid employees. It causes undue suffering among families, it dampens the potential of otherwise productive workers, and it places great burdens on those who wish to make a contribution and earn a living.

Driven as much by inadequacy as by the lust for power, oppressive officials define their self-esteem in relation to the lack of success of their work associates. They feel strong only because, and when their subordinates and other work associates are under their control. Oppressive people contaminate everyone with whom they come in contact. If they are in positions to influence others, they spread negativism to those who look to them for leadership and inspiration. They intuitively sense the power of decency and fairness among their work associates, and then begin an intense and insidious effort to destroy what threatens them most…the genuineness and integrity of others.

To be truly successful, we must all have an appreciation of life outside ourselves. And of course, that is what is so lacking in the posture of oppressive and incompetent workplace officials. Worst of all, they have forgotten so many of the people who are part of themselves, and so much of life that is meaningful. Their history, their present and future life, and that, they too, belong. They remember their wish for power all too well, and forget that they also need all the other people to make life worthwhile. It has been said so often that the road to success is through drive and competition. But, what value is there if I gain control and wealth, but I lose my world? Is the drive for power too great to remember the simple fact that "no person is an island," which is true now more than ever before in this world?

3

EMPLOYEES IN THE TROUBLED WORKPLACE

The Oppression Trap

Every oppressed employee has battled with the sense that there is something wrong deep inside them that causes oppressive workplace officials and administrators to abuse them. Although this belief is often held, it is never justified for powerful officials to take advantage of their positions of authority or an employee's vulnerability. In too many cases, employees arrive at work knowing that they will have little or no opportunity to achieve, or to receive recognition, unless they are willing to comply with the rigid expectations and unrealistic postures of oppressive and incompetent officials. A worker who submits to these conditions not only lacks feelings of fulfillment, but also becomes an extremely limited resource.

In an attempt to avoid conflict and risk, submissive subordinates make little effort to think or to contribute ideas for improvement. Instead, they remain silent and they do only as much as they are required to do to survive. If unchallenged, oppressive officials become increasingly involved in denial, and neglectful of the needs and feelings of subordinates. As long as abusive behavior is allowed to continue, conditions never get better, they always get worse over time. If these patterns are not successfully challenged, troubled organizations continue to move in the direction of reduced morale, diminishing productivity, and a climate of progressive workplace deterioration and stagnation.

It requires courage and realistic thinking to accept the possibility that your supervisor and in some cases, even the administrative levels of your organization may not really care about you. It is difficult to realize that beneath the superficial image of concern often expressed by officials to mask their oppressive and incompetent postures, the inescapable truth is that you must learn to survive on your own. Until you face the facts, you can be manipulated, dominated, and controlled. Once you face the facts, you can see through false promises and avoid the struggles that come to so many employees who believe them.

An insensitive supervisor who does things like taking credit for your achievements and criticizing you without valid justification will teach you two of the most valuable lessons of employment. Those lessons are...don't take it personally, and don't treat your colleagues that way. Successful employees do not dwell on such actions of supervisors. They learn, they grow, they do what they can, and if hope becomes lost, they move on. In almost all cases, once abused employees leave an oppressive environment, they start their new professional lives on a healthier plane. They just seem to blossom and become more dynamic and productive human beings.

The Struggle for Survival

Dependent employees who work under the supervision of an oppressive official will often endure such conditions in silence for years. This pattern may be the result of fear of retaliation. It may be due to guilt brought about by the manipulative postures of blaming and control. It may also be due to a belief that employees have no real choice in the matter. It will take still more time before these employees will leave their jobs. Some will endure oppressive conditions throughout their careers.

Oppressed employees will sometimes justify their decision to remain in a troubled work environment based on the love and sense of responsibility they feel to provide support for their families. They may then treat those loved ones with rejection and even cruelty, as a means of dispersing the anger and rage accumulated in their jobs. Others will stay at their jobs because of the illusive promise of security and retirement. Sadly these employees, perhaps largely due to the price they pay during their years of unresolved frustration, often die within a few years of departure from the workplace. They have spent their most productive years without a sense of true purpose or achievement, and in a very real sense, they have wished their lives away.

Employees who work in oppressive environments tend to be afraid to express themselves or to say what they think...or how they really feel. As a result, the problems that are caused by the oppression and incompetence are then perpetuated, and resentment and frustration take over. Teamwork and feelings of camaraderie are lost because workers become suspicious and untrusting of those around them. Employees become disillusioned and anxious. They often feel threatened because they fear that their associates will sacrifice them as a means of maintaining their own survival when pressures increase due to the controlling postures of oppressive and incompetent officials.

The result among employees is…

- Frustration and chronic dissatisfaction.

- Anger and rigidity out of proportion to circumstances.

- Repetitive behavior and preoccupation (Their discontent is all they think or talk about…it is the only thing that really matters to them).

False Labels

Oppressed employees are sometimes given labels in the troubled workplace implying that they are lazy or shiftless. In the vast majority of cases, that is simply not true. These employees are neither lazy nor shiftless. Workers who have been branded with the labels, lazy or shiftless, have simply sized up the operational patterns of the organization. It is vital for workplace officials to understand that almost all employees have a natural "radar system." This involves the ability to scan the "horizon" of the workplace, allowing employees to learn where the safe zones are, and where there is significant risk involved. As such, some employees quickly discover where they must remain conscientious and responsible, and under what circumstances they can do pretty much as they please. As a result, employees become opportunistic in their daily functioning and in carrying out their job responsibilities. They have realized that acting lazy or shiftless is one of the operational standards of the facility. Employees then waste time because workplace officials have provided an example that permits those assigned to do the same.

In a public sector facility on the east coast, upper level officials make it common practice to take a recreation break at 11:00 a.m. each day instead of taking a standard one-half hour lunch as defined by official policy. These officials then play racket ball (A racket in the true sense of the word) until 12:00 noon. They then of course, are sweaty from the activity and so, they spend another one-half hour showering and getting cooled down. After their showers, the officials spend another hour having lunch in the facility's dining room. (By the way, the meals are provided at taxpayer expense, and at no direct cost to the officials) Nice deal, huh?

After "lunch," the officials return to work, and counting coffee breaks and visiting, probably not too much of that. In other words, these officials make it common practice to spend a minimum of two and one-half hours of a designated, eight-hour workday engaging in their personal recreation and lunch activities at taxpayer expense. It probably won't surprise you to learn that these same officials frequently complain about staff members they have labeled as lazy and shiftless. These officials present a classic example of the abuse of power, negative modeling, and betrayal of the public trust, while blatantly displaying their unethical behavior.

Performance Appraisals in Oppressive Work Environments

In oppressive work environments, the performance appraisals completed by oppressive and incompetent officials provide yet another way for them to abuse the power of their offices. The appraisals are used only to serve the needs of the oppressive organization, and to support those who engage in treacherous, oppressive, or incompetent practices. The performance appraisals typically provide validation for the postures of oppressive and incompetent officials who wish to recognize and reward their snitches and cronies. In oppressive environments, the work of mediocre or treacherous employees who have been clever enough to align themselves with the oppressive regime is almost always rated as exceptional. At the same time, the performance appraisals are used as a device to diminish, control, and unfairly criticize the performance of effective employees. Or, they are used to shutdown those employees who have the courage to challenge the inept and unfair practices of the oppressive and incompetent officials, and their equally dysfunctional cronies.

In most oppressive organizations, an incredible amount of time and energy is spent in designing, administering, completing, and reviewing the performance appraisals that are initiated by oppressive and incompetent officials. Yet, they rarely, if ever, serve the purpose for which the concept of performance appraisal is legitimately intended. In fact, one measure of an oppressive organization is how often performance appraisal forms are changed by the controlling and incompetent officials in charge of the process. It is not at all unusual for these officials to hold a series of meetings to make changes in the form design or format every year or two. The whole exercise creates an atmosphere of "policies before people."

Officials of an oppressive regime strongly emphasize that performance appraisals are vital to the effective functioning of the organization. They also claim that performance appraisals are the only way that employees can be treated fairly. Yet, nothing really changes as a result of the performance appraisal revisions and review processes other than increased compensation and recognition for the cronies and favorites of the oppressive and incompetent officials. In the majority of cases, the truly effective employees, and those who have dared to challenge the oppressive and incompetent practices of officials are rated as ordinary and mediocre. This then leads to strong feelings of frustration and resentment among the effective and healthy employees who clearly see what is happening.

Meetings, Meetings, & More Meetings

And, speaking of meetings. As a general rule, the more oppressive and dysfunctional the organization, the more frequent it is that meetings are scheduled and held. In fact, in many oppressive and dysfunctional organizations, the primary function of some officials is to schedule and attend a series of meetings, most often on a daily basis. Yet, despite the frequency of the meetings, and the claims of their importance, little if anything of true or lasting value is accomplished.

Holding frequent and unproductive meetings is particularly common in oppressive public sector organizations. This occurs because the officials have forgotten, or they have ignored the fact that they have the responsibility to be "stewards of the public trust." A blizzard of discussion evolves during the course of the meetings, but that blizzard occurs without sufficient structure and leadership to provide an environment for effectiveness and productivity. As such no viable focus is established, and no meaningful movement occurs. Despite the incredible cost in time and energy that these meetings require, nothing of significant value occurs at an operational level. Or, if change does occur it is typically in the direction of more restrictive policies, or in support of the unrealistic and ineffective procedures implemented by the oppressive and incompetent officials in power.

Ryan Agenda

Ryan Agenda is an extremely inept mid-level official. Ryan started his career in the state of Oregon about twenty years ago through connections he had with the prominent and well established administrator of the social service agency in which he is employed. The somewhat inept administrator has made it clear that he strongly values his association with Ryan, therefore, he is essentially untouchable and cannot be effectively challenged or fired. Although Ryan has made only a very limited contribution to the operation and success of the organization over the years, he has gradually evolved to the position of "Director of Service Coordination." A position, by the way, that has no actual or meaningful purpose in the operational structure of the organization. In fact, the position was actually created for Ryan about six months ago. That occurred after Ryan had moved from assignment to assignment during the first nineteen years of his career with the facility. Practically every move that the management team arranged for Ryan took place due to his ineptness, and due to the frustration of the employees who worked under Ryan's supervision and management.

With each new assignment, the employees working under Ryan's direction became so dismayed by his ineptness, and by his lack of leadership ability that they threatened to quit. Adding, "insult to injury," major operational problems were frequently created due to Ryan's ineptness. In desperation, and on repeated occasions, the management team became compelled to act to correct the matter. Unfortunately, each action designed to correct the situation turned out to be a temporary "solution." Eventually, the managers simply ran out of departments in which to place Ryan. And so, the position of "Director of Service Coordination" was created. But, the officials then had a remaining dilemma. What were the managers to ask Ryan to do? After some deliberation, an agreement was reached. Ryan would become a "floating technical expert and adviser" with the primary duty of attending meetings. As such, it is not at all unusual for Ryan to attend or arrange, four to six meetings in an eight-hour work schedule. And yet, nothing of significance is achieved as a result of those activities. But, the problems created due to Ryan's ineptness have ended. However, when we look beyond Ryan's patterns of functioning we realize that many other officials of the organization are also attending those very same unproductive meetings.

E-Mail Wars

In recent years increasing numbers of public and private sector organizations have been equipped with various forms of computer technology and telecommunications networking. For the most part, these technological advances have increased the effectiveness of employees. When properly used, they have also enhanced the efficiency of the work environment itself. However, when oppressive or incompetent supervisors and employees become over invested in the use of these electronic communication systems, significant breakdowns in employee relationships and interaction begin to emerge.

In the midst of this electronic battleground, it is not at all unusual for two or more employees who are experiencing minor conflicts or disagreements to begin a bombardment of e-mail exchanges. In part due to the content and style of writing, and in part due to the accusing and abrupt nature of messages conveyed, increasing feelings of frustration and resentment begin to surface. What may have started as a relatively simple problem to resolve through thoughtful and solution-oriented discussion has now escalated to the point of open warfare. And, these patterns escalate without the need for either employee to leave the confines of an office or workstation. It is also not at all unusual for this type of electronic warfare to occur between employees who work in settings that permit easy access to each other. As a result, what was initially designed to be a system to increase effectiveness and efficiency has now resulted in the loss of meaningful encounters that could have provided a forum for effective conflict resolution and healing.

For example, Sue and Linda are administrative assistants who work in offices within twenty feet of each other in a public sector facility in Florida. In their most recent disagreement, Linda discovered that Sue had reorganized a filing system that they both use in carrying-out their individual duties and responsibilities. This action on Sue's part then triggered a barrage of increasingly negative and hostile e-mail messages. The tension between them became so intense that clients and co-workers issued complaints to upper management. As such, a time-consuming series of interventions became necessary to bring about resolution of the disagreement, and to again establish a reasonably effective working relationship between the two employees.

Some oppressive supervisors and managers use the e-mail system as a means of intimidating targeted employees. These oppressive officials often engage in the use of e-mail correspondence as a way to create a paper trail in building a case for firing employees who are a threat to them. The use of e-mail correspondence may also be used to counter the posture of an employee who has challenged the official about an oppressive or incompetent posture that has been taken.

When the e-mail system is used as a device for control and intimidation, rarely if ever, do officials meet directly with the targeted or resented employee to discuss workplace issues or concerns. Instead, these inept and callous officials rely on harsh, negative, and accusing e-mail messages as their primary means of communication with the targeted employee. When oppressive and incompetent officials use the e-mail system in this manner, it is usually a sign that they have personalized the situation to the point where opportunities for meaningful communication and negotiation of workplace differences have been lost. As such, an increasingly sterile and tense environment is created. That environment could easily have been prevented by the official's willingness to engage in solution-oriented action planning and negotiation in a "face to face" manner. Such action could have served as a means of resolving and bringing closure to the disruption and unrest created by the oppressive official's actions and posture. Unfortunately, once the use of the e-mail system has become the standard for supervisory/employee interaction in the workplace, the possibility of a return to a more congenial form of communication and problem solving becomes increasingly unlikely over time.

The "Loyalists"

Widely recognized as good workers, the "Loyalists" are the employees who keep the troubled organization going. They work hard, but in oppressive organizations, they often feel misunderstood and unrecognized. They are employees that want to do well and do so for a time. However, many of them eventually "burn out" or they develop physical illness when excessive oppression or incompetence is displayed in the workplace for extended periods of time. The result will be loss of innovation and talent that is never fully developed. After years of loyal service, this may lead to a deep sense of bitterness and resentment on the part of the otherwise loyal employee. These feelings are rarely, if ever, expressed to those officials who are causing the oppressive circumstances. Nor, are they expressed to those who are displaying patterns of supervisory incompetence. Instead, the bitterness and resentment are internalized and then displaced onto friends and family members who eventually tire of hearing the complaints. Or, those who are close to the employee develop deep feelings of resentment of their own due to the abusive and blaming behavior that is directed toward them.

In the work environment, Loyalists can be successful if given a fair opportunity. They work hard, but, if not properly recognized through effective supervision and guidance, they get left behind. Loyalists are not only victims of an oppressive system, but eventually they become their own worst enemies. Because they accept the oppression year after year, these employees often spend those years anticipating the joys of retirement, only to die within a year or two after their dream for retirement is fulfilled.

Doug Reliable

Doug Reliable can only be described as a really nice guy. Doug is conscientious, loyal, and dedicated to his profession. He rarely misses a day of work due to illness. Doug willingly carries out any assignment or challenge presented to him, and he is always cooperative with officials and co-workers. In my association with Doug during a nine-year period I never heard him swear, lose his temper, or express an unkind word to anyone. Yet, the work Doug is assigned to perform is almost always lacking in creativity and imaginative quality. The work will be done well, of course. His projects will be completed in a timely fashion. But, his efforts will also lack innovation or improvement above the ordinary. Doug is reliable, but mundane in his work and profession. On a number of occasions, newer and more innovative employees have looked at one of Doug's projects, and within a short time have devised a new and better way to accomplish the task.

Even in these circumstances, Doug will remain calm and consistent, readily adapting to the negative circumstances brought about by oppressive and incompetent officials without "missing a beat." He shows no indication of resentment, and he appears to readily adapt to the troubling circumstances. As such, Doug is a true "loyalist," and I might add, a valuable asset to his organization. It will, however, most likely always be necessary to look toward others for movements toward innovation and change.

The Creative & Dynamic Leaders

And, what about the truly effective employees? What about truly capable leaders and innovators? Healthy workers present themselves as genuine and flexible, expressing their views in a manner that conveys a sense of calm and self-assuredness. These employees take pride in their accomplishments and in their talents. And, they respect the accomplishments and talents of others. Creative and dynamic leaders commit themselves to their values. And, they seek to fulfill and defend those values when they are under threat. Healthy individuals find their life's work meaningful, with satisfactions and with some levels of accepted struggle. They do not apologize for being the persons they are, and so, there is an element of direction and of focus, to their existence. Their character and integrity are demonstrated by being authentic, decent, and fair.

Creative and dynamic leaders do well no matter how oppressive or dysfunctional the organization that they work in might be. And, they meet the challenge regardless of the level of difficulty or oppression that might come their way. But, they do not stay in oppressive organizations! It becomes very simple to see what happens to them. Creative and dynamic employees are often persecuted by ineffective supervisors because they are believed to be a threat. Eventually, they may find it necessary to leave the oppressive environment. And, what of their good works once they have gone? The oppressive management staff and the incompetent employees will reap the rewards of the good work they leave behind. Sadly, they will eventually distort that good work until it no longer has value.

Being a Creative & Dynamic Leader

Creative and dynamic leaders assure quality and purposefulness in life and in the workplace. To have such a mission requires a deep underlying belief in the ability of people to rise above negative circumstances, and to make a significant contribution to other people. In fact, most of us want to see ourselves as givers, but that is not necessarily healthy. People who give only on the surface are not genuinely giving human beings. They do so to prove they are okay, to prove they are right, to "show them!" They are typically very lonely and isolated people who are often angry and even hostile toward those close to them. They may also be filled with self-pity inside.

Takers, on the other hand, seem to almost always get the best of things, while the givers just seem to endure life much of the time. The taker's approach to life often brings significant reward without a great deal of time or effort. Their approach is fast, but shallow because they take care of themselves without regard for who might get hurt in the process. It may be then, that true credibility and leadership is reflected in people who can both give and take in balance and harmony with life, with themselves, and with their comrades. They are the ones with the courage to change…and to grow.

4

APPROACHING OPPRESSIVE WORKPLACE OFFICIALS & COLLEAGUES

Dealing with Conflict & Criticism

There are no guarantees that any approach to resolving conflict that I propose in this book will result in meaningful change in an oppressive work environment. However, when conflicts with oppressive supervisors, or problems with troublesome work associates are faced with courage and thoughtfulness, your potential to bring about improvement will certainly increase. And, you will gain strength and knowledge through your efforts.

Resolving conflict doesn't necessarily have to lead to open warfare. Nothing will be gained if you become angry and accusing. You don't need to attack. Positive and effective communication begins when you thoughtfully define the problem as you see it. It also involves trying to understand the other person's point of view. By talking things over, a minor difference of opinion or misunderstanding can be prevented from becoming a major disagreement or conflict. If you make demands and approach the situation from an accusing or blaming posture, your supervisor or colleague could become hostile toward you, and that could only make matters worse. But, if you remain thoughtful and fair-minded in your approach, even if the situation does not change, you will have the satisfaction of knowing that you have done the best you could. That could also give you an indication of the potential for improvement in your work situation, or whether you would be wise to begin the process of seeking employment elsewhere.

Responding to the Criticism of Oppressive Officials

When you are challenged or attacked by an oppressive official you have a greater chance of success and survival when you engage in thoughtful alignment and a search for solutions. With oppressive officials, you will rarely succeed by becoming defensive and by trying to prove that the official is wrong. When you make demands or threaten an oppressive person, you seldom achieve what you hoped to accomplish. Even if you do get what you want, you may experience retaliation later. Always remember, the oppressive official sets the scene through intimidation to maintain postures of power and control. Even if you disagree with what is being said, do not let your emotions cloud your judgment or cause you to behave in a demanding or otherwise unprofessional manner.

When an oppressive official directs criticism toward you, provide a professional response as you let the official know that you understand the seriousness of the situation. If you realize that the criticism is justified, inform the oppressive individual that you will do what you can to correct the problem. Close out the discussion on a positive note and then periodically inform the official of your progress as you proceed. Also be sure to keep the official informed of the approaches that you are using as you work toward correcting what led to the criticism.

Most oppressive officials present their criticism in a sarcastic, demanding or otherwise power oriented manner. This can cause you to become defensive and to offer excuses after encountering their unfair challenges. Regardless of whether the criticism of oppressive officials is presented with unfairness or with sarcasm, you will be wise to respond to the postures presented in a thoughtful manner. They may then respond more fairly when they see your sincerity, and when they recognize your determination to do the right thing. Try to understand the concern and do not take the oppressive postures personally. Instead, listen and let your supervisor do most of the talking. Before you respond to the oppressive official's criticism, get in control of your thoughts and emotions. If you believe the criticism to be unfair or inaccurate, calmly and professionally present the facts of the situation as you understand them. Then, suggest ideas that show your commitment to solving the problem even though it occurred through no fault of your own.

When you are required to participate in a meeting that is challenging your professionalism…

- It is okay to show some levels of vulnerability.

- It is never okay to attack, or to show anger or hostility.

- You may need to ask for time to think about the issues presented before you respond.

- With serious allegations, you may be wise to seek the advice of legal counsel to assist you.

Controlling Your Emotions

Oppressive supervisors and managers have two primary weapons. Employees must learn to defend against these weapons or remain subject to the controlling and manipulative postures of oppressive workplace officials. The first weapon is the ability to arouse anger or to provoke loss of temper. If the employee becomes angry or hostile, the oppressive official justifies the abuse of power and now has an additional excuse to abuse and criticize. The second weapon of oppressive supervisors and managers is the ability to arouse anxiety in those who must respond to the abusive postures. Therefore, employees feel compelled to yield to the unreasonable demands of oppressive workplace officials.

When you work in an oppressive environment, it is essential that you develop the ability to manage and control your feelings. The impact of uncontrolled emotions is almost always destructive, adversely affecting sound judgment and decisions. Uncontrolled emotions also tend to hinder the ability of oppressed employees to act promptly and wisely in times of crisis or challenge. But, if emotions are managed and controlled, and then reasonably expressed, they do not become troublesome. In fact, as I think of my own career, I cannot recall a single time that I made a significant mistake or behaved foolishly when I felt calm and self-assured. Yet, there were many times that I was both foolish and mistaken when I allowed my feelings to cloud my judgment.

The most common difficulty we have when we approach oppressive officials or other troublesome employees is that our emotions overwhelm our judgment and our ability to function with thoughtfulness and reliability. We become so filled with anxiety that we cannot think clearly. In a state of panic, we tend to rush the flow of our words. We then, say things that we do not want to say. Or, the comments we do make may not really be in our best interest. It is important to remember that in any exchange between two people, the one that is the least concerned about the other person's needs and feelings controls the situation. Therefore, it is always in your best interest to remain in control of your feelings. When you deal with controlling, manipulative, or oppressive individuals, display as little emotion as possible.

How do you keep your emotions under control? How do you maintain your composure during difficult encounters? When oppressive officials or troublesome co-workers become irrational and demanding, remain as calm and as silent as you can. Listen carefully and let them do the talking. Do not interrupt or respond until they have said what they want to say. It may be difficult to avoid overreacting by becoming defensive, but it can be done. It is vital to understand, if you convey anxiety, resentment or anger, you may then be providing the oppressive official or troublesome co-worker with an opportunity to use those reactions to further control and retaliate.

If you are in a situation where you know you might become too emotional, you may be wise to attempt to stall for time. You might consider saying, "I really feel the need to think about this further. I would appreciate it if we could take a ten minute break before I give you my response." Or, you might say, "I would like to take a break until after lunch before we continue." Then, allow yourself to regain your composure. Once your feelings are contained, you should be able to resume the discussion in a more effective manner. If you follow this approach, it is unlikely that the emotion you feel will be as overwhelming or difficult to control when you reconvene.

How effective you will be during a challenging encounter with an oppressive official or difficult work associate will depend on your ability to handle yourself with professionalism and self-assuredness. Learn to remain calm and thoughtful as you face stressful and anxiety producing circumstances. Once you have a clear understanding of what needs to be addressed, and you have a plan for getting the situation resolved, begin with a strong and solution oriented posture, and with an appeal to fairness and reason. Try to avoid making any comments that convey indecisiveness and uncertainty such as "I'm not sure I should be saying this, but..." or, "Maybe I'm over reacting about this, but..." Regardless of how hard you try to avoid it, if there is any way for oppressive or controlling individuals to misinterpret what you say, they are likely to find it and attempt to use it against you. So, express yourself with thoughtfulness, accuracy, decisiveness, and clarity. And, whenever you want to give your opinion, speak calmly. Do not reveal anger, frustration, resentment, or annoyance.

Having an oppressive supervisor or controlling colleague can be challenging and difficult. But, your ability to remain calm and professional will serve you well as you approach and respond to the troublesome individual. In fact, you can even improve your professional skills when you are required to respond to workplace officials or other work associates who are incompetent, oppressive, or controlling. The situation will strengthen your ability to work with people. It will also increase your ability to function more effectively while under stress. In particular, it is helpful to follow the three-step procedure outlined below:

1. **Slow yourself down.**

2. **Remember to breathe.**

3. **Think before you speak or act.**

The Role of Effective Breathing

Breathing effectively during stressful encounters with oppressive officials or other difficult work associates is vital. Through effective breathing, you permit your body to work more efficiently, thereby distributing nourishment and oxygen to various centers of the brain. Effective breathing permits more efficient use of adrenaline that is naturally produced in connection with our "fight or flight" response to danger and risk taking.

When you find yourself in a difficult encounter with a demanding official or troublesome work associate, try to pause briefly from time to time. As you do so, take a deep breath. Hold that breath momentarily, and then exhale as completely as your circumstances will permit. As you continue to find opportunities to breath deeply and to again exhale as completely as you can, the process should help you to think more clearly and help you to provide a more effective response as you proceed.

Speaking Out

You can use one of two approaches when you choose to challenge someone to whom you are professionally accountable. These approaches are particularly helpful when you fear the response of an oppressive official. The first approach involves determining, among several areas of conflict or concern, which of those might be the easiest for you to present. Then put the rest aside, and address the issue you selected. The second approach involves determining just the opposite. In the second approach, select the issue that might be the most difficult for you to talk about.

Why is this important? Well, each approach has it's own distinct advantage. For example, when you approach the easiest issue first, that action gives you new experiences and the realization that you dealt with the matter successfully. You will then know that you have survived, despite your fears. Therefore, you have developed new skills and resources for addressing the issue involving the next level of difficulty. Now, should you choose the most difficult matter you must take up with the oppressive or controlling individual, muster your courage and present the issue in a forthright manner. Once the issue is presented and worked through, every other issue will be less difficult in comparison.

The "Nixon" Approach

Never approach a difficult person from a point of weakness. The story is told of President Richard M. Nixon who, in the early days of his Presidency, was recognized for his ability to successfully work with the members of Congress. This ability, noted by the media caused one reporter to ask, "Mr. President, how is it that you have been so successful with the Congress when so many of your predecessors have been unable to do so?" The President's response, "Well, I never approach the Congress from a point of weakness." Indeed, that comment summarized Nixon's approach beautifully. He did his homework well, and knowing his adversaries, he approached them with success.

When we are positively assertive, we are not afraid to develop our abilities. We are willing to risk trying new things. If we do not try, we cannot grow. There is a wonderful song from the 1960's sung by Kenny Rogers that illustrates the importance of a positively assertive approach in circumstances such as those I have presented in this book. The song... ***"The Coward of the County."*** The fundamental message of the song is that there comes a time when we must all stand up for ourselves and for those we care about. If we do not stand up for ourselves and for those who look to us for security and support, those who abuse and take advantage of us will never stop. We then lose our right to live in peace and harmony with our comrades, and with those we love.

There is a related and powerful message presented by all strong and powerful countries in the world. That message…never yield to the ransom demands of the blackmailer. Why? The answer is both obvious and simple! If we cave in to the demands of the blackmailer, the blackmail will never end.

Following Through

Fight the fear of risk-taking when you know in your heart, and in your mind that it is the right thing to do. Whenever you are attempting to challenge the behavior and attitude of an oppressive or controlling person you are going to meet with strong resistance. In taking such risks, you may discover that the oppressive individual or difficult work associate will respond more positively to your concerns if you say what is on your mind in a firm and respectful manner. And, when dealing with oppressive officials you may need to stand on your principles even though it may be very difficult to do.

It is one of the peculiar truths of life that those people who are afraid of losing everything…usually have very little of true value to lose. Learn to confront and take charge. Most employees avoid confrontation due to unrealistic anxiety and the fear of losing their jobs. They then pay a bigger price in the form of lost self-respect and feelings of chronic dissatisfaction. They continue to experience troublesome circumstances under the controlling postures of oppressive and incompetent officials or difficult co-workers. Effectively confronting highly controlling and manipulative individuals involves being thoughtful. It also requires sound judgment as you challenge the behaviors, postures, and issues that are of concern to you. If you follow these standards, you will feel better regardless of the outcome. You will know that you did what you could to stand up for yourself, and for what you believe to be right.

The Power of Confrontation

All too often, we tend to believe that confrontation must be presented with a posture of offensiveness or even with attack. This is based on the belief that we can somehow say things in a way that is loud, demanding, and intimidating enough to change people. In my experience, that is simply not so. Witness the astounding number of arguments, temper tantrums, and screaming matches that occur in marriages, and between parents with their children everyday. Yet, very little, if anything of true value or change comes from those repeated exchanges.

So, what is it then, that promotes change in people? It is not our posture, our loudness, or the nature of the demands that we make. No, it is what we say and how we say it that makes the difference. If confrontation is to have an impact at all, we must express ourselves in a thoughtful and sincere manner, based on the standard of fairness for everyone involved. What we say may then trigger a sense of conscience or responsibility in the other person. In other words, what we say may cause those we confront to hear us, perhaps for the first time. They may then give thought to what has been said, and then perhaps...they will confront themselves in a meaningful way. The point is this. When you confront with the truth as you see it, regardless of how painful or difficult, the person receiving your message will make a decision about what you have said. That person will then respond positively to your concern, or simply disregard your message and continue with the same course. What this really means then, is that confrontation can be loud, angry, or even caustic...or, it can be soft, sensitive, and calm, and yet, either approach, or any level in between, can bring the same result, if the other person hears your message, and then decides to change.

Expect Your Supervisor to be Accountable

A frequent mistake of conscientious employees is to attempt to protect oppressive and incompetent supervisors from their own unrealistic postures and decisions. When effective employees become overly responsible, they then prevent ineffective and troublesome officials from facing the consequences for their actions and postures. When the anxiety and frustration of sincere employees becomes too intense, they take whatever corrective action might be necessary to ease the pressure and stress. This relieves the anxiety and concerns of oppressive supervisors, managers, and administrators who no longer feel compelled to act responsibly or to take corrective action. They then believe that they are free to continue the destructive course that they have set, feeling self-righteous and justified.

If meaningful change is to occur, effective employees must stop allowing their feelings of anxiety and frustration to compel them to do what the oppressive or incompetent official should be doing. The more competent effective employees are, the more that oppressive and incompetent officials take advantage of them. If these circumstances remain unchallenged by those who hold positions of authority in upper management, or at an administrative level, effective workers begin to feel angry and frustrated. These feelings evolve because the employees know that they are being used and manipulated. They begin to feel resentful because they know that they are being denied their rightful recognition as conscientious and effective workers.

When you work in an oppressive and dysfunctional organization, you will be wise to have a clear understanding of where your responsibilities lie, and to do your job to the best of your ability. Then allow the oppressive and incompetent officials to face the consequences for their ineffective and troublesome methods. This will help to place responsibility where it belongs when the decisions and behavior of these officials warrant corrective action.

The Role of Contracting

In healthy organizations, true professionalism always involves an unwritten contract, or an ongoing series of unwritten contracts between employees, administrators, managers, and supervisors at all levels of the organization, and in all circumstances. These contracts, either spoken or unspoken, become the basis for effective communication, understanding, and fairness. Professional relationships should always include an exchange based on sufficient information, agreement, balance, and fairness. All too often in oppressive organizations, these concepts are either not known, or they are disregarded and ignored.

After a significant period of soul-searching, Jason, a conscientious and effective employee found it necessary to terminate his employment with an extremely dysfunctional organization. Upon submitting his resignation, the young man was asked by an upper management official to participate in an exit interview according to policy. As the interview evolved, Jason acknowledged to the official that the primary reason for his departure was the highly unprofessional, and often unethical behavioral patterns of several employees of the facility. He also described the ineffectiveness, and sometimes, bizarre postures of two members of the management team.

Upon recognizing both the sincerity and validity of the departing employee's comments, the interviewing official asked Jason if he would be willing to put his observations in writing so that the information could be used as a basis for the official to challenge the oppression and incompetence of the staff involved. While making the request, the official even acknowledged to the departing employee that he had been quite aware of the troublesome, and at times unethical practices engaged in by the employees and management staff of concern.

Upon being approached with the official's inquiry, Jason became quite uneasy, feeling pressured and trapped by the request. However, he asked the official for an opportunity to give the request some thought. Jason then contacted me for advice. I told the young man that the most likely reason that he was feeling pressured and trapped was that is exactly what was happening. I explained, first of all, there was not a single element of contracting included in the official's request.

The official was asking the departing employee to assume all of the risks associated with putting his viewpoints and beliefs in writing. Jason was offered no assurance, whatsoever, that the information would be used ethically and responsibly. He was not told who might have access to the document. Jason was not given an explanation for why his involvement was even necessary. In other words, what was the point? Upper management officials were already fully aware of the shortcomings and inappropriateness of the staff members of concern. So, why didn't they just take appropriate action to resolve the problems being caused by the oppressive and unethical practices? After all, as stewards of the workplace, and by nature of their positions within the chain of command of the organization, it was clearly their duty, right, and responsibility to do so. And, by doing what was rightfully their responsibility to do, they may have had an opportunity to retain Jason as a valuable employee. They may have even prevented the loss of yet other valuable employees in the future.

This scenario, happens all too often in the oppressive work environments of today. The oppressive and incompetent officials, who have been designated to lead, simply do not lead. They appreciate very much the pay, prestige, and recognition they receive through their positions of power and authority within the organization. However, they really do not want to earn those rewards when there are any elements of risk involved. They fear challenges from inappropriate, but strong-willed and troublesome employees. They shun the need for accountability on their parts. And, they dread the possibility that they may be named in a lawsuit or otherwise held liable.

My response to Jason was quite simple. That response, "Don't do it." I recommended instead that he leave the responsibility where it belongs...with the officials designated to lead. In essence, I informed Jason that in some cases (and this was one of them) it is simply better to "Let the dead...bury the dead!" If the officials of the organization had not been willing to do the right thing based on information already available to them, his wisest course was to move on in the hope that his next work experience will be more productive and rewarding.

Productive Workplace Negotiations

One of the most common reasons oppressive officials refuse to change is that they believe they have their employees figured out. As long as victimized employees remain predictable and anxious, they also remain easy targets for dominance and manipulation by corrupt officials. Until predictable and anxious employees finally stand up to be counted, no possibility for meaningful change or efforts toward productive negotiation is likely.

When you wish to negotiate with officials in the troubled workplace, define the problems you encounter in a timely and forthright manner. Then, as you present your concerns, focus on solutions and avoid being critical. The ability to remain thoughtful, focused, and self-assured is the hallmark of a good negotiator. Do not resort to power plays. Give the oppressive or incompetent individual your attention and use questions whenever possible and appropriate. Acknowledge the troublesome person's point of view and his or her right to it. Even if you agree only on minor points, do what you can to build on them. Slow yourself down. Do not express your opinion until you are calm enough to consider all sides of the situation. Back up your position with sound reasoning and accurate facts to support your ideas and posture.

Effective employees keep their cool during negotiation, and they take the situation in stride. They get problems corrected without causing undue disruption, and without challenging troublesome officials or other work associates any more than necessary. They don't blame anybody and they don't attack. They just use their negotiating skills to explore the problem and get it resolved. And, they do so with the goal of achieving balance and fairness for all concerned.

Think of the truly great negotiators in public life. For me, the two who most often come to mind are Henry Kissinger of the Richard Nixon era, and George Schultz who served under Ronald Reagan. Do you remember their speech patterns and how they presented themselves? Neither of these men ever lost their composure in public. As they spoke, it was always in a soft, reflective, and self-assured manner. They frequently paused between sentences, and when dealing with difficult issues, they even paused between words. Although at times when I listened, I became a bit frustrated, wanting to hurry them, Kissinger and Schultz always conveyed a thoughtful presence. But, you see, although their manner of speaking may have been somewhat frustrating, that is also one of the reasons that they were superb negotiators. When opponents become frustrated during negotiation, they begin to act impulsively, and then, they diminish their own power and effectiveness.

To become more effective in workplace negotiations:

- Let the other person do most of the talking.

- Listen without interrupting.

- When the other person is finished, clarify what has been said.

- In presenting your posture, focus on only one point at a time.

- Whenever possible, let the "facts speak for themselves."

- If the oppressive workplace official or troublesome co-worker rejects your proposal, offer a viable alternative or ask the other person what he or she would suggest.

- Remain cordial, polite, and open to alternative suggestions or proposals.

- Avoid bringing up past conflicts or disagreements.

- Stand up for what you believe and emphasize the value and benefits of your proposal.

- Above all, do not lose your temper. Each time you do, you give away your ability to be effective with the oppressive official or difficult work associate.

Getting Oppressive Officials & Colleagues to Keep Their Word

If you believe that an oppressive official or colleague will not follow up on an agreement or plan, attempt to negotiate further until you arrive at a more solid and potentially successful understanding and contract.

- Do not rely on promises at face value.

- Tie the agreement or plan to a sense of personal integrity: "Do I have your word?" or "I know you want to do the right thing!"

- Confirm the agreement or plan by restating the important facts.

- Offer a proposal that the agreement or plan be put in writing to prevent future misunderstandings.

Choose Your Wars Wisely

One of the most common areas of difficulty in a troubled workplace is the lack of healthy professional boundaries. Don't overreact or make an issue out of minor annoyances. Recognize that oppressive and incompetent individuals frequently have prejudices and points of view that they never examine and never question. You can argue with them. You can tell them they should not have those beliefs. But, you will rarely persuade them to change their opinions or postures.

I recently heard a story that, although not directly involving workplace circumstances, illustrates this point beautifully. A female supervisor came to a work associate to ask the other woman her opinion about what she should do about her husband's wish to maintain an old car that to her, had become a real burden and eyesore. The female supervisor explained that each year the couple had been investing $150.00 to $300.00 to pay for replacement parts or labor to repair the vehicle. Triggering the woman's question was her husband's wish to invest yet another $200.00. This time, to replace the car's fuel pump. As the woman began the discussion, it was obvious that she had expected the female co-worker to readily agree that the couple should get rid of the vehicle.

On the contrary, upon hearing the female supervisor's concerns her colleague said, "Now wait a minute" followed by the question, "Does your husband get some pleasure by tinkering with this car?" Of course, somewhat reluctantly the woman said "yes," that was true. The colleague then suggested that what was really important was not the question of whether the couple should keep or get rid of the car, or for that matter, who was right and who was wrong. Instead, she suggested that the pleasure obtained by the husband, and the good feelings that would evolve between the couple by not insisting that he get rid of the vehicle were the issues of importance. In particular, when compared to the bad feelings that would evolve, should the woman insist that her husband get rid of the old car. In other words, what would be gained by agreeing to the $200.00 expenditure far outweighed the negative impact of having the vehicle remain available to the husband, but perhaps maintained in a more discrete location on the couple's property.

Despite the sound advice offered to the female supervisor by her work associate, the supervisor remained adamant in insisting that the vehicle be removed from the couple's property and sold for salvage. These circumstances, combined with a continuing pattern of disagreement and frustration, created by the female supervisor's rigid and demanding posture, eventually led to the dissolution of the couple's marriage. She now lives in an apartment alone. The woman remains angry, accusing, and bitter about what she describes (to the few who will listen) as the unreasonable postures and demands of her former husband.

This story illustrates why it is important to only fight those wars worth fighting. Winning the battle in some cases may be a rather shallow victory. Eventually, you may "lose the war!" Learn to distinguish between things that are worth fighting for and things that are less important. Stand firm on what you know is right, but do so calmly. Remain thoughtful and allow for the possibility that you could be wrong. Also try giving in occasionally even if you are completely right. If you give others the "benefit of the doubt," you will usually find that they will also respond more positively to your concerns. If you can resolve difficult problems, the results will bring feelings of satisfaction and a genuine sense of achievement.

"Blind-Siding" the Oppressive Official

It is not unusual for employees to attempt to challenge the behavioral patterns of an oppressive official or troublesome colleague after carefully planning what they intend to say, and how they will say it. Shortly after the challenge, however, the employees realize that they didn't say what they wanted to say. Sincere attempts by subordinates and other employees to confront the behavioral patterns of oppressive officials or difficult co-workers are rarely successful. They are unsuccessful because the challenged individuals control the situation. They do that through denial, defensiveness, threats, and intimidating remarks. The "blind-siding" approach can often be helpful in dealing with highly demanding and controlling persons. The approach is especially effective when oppressive officials and troublesome work associates are prone to easily become out-of-control.

When blind-siding an oppressive official or other work associate, it is essential to maintain your composure and to avoid overreaction. The key is to get the other person talking instead of you. As comments are made and views are expressed, remain silent or provide only a very limited response to what is being said. As the individual continues to talk, do not allow yourself to take any critical or unfair remarks personally. In other words, don't let the official or co-worker "get your goat!" Instead, breathe deeply. While the individual is raging, use the time to think. One of the first things to consider is whether the issue ("war") is worth fighting. Once decided, you then have the opportunity to respond in a professional and self-assured manner.

A number of years ago I worked with a manager who was remarkably predictable in his response to any situation or proposal he did not wish to pursue. Whether he believed the situation would expose his ineffectiveness as a manager, or whether he simply felt resentful that the ideas presented were not his own, Lou's responses were always the same. Before fully understanding the proposal and how it might be of benefit, Lou abruptly, and without the remotest concern for the feelings of his victims, would explode into a hysterical rage. Yet, as a mid-level supervisor, it was necessary for me to deal with Lou on a daily basis. Quite often those encounters were to present concerns of the staff I supervised, whom Lou had repeatedly offended. Following various attempts to talk with Lou at a productive level, and without success, I developed a remarkably effective approach. I simply used a "blind-siding" technique when attempting to negotiate issues vital to the organization, and to the staff who looked to me for protection and support.

With each encounter, as I presented the issue, Lou would of course, digress to his primitive postures of rage and accusation. As his expressions escalated, I learned to remain totally silent. Instead of attempting to defend or justify my posture, I would simply listen attentively while concentrating on my breathing as well as I could. I found this to be particularly important in attempting to deal with Lou. His tirades were so overwhelming that I would sometimes be unable to respond in a self-assured manner. However, through concentration on my breathing…taking a deep breath…holding it a few seconds…exhaling fully and then taking another breath, I was able to remain relatively calm and in charge of my emotions. Then, after what seemed like an eternity, (actually only about ten to fifteen minutes) Lou's raging behavior would subside. At that moment, I would muster my courage and implement the blind-siding maneuver.

Among comments I would use…

- "Gee Lou, this is so unlike you. You have always been so reasonable in the past!" (Knowing of course, that he had always reacted in an out-of-control manner.)

- "You know Lou, I'm surprised that you are so upset over something like this! You have always taken things like this in stride in the past."

- "Gee Lou, you sure seem threatened by this. That surprises me!" (Once this remark was made, it was essential that I left Lou wondering what I meant. It worked best when I remained silent or vague in my responses.)

- "Gee, I don't know Lou, you just sound threatened."

And with emphasis and a look of astonishment on occasion…

- "Are you mad at me, Lou?"

Throughout the years that I worked with Lou, I never heard him say he was wrong about anything. He did, however, frequently respond as I wished him to when I used a blind-siding approach. Upon hearing me ask, "Are you mad a me, Lou?" he would promptly respond with…"Oh, oh…oh no, I'm not mad. I was just trying to let you know my posture here." Upon hearing Lou's remark, and again with a "flair for the dramatic," I would say…"Wow, Lou, you have no idea how relieved I am. When I heard what you were saying I got the idea you were mad at me. I'm thrilled to hear you say you are trying to make things clear because that is exactly what I was hoping we could do. I think we both know this issue is important, and I don't think either one of us want to make the wrong decision about it."

By that time, Lou was relatively calm, and he may also have had time to compare his response to mine. Perhaps, feeling embarrassed by his loss of control, and noting my relatively calm exterior, Lou would invariably become more willing to explore options. He quite often agreed to exactly what I wished to accomplish. Should Lou hesitate to any degree, it was typically based on…"Well, Dick, I still think it's a stupid idea, and if you're going to go through with it, you're strictly on your own. If you screw up, I'll hold you fully responsible." My typical response was…"Sounds fair to me Lou. I'll just go ahead with it and keep you informed." Although I approached Lou many times through the blind-siding process during the years I worked with him, never was there a negative outcome. I think an important point, among many others illustrated during my encounters with Lou is that people who are inappropriate become increasingly predictable over time.

It was also during the years of my association with Lou that I learned the incredible value of the "left handed" complement. For example, whenever I said something like, "You know Lou, I'm surprised that you are so upset over something like this! You have always taken things like this in stride in the past," the remark would immediately put him at a disadvantage. At that moment, Lou had no viable way to disagree with the comment without discrediting himself. How could he possibly have said, "No I haven't, Dick. I've always blown these things out of proportion in the past." Or, when I said, "Gee Lou, this is so unlike you. You have always been so reasonable in the past," it was extremely unlikely that Lou would respond with something like, "No I haven't, Dick. I've always behaved like an arrogant jerk when you have brought these concerns to me." No, on the contrary, although I often used the "left-handed" complement in blind-siding Lou, he would typically respond by agreeing that it was his nature to be fair and reasonable when problems or concerns were brought to his attention. As such, an opportunity was created to engage him in a more productive and potentially successful negotiation.

The "Columbo" Tactic

If you wish to effectively use the blind-siding approach, it is essential that you learn to become somewhat of an actor, much like "Lieutenant Columbo" portrayed in the popular television series of the 1980's. Developing the ability to convey a "perplexed" or "astonished" look as was so admirably carried-out by the lieutenant is vital. And of course, having a sense of humor to keep things in perspective is of equal importance.

In summary then, to implement the blind-siding approach…

- Maintain total silence as the other person loses control.
- Keep eye contact and let the person run out of steam.
- Do not attempt to interrupt the person or defend your posture.
- Remember to breathe.
- Remain focused on your motives and mission.
- As your anxiety diminishes, think and plan how you will respond.
- When the rage subsides, make a blind-siding comment.
- Follow the blind-siding posture with a sincere effort toward negotiation.
- Calmly present your ideas and concerns.
- Remain firm, fair, thoughtful, and professional.
- Stay true to yourself and what you believe to be right.

- Display your resolve as you demonstrate that you will not back down.

When Mental Illness is a Factor

Tom is a 42-year-old corporate attorney who has skills that clearly demonstrate brilliance in the corporate world. Within a few years after starting his career as an attorney in southern California, Tom had established a lucrative practice. He had developed a sterling reputation among his colleagues, and he was recognized as a leader in the corporate community. However, what seemed to be was not necessarily so.

Despite his apparent success, Tom's personal and professional lives were in chaos. You see, Tom was also a victim of a mental illness, which he attempted to control through the use of alcohol and illicit drugs. With his staff, Tom developed a reputation as an unpredictable tyrant. During stable periods, his staff would relax and develop a sense of hope. But, inevitably, Tom's stability would dissolve into patterns of bizarre behavior and episodes of tyrannical rage. It was not at all unusual for Tom to go to the office in the middle of the night to rearrange furnishings in his staff's office areas. He would rearrange office supplies, legal files, magazines in the waiting room, pictures on the wall, and the locations of telephones, transcribing equipment and computers.

The next day Tom would hold a staff briefing, leaving strict instructions that his arrangement of items were as they should have been in the first place. He also made it clear that should anyone relocate the items, there would be "hell to pay." The disturbed attorney did this even though his staff had not dared to move the equipment from the locations that he had placed them during his previous outbursts. Tom regularly relocated the office equipment without taking the fact into account that the equipment would now be far more difficult to operate, and that staff efficiency would be significantly curtailed. He also totally rejected any attempts on the part of the staff to explain their concerns and points of view.

For the most part, Tom's staff adopted a posture of "roll with the punch" regarding his requirements for placement of office items. What they could not roll with, however, were his out-of-control tirades without provocation. Tom would suddenly erupt into episodes of explosive rage. The episodes typically escalated to the point where Tom's employees were reduced to extreme levels of anxiety and fear. This of course, led to an ongoing pattern of staff turnover with the exception of Marie. Marie who served as the office manager was extremely dedicated, as she endured Tom's abuse for years. Finally she too, could no longer deal with the outrageous behaviors displayed by the oppressive and out-of-control attorney.

And so, Marie asked for my advice. Following several less drastic measures to attempt to assist the office manager without success, I recommended that Marie write a letter of resignation giving fair notice of her intention to leave the attorney's practice. Once the letter was written, I recommended that Marie arrange an appointment with Tom during one of his relatively stable periods so that she could hand him the letter to read. I suggested if Tom accepted her resignation, Marie should then close out her employment in the professional and conscientious manner for which she already had a reputation. I also recommended, should the attorney ask her to stay on, as he had in the past, Marie should then indicate her willingness to do so. However, I also encouraged Marie to insist that the attorney agree to seek the services of a licensed psychiatrist, and that he discontinue his use of all forms of alcohol and other drugs unless specifically prescribed by the physician. I further suggested that Marie inform the attorney that, should another episode of abusive behavior be directed toward Marie or her staff, she will again offer her resignation, but without the possibility of reconsideration.

Marie followed my recommendations to the letter. Recognizing the value of the office manager to his practice, and realizing the sincerity of her message, the attorney responded positively. Within three days, the attorney was under the care of a psychiatrist who prescribed appropriate medication. Tom has discontinued all use of alcohol and illicit drugs, and his association with his staff is beginning to flourish with Marie's continued professional support and assistance.

Now of course, not every circumstance involving mental illness will be managed as effectively or result in the positive outcome that I have just described. Another factor to consider, of course, is the potential for violence to erupt during an encounter or challenge with a mentally ill or otherwise disruptive person. Therefore, safety and the use of sound judgment are always vital factors to consider. For further guidance related to effective management of circumstances involving mental illness or for managing the potential for violence, please see Chapter Seven entitled, "The Pressure Cooker Syndrome."

Respect the Chain of Command

Only in extreme circumstances of oppression, and only after all other resources have been exhausted, is it advisable to consider violation of chain of command structure. Short of those circumstances, do not go over your supervisor's head without first telling your supervisor. Should you be dissatisfied with decisions or postures presented by an oppressive or incompetent supervisor, arrange to discuss the matter privately and in a forthright manner. Should the official fail to respond to your concerns, or to your efforts toward negotiation, tell the official that you are dissatisfied, and that you wish to appeal the decision or posture that has been presented.

Even though you may know precisely how to file the appeal following established policy and procedure, ask the official how to go about it anyway. This illustrates your firm commitment to bringing about change. It also provides the troublesome individual with an opportunity to reconsider the decision and posture. Should the supervisor adopt a verbally attacking posture, or should the official refuse to provide guidance related to the appeal process, tell the official that you intend to follow through with the appeal anyway. In either case, invite your supervisor to attend any meeting you may arrange at the next level of management. Above all, remain calm and do not lose your temper. Keep in mind that the supervisor's manager may have no idea that a problem is occurring between you and the oppressive or incompetent individual. Therefore it is important to document the processes that occur in a factual and objective manner in the event that you will need them later.

During the appointment with the manager, do not accuse your immediate supervisor of incompetence or wrongdoing. Should the oppressive official elect not to accompany you, be sure to let the manager know that you have invited the individual to attend. Then, present only your concerns and the factual circumstances of the situation. It is also important to express your hope that the matter can be resolved in a fair and just manner. If your supervisor does attend and then resorts to false allegations, do not defend yourself or make angry or hostile remarks. Instead, maintain your dignity and professionalism as you present information relevant to the issue being discussed. Calmly describe your posture and viewpoint in a clear, concise, and factual manner.

Should you come to believe that your supervisor's manager is also responding to your concerns in an unfair and oppressive manner, calmly and professionally express your dissatisfaction with the positions and responses that are being presented. Then, ask the manager for guidance on how to appeal to the next level of authority and proceed to that level. If necessary, repeat this pattern until you reach the highest level in your organization's chain of command. Should you reach that level and continue to believe that you have not been treated fairly, only two potentially viable options remain available to you. You can seek the services of an attorney to determine whether legal remedy may be a possibility. Or, you can quietly look for employment elsewhere. Once such employment has been secured, you can then leave with dignity knowing that you have done the best that you could under the circumstances that have been presented to you.

Approaching the Chief Executive Officer

Knowledge has little value unless it is used with wisdom and courage. Don't allow yourself to be intimidated by a workplace official's position, approach, or reputation. Approach people in authority as though they are professional colleagues who are no more, or no less important than you. As you approach them, present yourself from a posture of strength and confidence. Be brief, factual, concise, and professional. For the most part, those in the higher echelons of power and authority are decent people. However, they are not always aware of the oppressive and incompetent postures of officials they have designated to manage under their command. If that is the case, decent administrators will usually respond in a positive manner when they realize that corrective action is necessary.

If you are challenged or criticized by the CEO, do not lose your temper or resort to unrealistic demands. And, do not make accusations or threaten to quit. Instead express appreciation for the opportunity to discuss your concerns. In closing the discussion you might say, "Thank you for your time. I will think about what you said and let you know my response." It may also be to your advantage to quietly look for another job, but don't announce that too soon. If you make threats, accusations, or prematurely declare your intention to quit, you may limit your options and jeopardize your future. Failing to use good judgment can diminish your chance to obtain positive employment elsewhere due to the networks and "grape vines" that often exist among oppressive workplace organizations and their callous and manipulative officials.

The Importance of Timing

Always take action on your own terms. In dealing with oppressive and incompetent officials, it is essential to be aware of the importance of pacing and timing. The Kenny Rogers song, "The Gambler" provides a wonderful description of what is needed. "Yah got to know when to hold them; know when to fold them; know when to walk away, and know when to run!" An important consideration is the time of day that is most likely to provide the best chance for successful confrontation of an issue with another person. For instance, the true measure of the character of people is how they handle themselves after a tough day, or in a crisis. Character, and the ability to remain effective and decisive under stress are not determined after a good day or when things are calm! Therefore, most of us handle ourselves better in the morning. It is more difficult to handle ourselves well during the afternoon when many battles have already been fought. Knowing this fact, the best time to carry out a confrontation of someone else is in the afternoon. Why? Because through knowing the principle, we can conserve our energy throughout the day so that we have the advantage. The person not knowing of the planned confrontation will most likely expend energy with the thought of getting things done, and without need to prepare for the event to come.

Motivating the abusive person to change is also best accomplished during the recent aftermath of a crisis...or during the remorseful period following an episode of out-of-control behavior. That remorseful moment rarely occurs on the same day that the negative incident occurred. Therefore, it is wise to avoid confrontation on the day of the incident. Instead, attempt to call a truce or otherwise diffuse the situation. Most often, the remorseful period evolves during the early afternoon, on the day after the episode, and continues into the evening. Typically, during the next morning, defenses remain intact, and the risk of escalation of defensiveness or renewal of out-of-control behavior is more likely. By the third day, postures of defensiveness, manipulation, and denial are again emerging, making chances for successful intervention increasingly limited as time passes.

The 4:20 p.m. Memo Approach

In an earlier chapter, I described an approach called, "Supervision by Memo," that involves the use of written directives by oppressive officials to control and manipulate staff members without making personal contact. Clearly, such an approach used by officials of an organization to avoid acceptance of responsibility for their actions is an ineffective way for them to relate to their employees. However, what may be an ineffective, and perhaps even unethical supervisory approach to dealing with workplace issues and concerns in one circumstance, can be a dynamic, effective and completely ethical way for employees to deal with the oppression and incompetence of workplace officials in another.

I once worked with a manager who was extremely impulsive in almost all aspects of his workplace functioning. When presented with a new idea, a request for change in procedure or policy, or the need for Murray to address a particular problem brought to his attention, he would quite predictability, "fly into a rage." Murray's immediate response to issues was so abrupt and so threatening that most of the employees under his supervision, and many of his colleagues, would simply find ways to avoid him. They would bypass him in chain of command structure, struggle with the problems on their own, or otherwise, "work around him." However, in my position, those approaches were seldom possible. Knowing Murray's predictable responses, I discovered an approach that was remarkably helpful. With the more vital decisions or issues to be dealt with, I would carefully develop a plan of action. In doing so, I attempted to anticipate Murray's objections and "cover all of the bases." I would then describe the plan in a memo. It was not unusual that the memo would be prepared as early as Tuesday of a given week. However, I would hold the memo until Friday afternoon at 4:20 p.m.

You see, not only was Murray predictable with his explosiveness, he was also predictable as a "clock watcher." Knowing that Murray would be anxious to leave for the weekend promptly at 4:30 p.m., I would arrive at his office at 4:20 p.m. with the memo and a well-thought out plan. I then walked into his office rather hurriedly with a comment such as, "Gee Murray, I'm glad I caught you. I've developed a plan on the travel policy. I knew you would want to review it carefully so I put it in writing for you. Since I know you want to act on it soon, I thought you would appreciate having it for the weekend. Well, I have several things to take care of this afternoon, and I know you're busy too, so I'll let you go." I then promptly left the office before Murray had a chance to read the memo. In talking with Murray's secretary later, she described Murray as "predictable as usual." She said, "As soon as you left Murray's office, there was a moment of silence. Then suddenly, Murray broke into a tirade, ranting and raging alone in his office. The sound then subsided, and Murray stormed out of the door at precisely 4:30 p.m."

Monday at three o'clock in the afternoon, I would again arrive at Murray's office. His typical response was to grumble momentarily, actively challenge several key points, then offer a somewhat reluctant sanction to go ahead with the policy or project. That whole process being far less volatile than what might have occurred with a direct confrontation. Now, why did the approach work with relatively little conflict, compared to what might have occurred in a direct verbal exchange? I think there are several key factors and lessons to be learned from this example:

- Thoughtfulness and planning (The memo will provide a buffer).

- A calm, self-assured approach (Not rushing or being overly aggressive).

- The importance of timing (Shortly before Murray's quitting time).

- An incubation period (Providing the weekend to think about it).

- A reality testing opportunity (Touching base with Murray's secretary).

- Knowing my adversary (Murray's predictable postures and patterns).

Putting your concerns in writing also calms your emotions and helps you to clarify the issues in a concise, professional, and diplomatic fashion. This works especially well with supervisors who may be highly controlling and impulsive during direct confrontation. Make sure you have a clear understanding of the facts before putting anything on paper. Then, stick to the subject and be sure to keep it simple. As you present your thoughts and concerns in written form be brief, fair, and accurate. Don't use confusing terminology or complicated language and explanations. If possible, include suggestions for how the problem or disagreement can be resolved in a manner that will be potentially acceptable to all concerned. And by all means, do not personalize the situation by engaging in accusations, or by attacking the oppressive official's integrity and character. Just focus on the factual circumstances involved, and present your ideas about how the problem can be resolved in a practical, professional, and productive manner.

Sometimes It's Just Best to be Nice to Them!

Some oppressive supervisors will be negative and hostile toward you, no matter what you say, or what you do to try to please them. They will be hostile and negative toward you regardless of how much you try to do the right thing, or how much you try to bring fairness and reason to the situation. If you are attempting to survive in circumstances like that, sometimes the only thing you can do until you find work elsewhere is to be nice to them. The solution to dealing with some particularly difficult workplace officials is reflected in what Elwood P. Dowd said in the wonderful movie of the 1950's called "Harvey." As Elwood, played by Jimmy Stewart, talked with Dr. Willie Chumley, the kindly psychiatrist in the mental hospital, Elwood said, "Years ago my mother used to say to me, she'd say, 'In this world, Elwood, you must be oh so smart or oh so pleasant.' Well, for years I was smart. I recommend pleasant. And, you may quote me."

Virginia, a former colleague, knew the value of Elwood's philosophy and applied it very well when we worked together in a particularly stressful environment years ago. The situation involved the oppressive postures of two upper level officials who created a rather overwhelming amount of anxiety, frustration and "office politics" in the facility. And of course, several of us were frequently, "called on the carpet" due to speaking out when we really would have been wise to keep quiet. However, that was not the case with Virginia. Somehow, Virginia was always able to remain above the fray. Throughout each day, Virginia appeared calm and relaxed. She never seemed to become emotionally distraught, and she never once became embroiled in controversial issues or discussions.

After once again being challenged for making a stand on a controversial issue, I asked Virginia how she was able to avoid similar circumstances. Without hesitation Virginia said, "Oh, that's easy! I just stay in my office, I do my work, I smile a lot, I'm nice to everybody whether I agree with them or not, and I do whatever they tell me to do. Then, when I am finished for the day, I get the heck out of here and forget all about it." Although I have never been totally able to avoid becoming involved in controversial matters in the work environment, there have certainly been times when following Virginia's approach has served me well.

Telling Your Supervisor What You Really Think

No one can put up with oppression and incompetence indefinitely without losing self-respect and confidence. But, it is very difficult for employees to challenge those who hold positions of power over them. It is even more difficult when they are employed in an oppressive environment under an oppressive administration. If you do choose to challenge an oppressive or incompetent official under such circumstances, you will be wise to remain thoughtful, and to use sound judgment. These officials almost always become defensive when being presented with criticism about their decisions or performance.

- Keep in mind that you will have a greater chance for success when you challenge a workplace official if you have a reputation for professionalism and a history of positive employment.

- Remain thoughtful during the encounter and do not become too aggressive or demanding. Otherwise, the official may feel overwhelmed or angry, and then become more resentful and defensive.

- Don't disclose your hand until you have to, and when you do, do it only on your terms. If an official tries to arrange a meeting on short notice, to discuss what you believe will be a volatile issue, ask for time to finish a project. Use that time to clear your thoughts and plan your comments.

When Formal Intervention is the Only Choice Remaining

Employees who believe they are in control of their work-related circumstances can withstand an enormous amount of pressure and even thrive on it. Employees who feel helpless in the workplace can hardly cope at all. You may find it necessary to consider formal intervention when all of your other resources have been exhausted. In situations involving extreme oppression or incompetence, to do nothing is the worst of all possible choices that you can make. The oppressive and incompetent individual who abuses power and authority will not seek meaningful change as long as that official maintains a position of power and control, and as long as the oppressive postures remain unchallenged in an authoritative manner.

The Administrative Role

Oppressive and incompetent supervisors are usually too deeply involved in themselves to consider change without authoritative intervention. Therefore, attempts toward intervention by subordinates must have the full support of higher officials if successful and enduring results are to be obtained. If such support is not forthcoming, workers are best advised to quietly build their strength, options, and resources. When those factors are in place, if improvement has not evolved, employees may then be best advised to submit their resignations in a professional manner after securing employment elsewhere.

When formal challenges are initiated, managers and supervisors who abuse the power of their offices must be dealt with through dynamic intervention. The course of action must include a well throughout and systematic approach, carried-out through the leadership, guidance, and full sanction of the chief executive officer. Even if such support exists, if the troublesome official refuses to respond positively, employees may have to leave their jobs due to the potential for undermining and revenge that may follow in the intervention's wake.

Christy Pious

Christy Pious in an extremely deceptive and controlling office manager who frequently describes herself to be devoutly religious. Yet, she routinely displays blatant disregard for the legitimate concerns presented by Ashley, one of her most hard-working and dedicated employees. Wishing to vacate Ashley's position to create an opportunity for one of her friends, Christy initiated a highly manipulative and insensitive scheme to force Ashley to quit her job. In implementing the scheme, Christy deliberately relieved several of her favorites from responsibility for performing portions of their assigned duties and responsibilities. Christy then assigned those duties to Ashley's already overburdened workload. Although Ashley displayed extreme dedication and effort in attempting to meet Christy's excessive demands, she eventually became so overwhelmed that she found it necessary to appeal for some level of relief. Upon hearing Ashley's appeal, Christy offered superficial excuses and blatant dishonesty, insisting that nothing could be done to provide relief because, "after all, everyone else is overworked too."

After struggling with her overburdened circumstances for several months, Ashley became compelled to appeal to the agency's chief executive officer. Upon reviewing Ashley's circumstances, the CEO required Christy to reassign her favorites to their original work assignments. Unfortunately, Ashley's victory was short lived. Christy remained extremely bitter and filled with the need for revenge. Knowing that the CEO was a rather distant and inattentive official, Christy simply waited for a few weeks. She then initiated a subtle form of departmental restructuring that resulted in Ashley being assigned even more work than before. However, the unscrupulous manager actively misrepresented the circumstances of her department to the CEO in advance. This time, the CEO did no investigation, whatsoever. Instead, the preoccupied CEO fully supported Christy's insensitive and unfair posture as she deceptively informed him that no options were available to relieve anyone's workload. As such, Ashley, then feeling even more overwhelmed and defeated, was left to endure the unfair circumstances, or to leave her job just as Christy had hoped would occur.

Letting the Chips Fall

Carrying out an intervention on an oppressive or incompetent supervisor can be one of the most difficult and challenging courses of action that you will ever have to face. You may be fearful of retaliation or of losing your job. You may realize that if the intervention fails, your circumstances could then be worse than before. It requires great courage for an employee to carry through with a plan under such threat. But, it may be necessary to take just such a risk if the troublesome or ineffective supervisor is to ever change.

If done with sincerity and professionalism, an intervention directed toward the controlling and troublesome behavior of an oppressive official can be successful. But, in doing so, it is essential that the process be carried-out with the full support of the chief executive officer. However, do not agree to engage in such action alone, even when the CEO proposes that you do so. Suggest instead, that all of your subordinates, and any other appropriate workplace colleagues should also be involved. Otherwise, you might find yourself being used as a scapegoat, and a readily available target for retaliation in a now, even more hostile work environment.

A thoughtful and well-planned intervention, carried-out by employees, along with the full support and sanction of the chief executive officer can be an effective way to help oppressive or incompetent supervisors and managers to see the troublesome situation more clearly. Unlike Christy Pious, they may then become willing to make changes that will lead to more positive and rewarding workplace circumstances for you, and for your colleagues.

Patterns of Defensiveness

Oppressive and incompetent officials are usually the last to recognize their own postures of excessive control and offensiveness. Elaborate defenses are an integral part of the make-up of these troublesome individuals. These defenses almost always render them resistant to exploring their oppressive and ineffective supervisory or management styles. Nor, are they willing to accept responsibility for the consequences of those postures. Oppressive and incompetent supervisors and managers continue their troublesome postures and methods despite overwhelming evidence that they are causing serious frustration and anxiety for the employees that they have been designated to lead.

Three Classic Defensive Postures of the Oppressive or Incompetent Official

1. Rationalization	*(I have to treat my staff this way. If I didn't, nothing would get done around here.)*
2. Projection	*(It's not my fault. My staff is always screwing up.)*
3. Denial	*(What problem? They're just a bunch of complainers.)*

When oppressive and incompetent officials first learn that employees and administrators expect them to give up their patterns of excessive control and troublesome behavior, they almost always become extremely angry. They typically believe that they are right and everyone else is wrong. It is usually useless to try to coax, to extract promises, or to threaten the troublesome official unless the employee making the threat is totally willing and able to carry it out. Idle threats will only give the supervisor or manager a renewed sense of destructive confidence. Such threats in fact, inadvertently give the oppressive or incompetent official permission to continue the destructive behavior and abusive activities. This pattern must be overcome if offensive officials are not to continue with their oppressive postures and troublesome practices.

Weighing the Risks

Despite the risks, change in the oppressive work environment must somehow occur. Sometimes the only way we can be treated fairly in important relationships and circumstances is to risk everything. Health in the workplace cannot exist without compassion and fairness. To accept employment without these qualities is to eventually destroy the morale of even the most capable workers. Employees in an oppressive work environment must come to understand and accept the concept "Half measures avail us nothing." Accepting the challenge will help employees to become more effective and confident, regardless of what the troublesome official might do.

Employees, supervisors, managers, and administrators must also accept the fact that change and innovation are essential to success in today's dynamic work environments. The starting point is in learning how to mutually solve problems and in developing an environment for talking and listening to one another. If employees and workplace officials are committed to these efforts, and if they are willing to make changes, an environment is created for individual achievement and for collective success. When a positive environment is created, there are great opportunities for individual growth and accomplishment in the workplace. If workplace relationships are to truly thrive, there must be commitment that is formed in an atmosphere of productivity, decency, fairness, and mutual respect.

5

PATTERNS OF SURVIVAL IN THE WORKPLACE

Weathering the Storm

During my professional career, I have known so many employees who have struggled with stressful issues in oppressive work environments. Among them, many have said, "You know, Dick, I just don't know what to do. I love my work, but I hate my job!" When I ask what they mean by the contradictory remark, some say, "Well, I really enjoy the work that I do, but my supervisor is just a tyrant. He finds fault with everything I do." Others say, "My supervisor acts as though she is the only one who knows how to do anything. When I suggest a way that I can do something more efficiently, she disregards my suggestions or belittles me in front of the rest of the staff."

Some employees say, "I am just at a loss. You see, I have three supervisors to report to and they all think that their projects come first. If I give one project a priority, the others complain. They come in screaming and demanding to know why their work isn't finished. It wouldn't be so bad if one person were making those demands. I could handle that and give priority to the assignment. But, that's not how it works. Instead, all three are ranting and raving at once. That leaves me frustrated and embarrassed. I would quit, but I need the money to support my family. Besides, I know I can do an excellent job when I have a fair chance."

Another circumstance described by employees is, "We have an employee at work that is so rude and obnoxious that it's impossible to work with him. He is always complaining or playing one person against the other. He undermines and back stabs every chance he gets. My co-workers and I have tried to talk to him, but he just blows us off. Finally, I couldn't put up with it anymore so I asked to talk to my supervisor. The supervisor listened to me, but then he said, 'Well, you know, that's just the way old George is. In fact, I have the same problem with him.' When I pressured the supervisor to do something, he came back a few days later and said, 'Look, I've thought about what you said about George, and there is nothing I can do. You will just have to learn to put up with him like I do'."

Of course, these dedicated employees will not put-up with this type of supervisory oppression and incompetence indefinitely. One day they will find an opportunity to leave. That, of course may be a good thing for the employees, but it will be a major loss for the organization.

In the Midst of Conflict & Discontent

Do you find yourself becoming increasingly resistant and frustrated as you think about going to work in the morning, or when your shift is scheduled to begin? When you are getting ready to go to work after a weekend, or after a few days off, do you begin to feel anxious and depressed? Do you become preoccupied with feelings of dread, and uncertain about what you will have to face next while you are at work? If these patterns are being experienced, and if they are allowed to continue, they will eventually lead to feelings of chronic dissatisfaction and discontent. When oppressed employees live with dissatisfaction and discontent, the problems are then perpetuated, and fear and resentment take over. This is why conscientious employees need to be thoughtful and strong if their circumstances in an oppressive workplace are to ever improve.

Positive and optimistic employees often have to deal with difficult and stressful circumstances in the troubled workplace. But, instead of constantly complaining, and taking their unresolved feelings out on their colleagues, friends, and families, they just keep doing their jobs in a responsible manner. Despite the difficulties and challenges that they face, they remain steadfast in their search for solutions, and they discover ways to rise above the troubling circumstances of the oppressive work environment.

Plan the Crisis

The idea of planning the crisis is not a contradiction in terms. Fire drills prevent disaster, and planning for crisis can do the same. It is not by accident that we have adopted policies in many public and private sector buildings that require regular fire drills. The purpose of the drill is to prevent accidents and death. And, it works. In facilities where fire drills are regularly conducted, property damage and loss of life are reduced when disaster does strike. So, if this approach will work to reduce the impact of disaster in an organization, why would it not do the same for us as individuals? If wise, we will conduct our own personal "fire drills."

Anticipating and planning how to handle negative experiences in the workplace provides feelings of confidence and a sense of control over events. It is also a good strategy to avoid overreacting in stressful situations. Crisis can be planned for by asking yourself, "What is the worst thing that could possibly happen in this situation, and what would I do to handle it?" Once your plan is in place, follow the British proverb "Hope for the best…as you prepare for the worst." In anticipating the difficult circumstances that you may encounter, planning the crisis will help you to approach the challenge in a more confident and effective manner. This is true even during those situations in which the crisis does not emerge as anticipated because you will have already envisioned handling yourself well in stressful circumstances. It is also helpful to realize, when crisis is planned for, rarely does the worst possible scenario actually occur.

Approaches to Survival

Knowing what to do is not enough if you have not developed your strength and self-discipline. Learn to say what you mean, and to do so in a thoughtful and professional manner. Do what you know to be the right thing to do. Positive assertiveness involves the ability to express your thoughts and feelings while allowing others to do the same. Workplace officials and colleagues will respect your firm postures and opinions more than evasive maneuvers that conceal your true feelings and concerns. You will respect yourself more too. If supervisors and employees engage in meaningful communication, and if they seek to resolve differences in an atmosphere of fairness and professionalism, individual and collective differences can often be overcome, however irreconcilable they may seem.

Mood Altering Substances

Although alcohol and other mood altering drugs can be used to relieve emotion and workplace tension temporarily, these substances do not remove the oppressive conditions or patterns of incompetence that cause the stress. Drugs in fact, may create more conflict and stress than they take away. They should only be taken in extreme circumstances, and then only with the full awareness and recommendation of your doctor. Chemicals, including alcohol, that mask conflict and the symptoms of stress do not help you adjust to workplace oppression and incompetence. They do not help you to resolve conflicts with co-workers. The ability to effectively resolve differences and handle tension in the workplace comes from within you. It does not come from something that you use to change your perceptions of life and the circumstances that you experience.

Burn Off the Aggression

When the anger and frustration that we experience on the job is turned inward, the results are depression and illness. When it is misdirected toward our families, friends and colleagues, anger becomes a destructive force that creates barriers and leads to further resentment and alienation.

When I entered the field of addiction counseling many years ago, the stresses of the two-year training and internship program were far greater than I had anticipated. Although discussion of those concerns was encouraged as part of the training curriculum, I chose to say nothing, fearing expulsion if the training officials were to discover how "screwed up" I really was. But, upon arriving home after a day at the facility, I would promptly size up the situation. Seeing that the evening meal was only partially prepared was enough for me to display a full-blown temper tantrum. With anger and rage I would say, "June, what's the matter with you? You know I have to study for a test tonight. I told you that I wanted you to have supper ready when I got home. Boy, what a wife you are. Here I am, struggling to get through this training program, working like a slave, and trying to stay afloat. I would think that you would be able to see that and be more considerate. But no...you don't even have a simple little thing like supper ready so I can study."

Of course, what I had not recognized was that June's life was just as difficult as mine, or perhaps even more so. June was also struggling. She was working full-time and trying to maintain home and children. And, she even had to put up with me, and with my irrational outbursts. On the other hand though, when I blasted June with my unkind remarks, it felt "fantastic!" You see, all of the pent up rage and anger that I had accumulated that day, and in fact, during a lifetime, came flooding to the surface, and out of proportion to circumstance. But then, within seconds I felt nothing but remorse and regret. As the anger and rage subsided, I saw the pain on June's face. I heard the hurt in her voice...and I felt ashamed!

Now, how was this pattern overcome? Actually, it was overcome quite by accident. You see, June and I lived with our children in a community located about nine miles from the training center I attended. As I left the facility one afternoon and approached the freeway, I was filled with anger and frustration as usual. At the same time, I felt a sense of remorse about my outbursts at home during the previous evening. While driving, and in the midst of my thoughts, I began to scream, holler, rant, and rage, pounding angrily on the steering wheel and dashboard of my car. By the time I arrived home, I felt free and calm, thereby providing an opportunity for June, the kids, and me to spend one of the most relaxed and enjoyable evenings we had experienced in quite some time. From that day forward, and continuing to this day, I have engaged in my ranting and raving routine alone whenever frustration levels begin to build. During more than thirty years, the approach has never failed to bring some level of stability and relief.

I must offer a word of caution, though. Have you ever been in a situation and really involved with something, when suddenly you get that uneasy feeling that someone may be watching you? Well, every once in a while, when I have been driving down the freeway, screaming and raging to my hearts content, suddenly, the sense of being watched has come over me. Sure enough, as I looked out of the side window of my car, there he was. Apparently in the midst of my tirade, I had failed to realize that a man had pulled up beside me. Seeing what I was doing alone in the car, the man was giving me one of those looks that sort of said it all. The look that the man was giving me conveyed the message, "What's with this character? Is he crazy or what? I better contact the Highway Patrol and ask them to check this guy out. Maybe he needs to be locked up in a psychiatric ward."

Well, I had a way of dealing with the intruder too! I would either, accelerate my vehicle to about ninety miles per hour and leave the man in the dust, or I would slow it down to about forty and let him get ahead of me. Then, as he continued into the distance, I would start in on him. "And you, you moron, what in the hell were you looking at? Besides, just what makes you think you have the right to snoop into somebody else's business when they are trying to stabilize their mental health?"

Now, why is it that something could seem so silly, and yet have such power to ease rage and frustration? Well, one theory suggests that we all have two memory systems. One memory system is said to center in the brain, and involves the ability to use our intellect, reason, and judgment. The other memory system is believed to be located throughout our bodies and serves as a "storehouse" for all experiences involving intense feelings. This system, called the "subconscious" memory system is believed to be only a storehouse. It does not have the ability to make judgments, therefore, it cannot determine right from wrong. It also cannot identify what is real and what is not real. Based on this theory, when you or I scream and holler about someone or something, from the perspective of subconscious memory, it is actually occurring. It makes no difference whether we are screaming into the wind, or whether the other person is there to hear it. As a result, when we engage in a verbal barrage, we are actually freeing the unresolved frustrations that have been stored in our subconscious memory. We can then explore the matter more realistically and deal with others in a more effective way.

Exercise & Physical Fitness

All too often when we are feeling frustrated and depressed due to oppression and incompetence in the workplace, we tend to do just the opposite of what we should do to make ourselves feel better, and to help us function in a productive and stable manner. For example, most of us have had "one of those days," when we have gone the extra mile, and somebody wanted us to go two more. When nothing we did pleased anybody, and everything we did to get things corrected turned out to be wrong. When we have such a day, we are likely to go home and sit in front of the TV. We remain distracted by our troubles at work, and we continue to feel sorry for ourselves. What we are doing is the exact opposite of what we really should be doing. Why? Because behaving this way only makes things worse.

When you hold unresolved feelings inside and then compensate for those circumstances through assuming a sedentary way of life, you are providing the same remedy for emotional exhaustion that is appropriate for physical exhaustion, and it just doesn't work. You are simply allowing the unresolved feelings to simmer and fester internally. When that happens, circumstances are created in which you will most likely take the unresolved feelings back into the work environment where they will continue to impact upon your ability to function effectively. Or, the unresolved feelings will accumulate to the point where you will take them out on yourself through developing physical or emotional problems. Another possibility is that the unresolved feelings will build until you begin to take them out in an irrational and unfair manner on those you care about.

If we still lived in a world where we spent fourteen hours or more per day working at hard physical labor, the natural, sensible thing for us to do would be to go home, rest, and let our bodies recuperate. However, most of us do not work that hard anymore, in a physical sense. No, most often our experiences in the workplace today involve emotional exhaustion, with only a relatively minor physical component. Because our bodies and minds tend to store the tension that comes from experiencing emotional crisis in our muscles, our bodies become tense and rigid. As a result, we are unable to truly relax. We are unable to defuse the emotional energy and frustration we have stored.

Exercise is an excellent way to reduce the workplace pressure and stress that is created and experienced in oppressive work environments. It gives you time to think through the problems and frustrations of the day. Exercise helps to lift your spirits while building strength and endurance. It increases your ability to be more thoughtful and alert. Instead of sitting around and doing nothing but dwelling on the frustrations of the troubled workplace, do something to diffuse the stored up energy and tension. It is almost always reported that stressed out employees who engage in twenty to thirty minutes of an aerobic type of activity feel rejuvenated in physical stamina and emotional clarity.

By diffusing bodily tension, you will be able to rest and sleep more soundly. As a result, it is less likely that you will unfairly burden your friends and family. A vigorous program of physical exercise will also help you to avoid taking the intensity of your frustrations back into the workplace where they may cause you to react in a manner that will only make matters worse. But, of course remember, before embarking on a strenuous exercise program of your own, seek the approval of your doctor.

The Benefits of Relaxation

Employees who work in oppressive work environments are often filled with so much tension and anxiety that they do not allow themselves time to relax, or to rejuvenate their energy and spirits. The pressures created by oppressive and incompetent officials can take a heavy toll on your physical and emotional well-being. When you ignore the need for physical and mental relaxation, stress builds up internal pressures like a corked volcano. And, the results become increasingly predictable. When the volcano erupts, so does the inappropriate behavior that contributes to physical and emotional disorders.

In oppressive work environments, stress is a fact of life. But, stress doesn't have to be a way of life. By using simple relaxation techniques, you will be able to reduce emotional anxiety and physical tension to a more manageable level. As you become familiar with these techniques, you can apply them whenever unwanted stress occurs. Using a systematic approach to relaxation will teach you how to relax your muscles and your mind. After practicing the approach for a few weeks, systematic relaxation will become a natural part of you.

By using techniques for muscle relaxation, effective breathing, and focused attention, you will develop a personal resource for control that will serve you well as you face stressful situations and circumstances in an oppressive work environment. With practice, your body will become more dynamic and flexible, and your mind will become clearer. As a result, you will feel more refreshed and energetic. Through commitment to the process, the benefits will then generalize to your daily activities and functioning. By taking the time to practice relaxation techniques on a regular basis, you will give yourself a chance to unwind, and to be ready for the next challenge that oppressive officials or troublesome colleagues might bring.

An Approach to Systematic Relaxation

Phase One:

In a quiet room dim the lights and play soft, easy listening music in the background. Allow your body to begin a movement toward relaxation as you sit in a comfortable chair. Once you are reasonably relaxed and comfortable, think of your feet and tense the muscles of your feet as tightly as you can and hold. As you hold the tension, think about how it feels for about ten seconds, then relax the tension and think about how that feels for about ten seconds. Repeat the procedure with your feet three times, then move to the calves of your legs and repeat the same pattern of tension and relaxation three times in that location. Continue with each part of your body and muscle groups in turn, moving from your calves to your knees, thighs, groin, buttocks, stomach, back, chest, shoulders, arms, hands, neck and ending with your head and facial muscles.

Elapsed Time—Ten to Fifteen Minutes

Phase Two:

While remaining comfortable in your chair, think about your breathing. Take a deep breath and hold for from five to ten seconds. Then exhale as completely as you can and hold for from five to ten seconds. Continue the process of deep breaths, holding, exhaling, and holding.

Elapsed Time—Three to Five Minutes

Phase Three:

Remain comfortable in your chair and continue to breathe deeply while thinking of two pleasant words. For example, you might choose the words peace and love. Note that any two pleasant words will do. If you wish, you can even choose to use two pleasant sounds. Then, as you inhale, think of one of the pleasant words or sounds and say it to yourself in timing and harmony with your intake of breath. Then as you exhale, think of the other word or sound and say that to yourself in timing and harmony with your exhalation of breath. For example, while inhaling slowly say, p_e_e_e_a_c_e, and while exhaling slowly say, l_o_o_o_v_e.

Elapsed Time—Seven to Ten Minutes

Overall time span for all three phases: Twenty to Thirty Minutes

Establish a Special Place of Your Own

A variation of focused attention on two pleasant sounds or words is to imagine you are in pleasant and relaxing surroundings. To do this, close your eyes and relax after completing phases one and two of the systematic approach to relaxation. Then, visualize yourself in a pleasant place. Perhaps floating in a mountain stream or in the middle of a peaceful lake. Or, you might try imagining yourself lying on the sand of a gleaming white beach, with wispy clouds drifting overhead in a clear blue sky. Choose whatever might represent a serene and peaceful scene for you. As you establish yourself in this scene, notice the incidental things in the environment. Listen to the quiet ripples on the water and other sounds that are present in your mind. Listen to the gentle rustling of the leaves. Feel the warmth of the sun touching your body. Notice the feel of the sand against your skin. Feel the soft breeze blowing across your brow.

The more of these incidental details you picture in your imagination as you engage in the process of systematic relaxation, the more effective you will be at using this technique as a way to manage the stress you experience under oppressive circumstances. Simply stay relaxed and allow it to happen. If unwanted thoughts or images occur while you are engaging in the process, observe them with detachment. Don't hold on to them. Just let them drift away. Regular practice of this approach to relaxation will cause the mental images to emerge in a clearer fashion and more readily with each session. Each of us needs a quiet place within our own mind, no matter how rough the waves may be on the surface. This quiet place within serves as a means of escaping from tension, worry, and pressures. It will refresh you and enable you to return to your world better prepared to cope. Just a few quiet minutes every day makes a big difference.

Patterns of Workplace Dissatisfaction

It is common for employees to disagree with each other from time to time as they perform their daily work assignments. However, chronic dissatisfaction in the workplace becomes a destructive force that quietly tears away the fabric of people and relationships, a little at a time. The process is a deceptive one in that at any given moment each person recognizes the problem, yet, there evolves a misleading belief that it is really not so bad. The true risk of chronic dissatisfaction in employment lies not in the ongoing situation. It lies in what is yet to come. When one chooses to do nothing, the price is paid in a future filled with bitterness and regret. "If only I had…" becomes the catchphrase for the future, and the standard for life itself. The oppressive workplace can be a particularly lonely place for a truly capable and creative person. This phrase, perhaps more than any other, describes the result of any creative and capable person's decision to remain in a state of chronic dissatisfaction in a workplace that is insensitive to the needs and feelings of employees.

Most of us are capable of resolving the difficulties we face in life, and in the workplace, if we become determined to do so. No one can ever let us down if we have not been leaning on anyone else. No one can make us unhappy, angry, or disappointed if we do not depend on other people for our welfare or motivation. An example is what happened the last time my computer needed repair. I took it to a service representative explaining what had gone wrong, and how important it was that I have the computer back within a week to complete a priority project. The technician said he saw no problem at all with having the equipment repaired and back to me in even less time then I had specified. I expressed appreciation and left.

One week later, I stopped at the facility to see how the work was progressing. Much to my dismay, the computer remained in the case in the exact location where I had left it. When I talked with the technician, he agreed that I was right, offered several excuses, and pledged that "Monday, at the latest" the computer would be repaired. He even said he would give it special attention by doing the job on the weekend. Imagine my reaction when I walked into the repair shop on the following Tuesday and found that the computer...you guessed it...remained in the case in the same location. Nothing had been done.

At that point I went to talk with the manager. The "manager," a swarthy and bullish man, listened to my comments then said..."You know, you are not the first one that told us this. Harvey does this all of the time. I don't know what we are going to do with him!" Wow! Talk about decisive "leadership." Upon hearing the manager's comments, I walked over to my computer, picked it up and left. I then purchased a book on basic computer maintenance and repair. I spent a few hours learning how to correct the problem, and never took the computer to a shop for repair again. I just fix it myself and remarkably, most of the time, it works!

Resolving Chronic Dissatisfaction

What can employees do to improve the quality of their jobs? The most important thing is to accept responsibility to make things more positive. Some questions that the chronically dissatisfied employee must answer, and then act upon include:

- What are you willing to do to make things better and make yourself happy?
- What are you willing to do to make your work more rewarding?
- Are you willing to take these actions in a spirit of cooperation and fairness?
- Are you willing to build on these principles with a posture of concern and professionalism even though others may not respond in a like manner?

Within the framework of these questions, their answers, and the initiative to take decisive action lay the solutions to the dilemma of chronic dissatisfaction in the oppressive workplace. If we have a legitimate complaint or concern, we can see if there is something constructive we can do to correct it. If we can do nothing, we need to accept it as one of life's conditions and move on.

Am I Better Off...Worse Off...or About the Same?

When you are struggling with circumstances in an oppressive work environment and there seems to be no way to resolve the situation, it is essential that you develop a means of measuring progress, or the lack of progress. An effective way to bring this about is to privately put your life on a time frame in segments of from one or two months into the future. For example, you might say, "It is now the fifteenth of the month. I am going to continue to do the best I can to resolve this situation until the fifteenth of next month. Then, on that day, I am going to ask myself the question, 'Am I better off...worse off...or about the same...as I was one month ago'." If you can honestly say, "I am better off than I was one month ago," even if that is only slightly the case, ask why that is and build on the positive response and direction suggested. On the other hand, if your answer is "I am worse off...or about the same"...ask yourself why that is and redirect your actions based on the answer.

This concept ties in with the three "A's" of all personal and professional growth. Those three A's are awareness, acceptance, and action. Although awareness and acceptance of oppressive circumstances are important components for achieving stability and success, they really do nothing to bring about meaningful change or improvement. It is only through adding the third component, action, that we realize movement toward an improved quality of life. Therefore, if you find at the conclusion of each time frame that your answer to the question, "Am I better off...worse off...or about the same..." is positive, you will know that you should continue to build on the positive course of action you have chosen.

On the other hand, should you realize with honest and straightforward assessment that you are worse off...or about the same, then clearly you must choose a different course. Should you discover after several time frames have passed, that your answer is worse off...or about the same, you can then reach only one of two possible conclusions. One is that you must change course as an attempt to bring about the desired change. The other possibility is that you have become excessively dependent upon the oppressive environment, and that you have in essence, become a chronically dissatisfied complainer.

Self-Esteem in the Workplace

"I'll never get it right."

"Anyone could have done it."

"I always mess things up."

"I should have…"

"I shouldn't have…"

It is all too easy to focus on our mistakes and shortcomings, and decrease our self-esteem in the process. Many employees have a compulsive need for attention and approval. They are unable to recognize and appreciate themselves as worthy and adequate individuals. They need confirmation that they are "okay," and that workplace officials and colleagues accept and approve of them.

Answering Questions Nobody Ever Asked Us

Employees with low self-esteem tend to spend a large part of their time at work answering questions nobody ever asked them. In other words, they frequently struggle with thoughts of how they are doing. They wonder what other employees think of them, and feel dread about who will be critical of them next. As a result, they carry out an internal dialogue in defense of their perceived limitations, mistakes, and failures. However, what they fail to realize is that they almost always look and function a lot better than they believe.

Looking at the Other Employee's Outside Through Our Inside

Workers with low self-esteem tend to look at the outside of other employees through their internal view of themselves. They constantly compare how they are doing with the behavior and attitude presented by those with whom they associate. These employees fail to realize that, although their co-workers appear quite confident and "put together" on the surface, most of them struggle with the same kinds of anxieties and turmoil on the inside. This has become clear on many occasions over the years as I have worked with corporate officials and public sector dignitaries who present themselves as powerful and capable in conducting the daily affairs of their offices. However, when these individuals discuss their personal lives and feelings, they appear quite different. When their professional image is set aside, I find them to have the very same struggles that I have encountered, and the same as those presented by my less distinguished or powerful associates.

There is Hope!

Loss of self-esteem comes when we act differently from the way we believe we should act. When employees believe they are inferior and inadequate, they look to others for respect and admiration. They are overly cautious due to the unfair challenges and unrealistic postures that have been experienced in an oppressive work environment. And, they are overly impressed by the success of other workers and the power that oppressive individuals may hold. Self-esteem can be improved. Don't permit the negative experiences of the past to hold you back.

Employees who view themselves in a positive light see difficult encounters with oppressive officials and troublesome co-workers as challenging and growth producing learning experiences. They recognize their worth is not solely a function of what others think of their work-related skills, their personal opinions and perceptions, or how well they handle their jobs. Employees with low self-esteem crumble when they feel inadequate or when they make an error. They avoid talking about important issues because they believe that they will feel embarrassed, and that they will have behaved foolishly if they say what they really think. They don't express their opinions due to fear of being ridiculed by their colleagues and supervisors.

The "Fragmentist"

During the first year of my training to learn the fundamentals of addiction counseling, there were many challenges presented to the six of us who had been selected to participate. However, being new to the field, with a program of development that was quite vigorous, none of us were certain that we would survive the year. Adding, "insult to injury" was a component involving a review of each trainee's progress *(or lack, there of)*, conducted without the trainees by the clinical director and staff. On the day of the first review, all trainees were subdued and preoccupied, fearing the possibility that any or all of us could be summarily expelled.

As the progress review closed, it was time for lunch. I was in the cafeteria, although unable to eat due to anxiety when the staff arrived. They of course, were quite upbeat and jovial, talking excitedly about events planned for the coming weekend. Then, as my clinical supervisor approached my table he offered the remark in passing, "Well, there's Dick. You know, it's unusual to have a 'fragmentist' with us. We really didn't have one around here until you came along." Now, perhaps you have heard the phrase, "a little knowledge can be dangerous." Well, that was certainly the case as I heard Ron's remark.

You see, we had been studying abnormal psychology during the semester, and I knew just a little bit about Schizophrenia. Knowing that Schizophrenics have difficulty with thought confusion, I, in my profound wisdom concluded that the staff was aware of my "fragmented" thought processes and had determined that I was a Schizophrenic. Surely on Monday, I would be called to someone's office to be told that I was to be dropped from the training program. Not only that, with such a serious condition, the staff might arrange my committal to a psychiatric facility.

Of course, my weekend was far from restful, but somehow I endured the agony. The next Monday I arrived at the training facility filled with dread, in anticipation of the ordeal to come. But, much to my surprise, nothing happened. It was just "business as usual" for the next several days. Of course, it was not business as usual for me. Inside, I was like a simmering volcano. Finally, I could stand it no longer. I went to my clinical supervisor's office and asked to speak with him privately. In the midst of expressions of anxiety and frustration, I told him of my dismay with having heard him tell me of my diagnosis as a "fragmentist." After blurting it out, I asked why it was that the staff had been willing to allow me to continue with the training, with me in my condition.

Ron was momentarily stunned. Then he said, "No, you dummy…I said pragmatist." Hearing and seeing his response with the typical touch of humor, I was somewhat relieved, but with a remaining dilemma. At that point I didn't know what Ron meant when he identified me as a pragmatist either. Of course, I certainly wasn't going to tell him that! Instead, I sat impatiently until Ron finished his mildly critical, and somewhat humorous mini-lecture on the virtues of trust as a tool for communication and healing. However, as soon as I was excused, I rushed to my dictionary. It was there that I discovered, in the context of Ron's remark, a pragmatist is simply a person who displays the tendency to retain what is practical and useful, and to discard what is not.

Postures for High Self-Esteem

- Believe in yourself and respect your own uniqueness.
- Act for what you believe to be right and don't be afraid to take risks.
- Be spontaneous and don't take yourself too seriously.
- Don't compare yourself to others, or worry so much about what they think of you.

- Be yourself. Do not attempt to be all things to all people.
- Maintain regard for others and reverence for life.
- Set your own standards and remain decisive under stress.

Most of us are stronger and more competent than we realize. Developing a positive self-image permits us to become more capable and confident as we rely on the abilities, talents, and strengths that are already available to us. Employees who feel good about themselves assume responsibility easily, tolerate frustration well and approach new challenges with confidence and enthusiasm. We must also learn to accept life as it really is. Everyone has ups and downs, good days and bad days. Instead of trying to be perfect, don't take yourself so seriously. In fact, even crisis can be a good thing! If we experience no meaningful challenges or struggles in life, we have little to offer, and we remain a limited resource for ourselves and for others.

The "Whiners"

Beware the helpless! Co-workers who claim to be helpless and frightened can be powerful manipulators. Whiners are also known as "squeaky wheels" because they constantly maneuver and manipulate as they attempt to get their way, or as they attempt to take unfair advantage of colleagues. Whiners frequently complain that they are overworked, and that they need more help. But, they rarely try to change their situation through their own initiative and effort. Instead, they typically ingratiate themselves with those they see as the most effective or powerful individuals in the organization with the hope that they will then be rescued and protected.

Whiners want to be supported and taken care of rather than to be asked to become more capable and self-sufficient. But, with whiners, there will never be enough. They are self-indulgent, and inconsiderate of others. Although they frequently pretend to be helpless and constantly seek reassurance, they can also be vain and demanding. Rarely do they follow through on advice that could bring about improvement. They merely want someone to blame for their problems, or they want to take advantage of someone who will assume responsibility for them.

Seductive Sirens

Whiners are sometimes attention-seeking employees who present themselves as seductive sirens. In Greek mythology, seductive sirens sat demurely on the edge of cliffs. Bare breasted and suggestive, they used their charms to lure the pilots of sailing vessels closer to the shore. But, much to the dismay of the ship's captain and crew, as they approached the promise of adventure by turning the ship closer to the shore, they struck the rocks beneath the surface, thus trapping the ship, its crew, and its cargo. In essence, this is the behavior of attention seeking whiners. They attempt to lure their co-workers with superficial promises that are rarely, if ever, realized. These are also the whiners who just love to be on stage. They fill the work environment with their presence as a way of gaining attention and reassurance that they are desirable and recognized.

Frightened Fawns

These Whiners send messages that they are weak, overwhelmed, and in need of constant reassurance and support. Frightened fawns are perplexing people who seem to be inadequate on the surface, and they give the appearance of asking for very little. Of course, they ask over and over again. Yet, they never do anything that is clearly and overtly hostile. How then, do you deal with someone who can so readily be hurt with even minor confrontation or criticism? These employees can use up all of the energy that their supervisors and colleagues are willing and able to lend in attempting to respond to unfounded problems, or to resolve the problems that the whiners have created through their own inefficiency. Employees who behave this way use their image of inadequacy against their co-workers and workplace officials because they know that there is great power in pretending to be weak and helpless.

Delicate Flowers

This type of whiner offers complaints of poor health as an excuse for frequent absences from work, or as an excuse for not meeting deadlines and other forms of workplace responsibility. They blow every little ache and pain out of proportion. These employees exaggerate physical symptoms, attempt to appear frail and delicate, and they display rapidly shifting moods. They constantly use their physical health and emotional crises with the hope that co-workers or officials will provide a magical solution for their problems. Employees who present themselves as delicate flowers often harbor secret wishes that their supervisors and colleagues will excuse them from responsibility, or that officials and co-workers will rescue them from the dilemmas that they have created through their own actions and inefficiency.

Carol Pathetic

During a fourteen-year period, Carol Pathetic systematically elicited the sympathy of a series of departmental supervisors. She created a system in which she had them all convinced that she was the most conscientious employee in the organization despite her frequent absences due to workplace "stress" and "health" problems. Eventually, a new and far wiser supervisor was assigned to head Carol's department. Following a competent and professional review of Carol's job assignment and history, the new department head very quickly became aware of the con game the whiner had been using.

Early in her career with the company, Carol began to complain about the level of work required by her position. Since the company had budget limitations, she discovered that overtime compensation in the form of time-off, could be provided at the rate of time and one-half. However, funding did not permit overtime payments, nor did the budget permit hiring for a second position. As such, Carol gained exactly what she wanted. Through constant whining, Carol created a situation in which she would do very little during the regular workday. Then, when complaints were received related to the work she was assigned to produce, Carol would go into her act, emphasizing her posture that the workload was simply overwhelming and impossible to maintain.

Carol would then offer the ultimate "sacrifice" by volunteering to come in on the weekend. While at work alone on the weekend, Carol would do only enough to make it appear that she had been productive, but not near as much as what could have been accomplished had she actually worked in a conscientious manner. By the way, upon further investigation, the new supervisor also discovered that the employee was not actually coming in on many of those occasions. And so, the scam was obvious. Carol would do little during the regular workday. She would do even less during times when compensatory time was approved. As a result of her scheme, Carol received increasing amounts of time and one-half compensation, thereby further decreasing her time on the job and building an increasing backlog of work to be done. Being relatively secure financially, this is exactly what Carol wanted.

By the time her maneuvers were discovered by the new supervisor, Carol was actually on the job less then twenty-four hours per week. Yet, she was receiving full pay and benefits for a forty hour per week position in addition to the many hours of compensatory time that she was using. When her new supervisor challenged the system, Carol became extremely hostile. She filed an informal grievance with the chief executive officer, claiming that the supervisor was insensitive to her needs. The incompetent CEO, being distant from the actual work activities of the facility then took Carol's side, chastising the conscientious supervisor, and disregarding her sincere efforts.

A revealing aspect of this story is that the CEO, being a rather bullying and macho character, one day rather patronizingly confided to Carol's supervisor, "You know, I don't see how you can put up with Carol's sniveling. If she were under my direct supervision, I wouldn't put up with her for a minute."

"Moonstruck"

Do you recall the movie, Moonstruck? One of the scenes involved Ronny Cammareri, the neighborhood baker, who was played by Nicolas Cage. In the scene, Ronny was pledging his undying love to Loretta Casorini, as portrayed by Cher. At that moment, Loretta really wanted nothing to do with him. In response to her refusal to continue their relationship, Ronny offered the plea, "But Loretta, I love you!" Loretta listened to the pleading momentarily, then moved her arm back, swung and slapped Ronny across the face with a resounding haymaker as she told him to *"snap out of it!"*

Responding to "Whiners"

- Although it is essential to remain professional and of course, to not resort to physical assault, the message of Loretta Casorini to the baker is exactly what is necessary to effectively deal with the whiners of the workplace. They need to be required to *"snap out of it!"*

- Refuse to pay emotional blackmail to the whiners you encounter. Keep them involved with as many challenges as you are confident that they can handle if they are required to make a reasonable attempt to do so. With whining employees, insecurity diminishes in proportion to each small success. The way to encourage that is to keep them busy so they don't have time to interfere with you or with other employees.

- When whiners come to you with complaints or for your support, briefly hear them out, but make sure the interaction remains on your terms. After you understand the concern, ask questions that point toward solutions and away from complaints. You might ask, "How do **you** plan to solve the problem, Carol?" or, "What are your thoughts about how **you** might get this resolved?" Rescuing them will only create a forum for continued frustration and unrealistic attention seeking to avoid self-reliance and the acceptance of responsibility.

- Avoid displaying sympathy to whiners. It only increases their manipulative behavior and complaints. By encouraging whiners to seek their own solutions, you help them to become responsible for their own success. Give them ideas for improvement and express confidence that they will be able to do it if they really set their minds to it. They can do well if they know that it is expected of them, and they know that you will not give them unwarranted attention or bail them out.

The "Stallers" and "Dawdlers"

"That's not my job, man." Stallers and dawdlers are procrastinators who bear grudges and take advantage of their work associates. Their favorite response when challenged, or when they realize they have trapped themselves with their own deceptions… *"Who Me?"* They blame other employees for any problems that surface and they avoid responsibility at every opportunity. Thinking only of themselves, stallers and dawdlers constantly scheme and maneuver as a means of avoiding responsibility and accountability. To compensate for their ineptness and for their lack of self-initiative, they achieve control by manipulating others.

Beware of False "Sincerity"

Stallers and dawdlers are experts at playing the game, *"Dumb Like a Fox."* They avoid obligations and responsibility by deliberate "forgetting" and inefficiency. When trapped by their own manipulations, they actively assure you that they will try harder. However, they never seem to do so. Stallers and dawdlers frequently display ingratiating behavior as a means of controlling effective employees and workplace officials. They often use people for their own gain, and they take undeserved credit when things go well. When challenged due to their inappropriateness or unprofessional behavior, stallers and dawdlers accuse and blame others for their lack of effectiveness. If officials and colleagues refuse to accept their alibis and excuses, they become abruptly angry and sullen.

"I only want to please you" is the surface message that stallers and dawdlers attempt to convey. But, "I want to control and take advantage of you" is their internal motivation and posture. Sullen compliance is combined with deliberate undermining of workplace activities and projects. Stallers and dawdlers are expert at putting things off until someone else takes over and gets the job done. In fact, working with stallers and dawdlers is often like trying to plug the holes in a sieve without having the right materials to do so. As soon as you get several of the holes plugged, some of the first that you worked on will start to leak again. Just as it is with the sieve, when you start to believe that stallers and dawdlers are going to become more productive, they will find another excuse for their ineffectiveness, or they will deliberately cause something else to go wrong.

Martin Gotcha

Martin Gotcha is a sour and negative individual who has changed jobs on frequent occasion during the fifteen years of his professional career. With each new job, Martin initially presents himself as a willing and conscientious worker, actively agreeing to perform any function and cheerfully presenting a, "happy to help you" posture. However, as soon as he is established in his position, Martin begins to size up the power base of the organization. Once that base is determined, Martin actively caters to the CEO and management staff as an attempt to convey the message that he is a dedicated and valuable employee. By the time his probationary period is over, Martin is well established in the organization, putting on his, "happy to help you" face whenever it is to his advantage. Martin then, deceptively defies the rightful authority and concerns of his immediate supervisor and colleagues as he progressively demonstrates increasingly troublesome patterns of inefficiency and procrastination.

How to survive…"Stallers and Dawdlers"

- Don't play their game. Keep in mind that stallers and dawdlers are trying to control you with their troublesome behavior. Stick to issues instead of reinforcing their behavior by impulsively reacting to their manipulations.

- Insist that stallers and dawdlers cooperate and then back up that posture with a reasonable amount of "clout." Don't let discussions turn into arguments. Stallers and dawdlers are almost always argumentative and poor listeners. Most often, they are too busy thinking up defensive arguments. Therefore, when concluding your discussions with stallers and dawdlers, ask them to summarize your main points and expectations. This will help you to limit the opportunity for them to deny the agreements or understandings that have been established, and to make sure that you have been heard and understood.

- Encouraging initiative from stallers and dawdlers can be a frustrating experience. When their provocative and undermining behaviors irritate you, avoid impulsive reactions. If they challenge you or accuse you of unfairness, don't counterattack. Instead, tell them you know what they are up to and point out the troubling or inefficient behaviors you see them display. Stallers and dawdlers will usually comply with your expectations and become more productive if they realize that you are unwilling to accept their inefficiency and excuses, and that you will not back down.

Don't Fight the "Wars" of Your Work Associates

"Let's You and Him (Her) Fight" is a very popular game that is played by highly manipulative, and somewhat sadistic employees in the workplace. It was first identified by Eric Byrne in his book, "Games People Play." In the workplace of today, as it was in Byrne's time, some employees just love to stir up feelings or issues between otherwise friendly co-workers. They often do this just to create excitement and to have a chance to watch the action. Be careful of people who come to you with inflammatory information or suggestions of what other employees may be saying or doing. It might be that the person providing the information is just trying to get to you, but the person does not want to be involved or held accountable if things go wrong.

In a variation of the game Byrne identified that I call, *"We're Behind You All the Way...Right!"* certain power-oriented or manipulative employees create a stir by encouraging collective action to challenge some real or perceived injustice in the work environment. Once the "seeds of discontent" are planted, the instigators cleverly select a "spokesperson" to represent the group's posture and present the case to higher management.

For example, Tim, a capable and conscientious employee was asked by the administration of a packaging company to assume responsibility for first level supervision of a seven-person crew assigned to carry out an evening project. After several weeks of successful operation, the crew began to grumble and complain to Tim about their levels of compensation. Since their efforts were increasing the company's profit margin, the members of the crew expressed their view that they should be entitled to a greater share of the profits. As Tim met with the crew, they asked him to represent them by talking with the company's general manager to request a 15 percent salary increase. The crew also stated their intention to request to be relieved from the project if the increase in salary was not forthcoming. In good faith, Tim approached the designated official to present the crew's message and posture. The official then informed Tim that he would look into the matter.

Following the official's meeting with Tim, he met individually with each member of the crew. Being a rather imposing and intimidating individual, the official approached each employee in a sarcastic and bullish manner. As a result, each member of the crew backed down. They told the official that they were quite willing to continue with the assignment at the level of compensation already established, and that they had no problems with doing so. The employee who inflamed the discontent in the first place, even falsely reported that the idea to demand a salary increase had been initiated by Tim, and that he was quite content to continue with the established level of compensation.

Upon hearing the crew's response, the official called Tim into his office and summarily accused him of creating unrest among the crew. The official also forwarded a memo to the CEO, chastising Tim for his alleged "undermining" of staff morale, and recommending sanctions, should future incidents be reported. At that point, Tim could do nothing to defend or clear himself from the accusations since all members of the crew, threatened by the posture of the oppressive mid-manager, stuck to their misrepresentation of the circumstances.

Speak for yourself. Do not allow yourself to be a spokesperson for the complaints or problems of other employees. Avoid such behavior even when you are angry with a workplace official, or when you have a wish to get back at a co-worker for some reason. Instead, encourage your work associates to speak for themselves, and don't defend or refer to absent or anonymous employees or workplace officials. Avoid such references as "The boss doesn't like it when you…" or, "A lot of employees are upset with you because…"

Never be a "Company Person"

When I first became involved with the world of employment many years ago, the image of the, "company person" was quite different from the image that is considered today. In those days, the person who had the reputation of being a company person was someone who had gained the respect and admiration of workplace officials, colleagues, and customers. The individual identified as a company person had the reputation of being a dutiful and loyal employee who had made an outstanding contribution to the workplace. The individual was rarely, if ever, late for work. He or she used little or no sick leave. And, the employee worked with minimal supervision in a totally conscientious manner throughout the workday.

The company person of those days was typically hired by an organization as a young man or woman. The individual then stayed with the company for thirty or forty years until he or she could finally collect a retirement benefit and be awarded a gold watch. The former employee would then spend his or her leisure years in comfort and serenity, having gained the respect and admiration of the organization, and of the community at large.

However, as the nature and flavor of the workplace has evolved over the years, so has the image of the individual that we call, "a company person." The image of today's company person has undergone a drastic transformation. The company person of today is generally seen as someone who is an opportunist by nature. The individual typically chooses the route of least resistance in the work environment. Company people in today's modern workplace are individuals who cling to the "status quo" in the organization, doing only what is absolutely necessary to get by. These are the employees who accept a position in the early phase of their careers and then stay with it, looking forward to retirement for the next thirty to forty years.

Although company people may frequently look good due to the impression of loyalty that they convey, they offer little innovation, creativity, or outstanding achievement. They are just there. Company people actually begin their retirement within the first year or two of employment. They just don't make it official until they can finally quit and have a guaranteed income for life.

Three Classic Characteristics of Today's "Company Person"

1. They are clock watchers and procrastinators who do only what is needed to get by.

2. They use people for their own gain, and they blame others when things go wrong.

3. They take undeserved credit when things go well.

Before you can receive respect from yourself, or from your colleagues and workplace officials, you must have credibility and integrity. To avoid the "company person" image, believe in your mission. Do not require of others what you are not willing to accept for yourself. If you have made a mistake, admit it. Don't try to shift the responsibility to someone else. If employees are to survive the pressures and complexities of the oppressive workplace, they must accept responsibility for their actions, work together, and make a meaningful contribution. Attempting to function in an oppressive work environment becomes far too difficult and unrewarding when you attempt to do anything less. Always remember, in any given group or organization…the followers always take on the characteristics and qualities of the most dynamic leaders.

The "Civil War" Concept

When you find yourself experiencing a "civil war" inside of yourself, it is a clear indication that you need to speak out in response to a perceived injustice or other form of conflict. The civil war is evident when at one point you are saying to yourself, "I really need to say something to him (her)." Then in the next instant you are saying, "No, I better not. If I say something, he (she) will just get mad." Or, you might tell yourself, "There is no point saying anything. If I do it will just make matters worse." When you find yourself vacillating back and forth between these and similar postures, it is almost always an indication that you need somehow to resolve the matter. This resolution can come about in a number of ways involving direct or indirect confrontation, or a combination of both.

The Basic Survival Mode

A conscientious private sector official recently told me about the pressures she was experiencing in her job as a manager for a local business firm. In the midst of accounting deadlines, and at the busiest time of the year, her best employee, a young accountant and computer programmer announced his resignation. The employee was leaving the firm due to his unwillingness to continue to endure the oppressive environment created by the firm's president. The position the young man held was highly technical, and involved a number of interrelated functions. As such, the manager questioned whether she would be able to maintain continuity with the daily responsibilities of the position held by the accountant and programmer after his departure. She reported herself to be overwhelmed with the amount of time she would need to expend to advertise and hire for the position. She expressed concern about the energy and effort that it would take to provide the necessary orientation and training to bring the new employee to a reasonable level of effectiveness and productivity. The manager also expressed doubt about her ability to continue to meet the demands of her own already overburdened work activities. To add to the dilemma, the young woman had invested strongly in the development and viability of her department. She needed her job and she was not able to leave her position with the firm.

In response to the manager's concerns, I introduced her to the concept of "basic survival." I explained that she might never be able to please the firm's president, but that she could please herself. Being bright and perceptive, the young woman readily identified with the benefits of the approach. She simply mapped out a comprehensive plan of action. Then one step at a time, she began with the development of a position announcement that she dispersed through employment services and the media. Within weeks, taking each step in turn, handling what she could on a systematic and prioritized basis, the manager handled the crisis in a far more efficient manner than she had even dared to imagine.

Adopting a Basic Survival Mode

In assuming a basic survival mode, make a commitment to start your job each morning with the firm intention to do the best work that it is possible to accomplish. Do this by concentrating on the task at hand and by devoting full and focused attention to that activity. Complete the project in a timely manner. When one job is finished, go on to your next level of priority and area of responsibility. Throughout the day, adhere to break time limitations to the letter. Totally avoid gossip and office politics, but engage in occasional and brief socialization to convey a posture of friendliness with co-workers. Base your entire workday on the philosophy, "An honest day's work for an honest day's pay."

Once your scheduled workday is completed, whether the work is completed or not, close out all work-related activities. Then, leave the work environment and insist upon having a life of your own. Do that by actively separating from any thoughts of the workplace and projects yet to be accomplished. Focus instead, on the "here and now" activities of home, family, and social life. At the close of the evening, get a good night's sleep so that strength and stamina will be restored for the next day's challenges in the oppressive environment.

"All Things in Balance & Moderation"

Most of us have enough to deal with in our personal lives without taking the problems created in an oppressive work environment home with us. We had lives before we entered the world of employment, and we should continue to have our lives while we work in our professions. It is important for us to remember that we all live in three worlds. We live in the world of home and family. We live in the world of work and productivity, and we live in the world of social processes.

Whenever we "short change" ourselves in one of these worlds, by over-investing in another, we become out-of-balance and in trouble to some degree.

Moderation and balance can be beneficial in virtually every aspect of life. If you are feeling stressed at work, keep the other parts of your life simple and stable. Don't expect so much of yourself, especially during unsettling or difficult times. Too many employees make their work the most important thing in their lives, thereby neglecting the world of home and family, and the world of social processes. Then, whenever anything goes wrong on the job, it is magnified and responded to in an out-of-proportion manner. A small disagreement with a co-worker or supervisor can become the most important issue in our lives. On the other hand, if we develop other interests, and if we maintain balance in the three worlds that are available to us, we are more likely to respond more thoughtfully and be able to keep things in perspective. If we expand our personal experiences, we will then also be able to work more effectively and interact more satisfactorily on the job.

Whenever possible get out of town during weekends and holidays. As you begin the outings, make a firm commitment that you will actively avoid all thoughts and discussion of your work-related activities and concerns. Should intrusive or work-related thoughts or issues emerge, close them out as quickly as possible as you focus on the pleasurable elements of here and now activities and relaxation. If you are able to truly escape during weekend and holiday outings, you will greatly enhance your ability to face the difficult workplace challenges of the coming week with renewed vigor and stamina.

Knowing Your Adversaries

Maintain a realistic view of others. If oppressive people believe you are strong and confident, they will be less likely to be a threat to you. An inspiring story of political prisoners of the Stalin regime in the Soviet Union illustrates this. Officials of the forced labor camp set a daily quota for the men to lay 375 blocks per day to build a wall that would serve no useful purpose. The work was required to be carried-out in the bitter cold of winter, without sufficient rest, and without adequate food or clothing.

In a gesture of solidarity, and aware of the motives of their captors, the residents decided to lay 425 blocks instead. Seeing what had taken place, the camp commandant became spiteful, then requiring the residents to lay 475 blocks. Of course, the captives responded with the placement of 525 blocks. Upon learning of the action of the captives, the commandant became enraged, vowing to stop them at any price.

As the escalation of postures continued, a fascinating pattern began to emerge. The captives became stronger, more united in their determination, and in their camaraderie and efforts. And so, the quota reached 925 blocks. Although requiring great effort and sacrifice, the captives did not falter. The commandant, however, began to lose his grip, eventually becoming psychotic and requiring placement in a mental institution. His frustration and rage had overcome him. Unable to understand the motives of his captives, the commandant had become obsessed, leading to a full-blown state of paranoia.

People who are mean and cruel are ultimately mean and cruel to themselves! We are emotionally upset, not so much by our work associates or by what they say or do, but by our own attitudes and our own responses. Oppressive and incompetent officials are often overly sensitive to other people's opinions and responses. They harbor secret beliefs that they are unworthy and inadequate. Oppressive and incompetent officials also have a strong fear of being rejected by those who hold positions at the upper levels of power and authority. They fear that if their inadequacies are detected, it will discredit them and diminish their potential and authority. These inadequate officials fear that if they admit that they have been wrong, they will then be seen as weak. And so, they abuse power, and their compulsive need to be right, and to "win at any price" destroys them. Despite what might be painful in our lives, despite the wrong that others might do to us, it remains a fundamental truth…it is what we believe about ourselves that is of the greatest importance. What happens outside of that is really only a matter of the passing scene.

Watch for Manipulation

Never rush an answer to a difficult question. Not only is a pause for breath between question and answer an acceptable thing to do, you can give yourself time to think more clearly by commenting on the fact that it is an important or interesting question. When you have demands placed upon you, it is almost always certain you are being tested. So, what should you do? The best response to a vaguely-worded or otherwise unclear demand is to say "That depends…what do you have mind?" You need to know when you would be wise to agree, and when it would be best to say no. When you are confronted with, "Give me an answer right now" or "Decide immediately," your best response is "No, I will have to think about that." After you have had a chance to think, you can then respond in a number of ways. For example you might say, "What you present is not acceptable, what else do you propose?"

If needed, ask for more information or clarification when you believe that excessive demands are being placed upon you. In a professional manner, request time to discuss the issues, and to more thoroughly explore expectations and consequences. Do what you can to examine any differences of opinion that may exist. When you understand the demands or unreasonable expectations, provide a response in a manner that you believe will be most likely to bring about a positive result. Do not let oppressive officials or unfair co-workers control you with threats, or with "guilt tripping" maneuvers. Resist the temptation to apologize or to feel responsible when a manipulative work associate makes a demand, gives you a hurt look, or assumes an angry posture. Remember…you will be treated the way you teach your work associates to treat you. If you adopt this as a guiding principle, you will be on your way to more successful and rewarding experiences with workplace officials and colleagues.

Beware of Messengers Bearing Bad News

The rumor mill and office politics have no place in a healthy workplace. Effective organizations run on trust, and they thrive on teamwork. Intruding into the business of co-workers, and conveying false information about the activities or remarks of colleagues destroys trust. Casting doubt on the motives and intentions of other employees reduces their ability to get along with you, and with each other.

In a troubled work environment there will always be manipulative employees around who will try to convince you to agree with them about the disagreements that they have with their co-workers, and with the officials of the workplace. You will readily encounter those who can hardly wait to share the bad news with you about someone else. You will also find those who eagerly seek an opportunity to spread the bad news about what an employee or official has said about you. When you encounter these circumstances and then explore the issues further, you will most often discover that the gossip is conveyed from very limited and manipulative personal postures. You will rarely discover that the information has been conveyed from the larger dimension of what is really going on, or from what someone else has actually said about you. Even when the information that has been conveyed is accurate, it will most likely have been shared to promote resentment and discontent, rather than to encourage understanding and positive interaction among colleagues.

If you want to stay out of the "gossip loop" and "office politics," develop standard phrases that allow you to take charge of the situation when the gossips stop by to spread the bad news, or to tell you about the latest scandal that is brewing. If you do not want to offend these individuals, you can simply say, "It has been good to see you, but, I have several deadlines to meet and I must get back to them." If they do not leave with that type of comment, just proceed with your work and ignore them. It may take a while, but they will eventually get the message if you maintain your posture and remain unresponsive to their remarks.

On the other hand, if you are not feeling that kindly when Harry says, "Hey, do you know what Joe just said about you?" A good response would be, "Is that right? You know, I would like you to come with me so that we can check it out with Joe right now!" When you arrive at the other employee's location you might say, "Hey Joe, Harry just told me…" I can assure you Harry will be extremely uncomfortable about that time! If Harry refuses to come with you just say, "Since you don't want to deal with this issue, I am going to assume it is you that is doing the talking. It's pretty obvious that you don't have the courage to accept responsibility for your actions, so I believe that you're just trying to lay it on Joe!"

When you encounter annoying and manipulative work associates, let them do most of the talking. Do not lower yourself to their level, and try not to become defensive or overly reactive when they make their inflammatory remarks. Just listen, and keep calm and self-assured. Remember, you do not have to buy into the power plays or insensitive patterns that manipulative co-workers display. Knowing when to stand up for yourself and what you believe to be right requires patience, commitment, and practice. But, you will find that you will be able to accomplish more, gain pride in yourself, and respect from others once you master the ability to do so. One thing for sure, you will be out of the "gossip loop," and you will be excluded from "office politics" in short order. And, that may actually be a blessing in disguise.

The "Uproar Players"

Uproar Players! Almost every organization has them. Even small organizations or departments can have one or two. Also known as *"busy bodies,"* uproar players are the employees who just live for office gossip and office politics. In oppressive organizations, they are agitators and the "bearers of bad news." Uproar players love to talk about other employees and the problems that they may be experiencing. They find great delight in stirring up trouble and then watching to see what will happen next.

Although uproar players have little loyalty or concern for others, they almost always closely attach themselves to one of the more gullible employees in the oppressive work environment. This individual then serves as an accomplice. The employee that has been selected becomes a "stooge" to validate the uproar player's dishonesty, and to "take the rap" when things go wrong. The accomplice is claimed to be admired and respected but, is really only there to be used by the uproar player. The accomplice also serves as a defender of the motives of the uproar player when troublesome behaviors are challenged. Despite the manipulative nature of this relationship, the accomplice is typically quite sincere in the belief that the behaviors of the uproar player are honorable, and that the uproar player's motives are just.

Uproar players are intensely interested in office politics. They are typically involved in gossip about the workplace conflicts of fellow employees, and they love to talk about the personal problems of employees outside of the work environment. They often secretly undermine the positive efforts of successful employees, while at the same time they may be wishing them success on the surface. Uproar players prefer to talk behind a targeted employee's back rather than to meet with the person in a direct confrontation. They often envy the success, intelligence, and abilities of workplace officials and other work associates. Uproar players also resent the closeness and warmth other employees may share with each other. Since uproar players cannot live comfortably with themselves, they also cannot live comfortably with others. And so, they adopt an overwhelming need to diminish the lives of their associates through gossip, deceptiveness, and manipulation.

Oprah Butinski

Oprah Butinski is a superficially charming and highly manipulative uproar player who holds a strategic position as personnel officer in an oppressive organization in Arkansas. She is an absolute master at hiding her shallow internal posture as she caters to those in authority to strengthen her own base of power. In her role as personnel officer, Oprah has frequent opportunities to solicit the confidence of employees who may be having difficulties in the workplace or in their personal lives. And of course, she actively seeks their comments under the pledge of "absolute confidentiality." Then, with the information still filtering through her ears, she is off to share it with whomever in authority that will listen.

You see, Oprah is actually quite selective with whom she will confide. Her comments are made only to those who will somehow look up to her due to her access to information, or to someone who will be in a position to further her career. It is interesting to note that Oprah has been employed at the same corporation for more than fifteen years. In that time, she has produced only an extremely limited amount of actual work. She frequently attends professional workshops at company expense, she takes excessive amounts of "sick" and "family" leave, and Oprah regularly arrives at the office late and leaves early. Yet, despite these patterns, her salary has doubled every five years. This is a true testament to the effectiveness of Oprah Butinski's manipulative character and deceptiveness.

Milton Butinski

Oprah's ex-husband, Milton, is also a classic uproar player and a true "busybody" in the workplace. He is always on the alert to gain the latest news about the problems of other employees. Once Milton has the information he wants, he finds great pleasure in spreading it around. Whenever Milton stopped to "visit" during my association with him several years ago, it was always very obvious that he was actively searching for the latest gossip to spread around. As a countermeasure to his excessive curiosity, I would simply change the subject. My typical response to his inquiries, "Gee, I don't know, Milton, but have you heard about the new computer software program that will…?" Or, at other times I would say, "I don't know, Milton. You know me. Nobody tells me anything. I'm always the last to know around here." Eventually Milton got the message, and he stopped coming around. To tell you the truth, I really didn't miss him.

How to respond to…"Uproar Players"

- Some uproar players chronically complain about their employment circumstances, and about the behaviors of workplace officials and other work associates. They do this as a device to encourage you to feel sorry for them. They also do it as a manipulation to encourage you to share what you know about the problems of officials and employees. They then, quickly divulge that information to make them feel important and powerful. Don't provide uproar players with the information or unrealistic support that they wish to receive, and tell them nothing of what you know of the problems of others.

- In some circumstances, the complaints of the uproar player are designed to persuade you to come to their defense when they are in trouble due to the problems they have caused. They love to solicit your help so that they can play the game "Let's You & Him (Her) Fight!" Don't take on the uproar player's problems or responsibilities. Instead, redirect them to solve their own problems. It also is helpful to do what you can to keep them busy. They are almost always under challenged in oppressive work environments.

- If uproar players ask about any difficulty that you may be having in a relationship with another employee or workplace official, tell them nothing. If you wish to provide a response, you might say, "No problem that I know of…why do you ask?" Then, no matter what they say or ask, deny everything! Or if you wish you might respond with, "Maybe you should check it out with him (or her)."

- In dealing with uproar players, it is important to remember that they have an intense desire to share any secrets that they may come to their attention. Therefore, it is wise to never talk about confidential matters with them. If you must associate with uproar players, say as little as possible about sensitive matters and don't react in response to their manipulations or play their games. In other words, deal with only here and now behaviors in a direct and firm manner, and on a need to know basis.

- For the more malicious uproar players, avoidance may be the only viable solution. If they ask you why in a public setting you might say, "I have no idea what you mean." Then refuse to discuss the matter further. If you wish, tell them in private that you know exactly what they are up to and why they are doing it. Therefore, you prefer not to associate with them. That will usually take the pleasure out of the games that they are playing. As a result, you will no longer be of interest to them as a resource for their disruptiveness and manipulation. You might, however, then become a target for the gossip that they wish to spread. If that should occur, it will typically be short lived and a relatively small price to pay.

Bloom Where You Are Planted!

Nothing is more rewarding than exploring our true potential by leading creative and purposeful lives! But, highly disruptive, negative, and manipulative employees base their destiny on unhealthy circumstances, the misfortune of others, and on the legitimate efforts of their work associates and supervisors. They believe the workplace owes them a living and that officials and colleagues should provide them with consideration, appreciation, and happiness. They make unreasonable demands and claims on their co-workers and workplace officials, and they feel cheated and hurt when those expectations are not fulfilled. These individuals fail to realize that when we are self-reliant, we are able to meet life's challenges with confidence and power by looking at each situation based on individual merits and characteristics. We then see things as they are, not as we would like them to be. And, we refuse to let our lives be dominated by wishful thinking and unethical practices.

All indications are that incompetence and oppression in the workplace will continue. This is not to say that we are not entitled to have more of our basic needs met by workplace officials and colleagues…the need to be supported in our professional growth, the wish to be recognized for our responsible efforts, and for our positive contributions. But, when we are not handling our lives, no amount of support and recognition will ever be enough. We become a bottomless pit. The important people in our lives could sacrifice everything…but it will never be enough. In the final analysis, we can only please ourselves, and we are the only ones who can. We do that by the way we live our lives. And, the way we live represents what we believe. When we understand that, we are experts on ourselves, and in that sense, we are experts on everyone.

6

ANSWERING YOUR CRITICS

So...Shoot Me!

A number of years ago a major research project was being conducted at a top-secret military installation. After months of intensive and painstaking effort, the mission was nearing completion. The success of the project depended on precise scientific timing and the bringing together of key elements within a fraction of a second in time. The plan of the research team was to bring all components together, and at that precise instant, a photograph would be taken to record the event. The event, recorded on film would then be the permanent and only available evidence to justify the entire investment. Due to the physical delicacy of the project itself, and due to the extreme limitation in space, only one camera could be positioned to record the event.

Because of the project's importance to national security, the President of the United States was in direct communication by telephone as the moment of completion was at hand. With everything in readiness, the Chief of the project requested his leave of the President so that he could personally supervise the event. The President agreed to remain on standby as the CEO ordered the staff to proceed. The chief gave the signal and the technicians initiated the procedure. At the precise instant of critical importance, the procedure was carried-out to perfection. The camera functioned with precision. The event was a total success!

As the procedure came to a close, a cheer rose from those in attendance. The CEO rushed to the telephone where the President was on standby. He said, "Mr. President, it is my honor to report to you that the experiment has been a total success." The President then offered his congratulations to the CEO and his staff, inviting them to come to Washington the following week to share the good news with a select congressional committee. Following the conversation with the President, the CEO signaled for a champagne celebration to begin. At the same time, a photographic specialist hurriedly prepared to process the results of the project in the darkroom.

As it turned out, the photographic specialist was deeply involved with a female laboratory technician who was also assigned to the project. In her excitement, and under the influence of the champagne that had begun to flow, the technician impulsively decided to suggest to her boyfriend that they spend an evening on the town to celebrate the success of the mission. In her excitement and in her enthusiasm to share her plan, the young woman rushed to the door of the darkroom where her boyfriend was engrossed in processing the filmed results of the experiment. Despite a brightly colored sign warning against entry when a red light was flashing, the young woman burst into the room, exposing the film and destroying the results of the delicate experiment. When they realized what had occurred, the couple stood frozen in shocked anguish and silence. As alarms shrieked their ominous alert throughout the facility, the CEO rushed to the scene. Filled with rage, he began shouting, belittling and degrading the young woman for her impulsive actions, knowing full well the repercussions to follow. The CEO would now need to contact the President to inform him of the disaster.

Still filled with rage, the CEO ordered the young woman to his office where he continued with his barrage of criticism and condemnation as other administrative officials arrived on the scene. Upon arrival, they too joined in on the tirade directed toward the technician. All the while, the young woman remained composed and totally silent, standing almost motionless as the verbal attacks continued. After several agonizing minutes of rage and disgust expressed by the CEO and the other officials, the room fell silent. The CEO soon broke the silence as he caught his breath and contemptuously inquired, "Well young lady, what do you have to say for yourself?" The young woman paused in reflective silence for a moment, and then said calmly... ***"So, shoot me!"***

Now, that was class! With those three words, this young woman brought everything of importance into perspective. In the words of the young woman at that moment, everything of importance had been said. Nothing of value could be added. No amount of raging would matter. Nothing could be said or done that would change a single fact of what had occurred. The result of the experiment was lost forever. So, what was the point of the "grand inquisition?"

Answering Your Critics on Your Terms

Are you easily hurt by what others say and do? Do you have trouble saying what you think? Do you go along with what someone else wants because you are afraid to say "no?" When you are being mistreated, or when you are being taken advantage of, what should you do? Some form of response is necessary, but not an abrupt display of anger or defensiveness on your part. That hardly ever accomplishes anything constructive, and often escalates feelings of anger and frustration all around.

You have the right to take care of yourself. You don't have to allow yourself to be abused or disrespected. An assertive style allows you to stand up for yourself, and to be less vulnerable to the troublesome postures of oppressive supervisors and manipulative co-workers. A basic human right is to say, "This is what I think…this is what I believe!" You also have the right to be different, to be wrong…and to make mistakes. When you do make mistakes, the only essential is that those mistakes be honest mistakes, and not of a deliberate nature. You also have the right to decide how you will live your life, as long as no one is hurt in the process. Being assertive allows you to act in your own best interest without feeling guilty or wrong, and without making others feel resentful and discounted. Assertive people express themselves firmly and clearly without making insulting or degrading remarks. They understand the value of negotiation and the benefit of compromise while resolving differences.

Fundamental Clues that Positive Assertiveness may be Necessary:

- Do you believe that you must accommodate your work associates because you fear that you will somehow offend them?

- Do you feel compelled to allow supervisors and co-workers to maneuver you into situations that you don't want?

- Do you feel cornered, pressured, or trapped in your associations with workplace officials or colleagues?

- Do you believe you have no choice or alternatives during important workplace negotiations?

When you experience these signals, it is most likely time to set limits or to stand up for yourself in a positively assertive manner!

A Hallmark Clue that We Are Not Being Positively Assertive

One of the hallmark indications that we need to be more assertive is when we are unable…or unwilling to look another person in the eye. In my experience, there are really only two reasons that we cannot look someone else in the eye! One reason is anger. The unspoken message we are sending either consciously or unconsciously is, "I am so angry with you that I want you out of my sight!" The other reason we have difficulty looking another person in the eye is shame. In this case, the unspoken message is, "I am so ashamed of what I have done…(or) what I am doing…(or) what I have not done…(or) what I am about to do…that I can't bring myself to face you."

Becoming Positively Assertive!

To avoid being controlled by oppressive and incompetent co-workers or authority figures, we have to see them as no more and no less important then we are. Each time we elevate others in response to their abuse of power, we diminish ourselves. We cannot give any person more recognition than we give ourselves and expect to feel good about ourselves. If we do not insist on our right to be treated as equals, we must look up to others. We then find it necessary to seek approval, to ingratiate ourselves, and to cater to the whims of those we grant authority over us.

To be assertive, speak up for yourself when you know the issue at hand is important. To gain strength and power in relationships, stop personalizing the negative reactions of others. You have the right to express your concerns about situations that are interfering with your effectiveness at work. But, what is the best way to handle the situation? Part of the answer is to not let the tension build. Storing up complaints produces more irritation and agitation as time goes on. Pent-up anger and frustration can cloud the issue and affect your judgment. The answer is to rise above the situation to become the best and most effective person that you can be. Assertive behavior promotes equality in relationships. It permits you to act in your own best interest, to stand up for yourself without undue anxiety, to express honest opinions, and to exercise personal rights without denying the rights of others.

Sometimes We Get What We Ask For

Many years ago, C. B. DeMille, the renowned Hollywood director is reported to have frequently lectured at length from a platform through a microphone. The story is told that during one of his lectures Demille noticed two cast members talking. "Stop" shouted DeMille, as he pointed at them…"Ladies, you two, come up here please." The two women mounted the platform. "If what you have to say is so important," said DeMille, "please tell everybody over the microphone." One of the women took the microphone and said "I was just asking my friend 'who is that old bald headed S.O.B., and when is he gonna let us have lunch'?" It is said that the great director was silent for a moment. He then grabbed the microphone and yelled, "Lunch!"

Positive Assertiveness in the Workplace

Assertiveness can be direct and confronting, or it can be soft and gentle. Hostile and attacking people who claim they are being assertive give the concept a bad name. You don't have to be mean…cruel…or a bully to be assertive. In fact, that is not dealing with anything, really. That is just being mean, cruel, and a bully. It is important to remember, people who are mean and cruel are ultimately mean to themselves! Positive assertiveness is not winning at any price! It is not self-gain at the expense of others. To be truly effective and positively assertive, we need to remember the words of Leo Rosten, author of the book, "Captain Newman, MD." In the book, Rosten tells the story of casualties of the Korean conflict who spent time after their combat experiences in a military psychiatric unit to heal their emotional scars. In a scene reflecting the posture of Captain Newman, he said the most important thing he learned from his experiences is that *"Only the weak attack, the strong don't have to prove a thing!"*

If people respond negatively to genuine effort, it also helps to remember another of Rosten's comments, *"The reason we live is not to be happy. It is to matter to someone that we lived at all!"* Those who attack others never really understand that. They are empty and shallow. They pay the price for their insensitivity and greed. For their abuse of power and their selfishness, what goes around truly does come around!

Oppressive organizations are often filled with employees who have lost their sense of optimism for the future. These oppressed workers have given up because they believe that they no longer have viable alternatives available to them. There are no guarantees in life, but without courageous action there can be no hope. It is hope that sustains us through petty crises and real adversity. If we live without hope for too long, we will wither away and grow old before our time. We then live with a sense of regret that we really didn't take the risks that were necessary to make a difference. Don't be afraid to take control of your life. It can be one of the most important things you will ever do.

The Soft Approach to Conflict Resolution

When you are aware that you must face an oppressive official or difficult circumstance, it is best to do it from a thoughtful approach to negotiation and problem-solving. In applying the soft approach to conflict resolution you appeal to reason and to fairness. And, you issue that appeal in a non-accusing and non-blaming manner. Your primary message should be, "We have a problem in our relationship that I would like to work out with you." One of the best ways to do that is to use the formula:

I'm feeling _____.

What I need from you is _____.

Will you _____?

You might say…"I'm feeling very anxious and uncertain right now, so I appreciate having a chance to talk with you. This is difficult for me to talk about and it would help if you would just hear me out. If you would do that, when I'm finished, I would like to hear your thoughts on what I have to say…or if you wish, you don't need to say anything at all."

One of the most effective phrases for negotiation of workplace conflict is the phrase…"As you know!" Negotiation can be remarkably effective if it is started with this simple statement, followed by a brief description of the history of your relationship with the other person. For example, a soft approach to conflict resolution might begin with…"As you know, you and I have been friends for a long time. In fact, I remember when we first started working here. We had some good times back then, and some tough times as well. Do you remember the time that…?"

The focus might then be shifted to the present concern by saying…"Now I don't know that it's me…I don't know that it's you…In fact, maybe it is neither of us. Maybe someone or something else is contributing. I just know we are not as close as we used to be…and, I would like to talk it out to see if we can resolve whatever might be happening between us."

In essence, the soft approach to conflict resolution involves:

- A contract and forum for communication…
  "It would help if you would hear me out."
- Identification and alignment with the other person…
  "As you know."
- Neutralizing the situation…
  "We have a problem in our relationship."
- An opportunity for discussion and negotiation…
  "I could be wrong about this."
- A search for solutions…
  "I would like to talk it out with you."
- Conveying non-blaming and non-accusing messages…
  "I don't know that it is you…"
  "I don't know that it is me…"

In using the soft approach to conflict resolution, your role is to convince the other person that your position is decent and honorable. By going along with you, the person will show that he or she shares those values. Even oppressive and incompetent people would like to be seen as decent and fair-minded. Deep inside, many of them would like to "do the right thing." However, they have lost their sense of decency and fairness due to ineptness and their lust for power and control. It is your job to help them to get in touch with what is the right thing to do, and to understand the value in your position. Your message will then cause them to be more likely to align with you so that they will want to correct their actions and "make things right."

When you approach a difficult situation with a colleague or workplace official by using the soft approach to conflict resolution, it is possible that you will hear one of two responses to what you have to say. One possibility is that the work associate will respond with, "Oh no, there's no problem that I know of between us! In fact, now that you mention it, you have made me realize that I have been kind of distant and irritable lately. But, it has nothing to do with the two of us. You know, I've been having a lot of problems in my marriage lately, and that has caused me to feel really overwhelmed and frustrated. Thanks for mentioning it. I'll try to watch myself closer, but again, there is no problem between us."

On the other hand, when you approach the colleague or official with the message, "We have a problem that I would like to work out with you." you just might hear something like this. "You darn right there is a problem between us! I don't know if you realize it but about two months ago we were in a staff meeting together. During the meeting I was trying to explain my thoughts about how to handle the workflow problem. Before I had a chance to explain the whole plan, you interrupted and took over the discussion. You acted like it was all your idea. Then, whenever I tried to say something, you just blew me off. I felt really put down and angry when you did that. In fact, a couple of the guys have been laughing about it ever since it happened."

Now, when you hear a response confirming the possibility that you have created a conflict due to your own behavior and actions, it will most likely be very difficult to listen to. It is also likely that you will become defensive and wish to retaliate. But, I encourage you to slow yourself down and remain thoughtful in your response. At least now, the problem is out in the open where it can be dealt with in a positive manner instead of being left to simmer and escalate to an even more troublesome level. Do your best to avoid defensive responses as you join the colleague or official in a search for solutions.

If you realize that, indeed you have been wrong in how you have behaved, one of the most helpful and cleansing responses you could offer would be to make an apology. Then accept responsibility for your actions, along with asking the question, "How can I make it right with you?" Providing an offer to "Make it right" when you know that you have done someone wrong is a powerful tool for bringing about positive feelings and healing between work associates who have been in disagreement or conflict with each other.

The Direct Approach to Conflict Resolution

Should the soft approach to resolving conflict fail, or if the posture of the other individual is too obnoxious and belligerent to permit the soft approach to be used, you may then need to shift to a more direct approach to conflict resolution. In using the direct approach, you point out the troublesome patterns that you see. You then give the person a chance to decide whether he or she wants to honor the expectations that you present.

When you initiate the direct approach to conflict resolution, first, take a moment to collect your thoughts, and to plan what you will say or do. Then, take a deep breath, and remind yourself to speak in a calm and self-assured manner. Describe, in specific terms, the behavior that distresses you. Then, suggest a solution to the problem. Or, ask the person to change the behavior that is causing the difficulty. Clearly in this approach, the messages are quite different from the messages conveyed in the soft approach to conflict resolution. In using the direct approach your primary message is, "This is what you are doing (or have done) and, this is how I feel about it." You also let the troublesome individual know what it is that you expect him or her to change. In using the direct approach to conflict resolution, you develop the strength and courage to confront the issues "head on."

During Lynden Johnson's administration, the President had a great deal of difficulty getting the support of congressional Democrats as he attempted to implement one of his programs for the Country. A nationally syndicated cartoonist defined the problem nicely with a characterization of President Johnson. The President was depicted holding a heavy wooden club in his hand. President Johnson was standing near a donkey symbolizing the Democratic members of congress. The message of the cartoonist was clear. The donkey was portrayed slumped back on its haunches with stars radiating out of its head after having been struck by the President. The caption read…"Sometimes, Mr. President, you just need to get their attention first!" The President's dilemma as portrayed in this cartoon illustrates what is necessary to convey in the direct approach to conflict resolution. In the direct approach, the message is no longer, "We have a problem in our relationship." In the direct approach the message is, "Yes, there is a problem, but…it is not about us. It is about you! Your behavior is the problem and I expect you to do something about it!"

When using the direct approach to conflict resolution, it is best to confront troublesome behavior in specific terms, and to then level with how you feel about what the other person has done. In a confrontation with another person, if you are too vague or too general in your statement or posture, you leave an opening for the other person's defensiveness. When people are defensive, they almost always search for loopholes. For example, should you say, "You know, the problem is that you are late all of the time and that leaves me to cover for you during the morning rush," you have already weakened your posture by being too general and vague. The fact is, it is unlikely in long term associations that someone does something "all of the time." Should you offer this opening to the other person, unless it is absolutely accurate, you will likely hear something like…"Now, wait a minute. Don't you remember the winter of 1998 when your wife had the operation? You spent a couple of days stopping at the hospital before you came to work? When that was going on you know very well that I covered for you. I was here fifteen-minutes early and I handled everything by myself. What do you mean, I'm late all of the time?"

During the direct approach to conflict resolution, let the other person know how you feel about the situation or about what has been happening. "I feel angry when you come to work late and leave me to handle the morning rush alone." Avoid making comments like, "You're such a thoughtless jerk!" Such comments will only lead to resistance and resentment. Once you have made your point, offer recommendations for change. Ask for a response to what you have proposed. When the answer is provided, listen quietly and attentively so that you will be able to hear and understand the response. At an appropriate time, reassure the other person that you do value his or her friendship, and that you hope your relationship will move in a direction that is satisfying for both of you.

The "I'm at a Loss" Approach

An alternative to the soft or direct approaches to conflict resolution involves approaching the oppressive or incompetent official, or a troublesome colleague with a perplexed manner and tone. The technique incorporates such messages as, "You know, I just don't understand," or "You know, I'm just at a loss to understand." The messages must then be supplemented by a factual review of your perception of the unfair or incompetent posture of the oppressive official or coworker.

For example, Lorraine, a sincere and hard-working employee was undergoing an annual performance appraisal at a public sector facility in Ohio. The oppressive supervisor had rated the employee as significantly lower on a numerical scale in three key areas of the employee's performance than he had during the previous year. Fred had provided the lower numerical ratings despite the fact that he had also provided written narrative indicating that Lorraine had displayed marked improvement in carrying out her duties in those very areas. Upon receiving a copy of the appraisal, Lorraine approached her supervisor with the message, "You know, Fred, I'm just at a loss to understand how it could be that you rated me lower in these areas than last year. In particular, since you also indicate that you have noticed significant improvement in my performance during the year."

In attempting to justify the lower ratings, the oppressive supervisor said, "Well, that's right, but I rated you lower than last year because I want you to realize that these areas have been a problem for a long time. I just want to make sure you understand that." Feeling dissatisfied with Fred's response, Lorraine decided to appeal the oppressive supervisor's decision and posture. She then requested a meeting and invited Fred to accompany her to review the appraisal with the department's manager. During that review, Lorraine again presented the posture that she was at a loss to understand how the lower ratings could be justified. The manager, being at least to some degree a more fair-minded person, required Fred to change the ratings to reflect a more accurate picture of Lorraine's current performance. He required changes that more fairly recognized the extraordinary effort that Lorraine had demonstrated in improving her performance and in carrying out her duties during the year.

Clearly, as is so often the case with oppressive or incompetent officials, Fred failed to understand the basic principles associated with shaping behavior and performance in a positive direction. Those principles are that negative reinforcement promotes resentment and mediocre performance in employees. Positive reinforcement promotes extraordinary effort and exceptional achievement in people.

The "Redirection" Technique

Using the redirection technique permits you to keep the focus on a key issue when you are in the midst of dealing with conflict. The approach involves the use of phrases such as, "That may be the case, but…" or "I'm not so sure about that, but…" For example, you may be required to address the inappropriate behavior of a work associate. As you approach the issue, the person may then respond with, "Hey, I don't know why you're picking on me about this. Everybody else does it too." In using the redirection technique, you might respond with, "I'm not so sure about that, but, right now I am talking about your behavior."

In some cases, when you challenge the inappropriate behavior of someone else, the person may respond with truly heart wrenching comments. The response may be due to actual circumstance, or it may just be a manipulation to get you off track. What you might hear is, "You know, you're right. I really haven't been myself lately. But, we found out a couple of months ago that my wife has cancer. Not only that, our oldest son just got caught shoplifting. We don't know what is going to happen with him. With that, and the hospital bills, I just haven't been able to concentrate." Now of course, hearing those words, your heart might just "go out" to the person, and rightly so. But, you might be wise to consider two possibilities. One is that this might just be a "con job" the employee is using to "get off the hook." The second possibility to consider is that the story might actually be true, or the truth might be even worse than portrayed. So, what do you do? Now of course, you will want to respond more sympathetically to employees who appear to be sincere in telling you their problems, compared to how you might treat employees who become belligerent and attacking.

With the struggling employee you might say, "I'm sorry to hear about the difficulties you are having. Perhaps we should talk about resources that you might have to deal with these things. I know that hospitals and juvenile service agencies usually have counseling programs available to help families in your situation. However, we also need to talk about how to approach the problems related to your work." Then, just take it from there in supporting positive ideas the employee might present, and challenging those you see as not workable. In taking this approach, you have responded to both issues in a sensitive and professional manner. You have given the employee information on possible resources to resolve the family concerns. You have also given the message that you expect the employee to change the troublesome behavior. Of course, continue to keep the discussion moving in a sensitive and straightforward direction. When people are confronted for doing wrong, they can be real sticklers for detail, and will grab at any "loop hole" they can find. The simple answer...know the facts, stay focused, be sensitive to legitimate concerns, and do not use generalizations.

The Godfather Legacy

In "The Godfather" movie series, although the behaviors and life styles of characters portrayed were repulsive, several of the methods illustrated can also be superb tools for positive assertiveness and negotiation if used with decency and integrity. For example:

- **Keep your enemy close to you.**

A policy of don Corleone was to invite people he knew to be treacherous to associate closely with him so that he could keep them puzzled about what he was up to. At the same time he had an opportunity to arrange close monitoring of their activities. The message that the Godfather conveyed was, "Keep your friends close to you. But, keep your enemies even closer."

- **Never reveal your plan to your enemy.**

Do you remember the powerful scene in the first episode of the Godfather movie series when don Corleone invited his oldest adult child, Sonny, to join him in meeting with the leaders of the other gangland families? As negotiations evolved, the don said very little. Sonny, in reaction to the deceptive manipulation of those present, lost his cool and blatantly revealed plans he believed his father to be considering. All the while, the don remained silent. Then, as the don and Sonny left the meeting, Sonny was harshly reprimanded by his father. "Never reveal your plan to your enemy" was the essence of the message that the don conveyed to his son. As an illustration of the extent that the Godfather applied that principle, what Sonny had revealed to the enemy was not even the actual plan his father had in mind. The don had recognized Sonny's youthful zeal and lack of sound judgment. Therefore, he had provided his own son with false information, knowing that Sonny could not be trusted to use the true information wisely.

- **"Make them an offer they can't refuse."**

Of course, the hallmark message of the Godfather series, "Make them an offer they can't refuse," requires no elaboration. Following release of the first Godfather episode, the phrase swept the country in popularity, and today, it remains well known and widely used to depict a posture of resolute strength and power.

Display a Professional Presence

Presence has nothing to do with size. Adolph Hitler, for example, was the most notorious paranoid psychopath the world has ever known! Despite standing only a little more than five feet tall, Hitler struck intense fear in the hearts of men who were physically, "mountains of steel!" This occurred, of course due to Hitler's iron will and due to his maniacal abuse of power without conscience.

Now, in no way am I advocating that you become like Adolph Hitler. I refer to him only because of his notoriety, and the lack of physical stature of this pathetic little man. Yet Hitler too, conveyed a powerful presence despite the atrocities to humanity he committed. Rather than encouraging you to be like Hitler, what I wish to convey is that physical size and sexual gender have no bearing on presence. To convey a professional presence you need to present yourself as a person in charge. Even when you feel nervous inside, you will gain confidence by standing up straight and not being evasive or wishy-washy. Stand with an open, well balanced, and self-assured posture. Once you get used to this posture, it will be your natural way of behaving.

Years ago, Alfred Adler, a renowned physician, and former colleague of Sigmund Freud explained the power of adopting a professional presence. He called the concept, "Acting as if." In presenting his views on the subject, Adler suggested, whenever we wish to overcome a perceived shortcoming or sense of inadequacy, improvement in our patterns of functioning and self-image will be accomplished by simply acting as if we have already overcome the shortcoming or inadequate feelings. Adler proposed that by behaving in a strong and assertive manner, the strong and assertive behaviors will evolve to become a true part of our character and functioning.

Remember the Power of Silence

When in doubt...remain silent! The silent person always has the power. Also remember, after a question is asked...the person who remains silent the longest controls the encounter. Do not rush in to rescue the other person or to ease your anxiety. Learn to endure the silence. Let the other person talk. One of the most useful negotiating skills is silence. Most people feel uncomfortable when nothing is being said, and they will make a comment just to say something. Keeping silent and letting others speak will help you find out what they really want so you can negotiate a more satisfactory agreement.

An example of the power of silence was provided during an incident involving Bill Gates, one of the wealthiest men the world, and the founder and chairman of the board of Microsoft Corporation. A few years ago, Mr. Gates was being covered on television by the major networks as he was climbing the steps of an office building to attend an important meeting. As Bill reached the landing at the top of the steps, and as he was about to enter the building, some sleazy character rushed toward him from out of the crowd that had gathered, and he abruptly threw a pie in Bill's face.

Now, what was the point of that? In my opinion, the sleazy character did absolutely nothing to advance his cause. Whatever message he may have had was lost in the pettiness of the behavior he displayed. But, at that moment, Mr. Gates was magnificent. I don't recall for certain what he did first. He either wiped the pie from his glasses, or he simply removed them. Bill then calmly looked at the sleazy character for a brief moment, as he said absolutely nothing. Mr. Gates then returned his attention to the business at hand, and he walked into the building to continue his important work.

Here we have one of the most powerful men in the world, demonstrating superbly, the power of silence. Bill could have easily lost his cool. He could have retaliated with a barrage of obscenities. He could have verbally reprimanded the individual. He could easily have sent his bodyguards to "take care" of the guy. He could have called for law enforcement intervention. He could have created more of a scene. And, yet, Mr. Gates did none of those things. Clearly, at that moment, Bill Gates knew the power of silence.

Mr. Gates also indicated his understanding of power in another way. During that incident, Bill demonstrated his understanding of what Oskar Schindler knew as he engaged in his efforts to save the lives of innocent men, women and children during the holocaust. What Bill Gates demonstrated at that moment on the steps of the office building is that true power is not actually reflected through the exercise of power in some circumstances. In some circumstances, true power is best demonstrated when you have the power to destroy, but you choose not to use your power in that manner. It is demonstrated instead, by having the intelligence and the courage to rise above the situation. In that moment, during that day, Bill Gates demonstrated both of those principles magnificently!

Listening With the "Third" Ear!

When conflict occurs, most of us do not really listen well. Too often, we just take turns interrupting! We are too busy defending our position and preparing our response. Eventually, some of us begin to realize that we really should listen to others. Unfortunately, we then listen and react only to the words that are spoken. To listen effectively, we must learn to listen with our "third ear." We need to listen to what people are saying…through their behavior, their facial expressions, their movement…and even through their silence! We also need to listen to what is being said in words, and to what is being avoided.

- Do facial expressions and gestures match the words?

- Are they verbally agreeing, but gesturing with a shrug or some other form of body language?

- Are they agreeing with you while displaying an artificial smile that suggests dishonesty or manipulation?

- Why do they remain silent?

- Is there an implied meaning to comments like, "You will never know what this means to me?"

Positively assertive persons have learned to listen without prejudging or jumping to conclusions. They listen to what is being said without necessarily believing it, until the truth has been established. When you develop your own assertive skills, you will learn to rise above the ordinary aspects of listening. You will learn to listen to yourself. How do you sound? What do you reveal? Are you over or under reacting? Do you sound angry, frustrated...vulnerable? When you and I have mastered the ability to be positively assertive we will have learned to listen to the silence of others! We will be able to sense what others say through their silence...of their hurt...of their loneliness...their hopes...their dreams. Silence can tell us these things. Silence speaks eloquently when we really listen!

"Louise"

An employee, having become extremely upset during a difficult meeting with an oppressive supervisor came rushing to my office to talk. As I invited Louise to join me, I was in the midst of writing a priority letter on my computer. The young woman agreed to wait while I finished the last few lines. Upon completing the letter, I looked up. Noting that Louise appeared to be deep in thought, I decided to remain silent until she was ready to speak. I sat quietly, wondering what may have been of such great concern to Louise as she sat there displaying such intensity. After about five minutes of total silence, Louise stood up and walked quietly out of the office. I said nothing as she departed. About 3:00 p.m. the next day, the young woman again knocked on my door. As she entered the room, Louise said, "Dick, I just wanted to stop in to thank you for yesterday. You helped me so much by what you said. I really appreciate your willingness to take the time to talk with me!"

Responding Constructively to Criticism & Conflict

How do you respond to criticism? Do you become angry? Defensive? Do you seek revenge? Do you try to prove that the other person is wrong and that you are right? There are more effective and powerful ways to respond. Criticism comes with every job. However, you can look for what might be learned from the criticism and use that information to enhance your skills and abilities. When criticized, ask questions to make sure you understand the concern and what you are being told. The things we resist most are the things we most often need to hear.

What bothers us most are the things people tell us that we already know inside, but do not want to admit, and certainly do not want other people to know. A fundamental principle for success in life is:

"Whenever I have a conflict in a relationship with someone else, it is always best to start with me first…to see how I am contributing!"

As you pause to reflect on the criticism that you have received, and how you may have contributed to the conflict, you may also be wise to consult with trusted family members, friends, or colleagues. Consultation with trusted individuals provides an opportunity to determine their views and perspectives on the issue that you have been struggling with. If, after thoughtful reflection and consultation you realize that you have been wrong, you may then recognize that the only right thing to do is to accept responsibility for your actions and decisions, and then take corrective action in the matter.

After you have paused to reflect on the criticism, you may also come to realize that you have been entirely on the right track. After you have taken time to think about how you may have contributed to the conflict, you may become aware that you have been free from wrongdoing in any manner, whatsoever. If that is the case you will then know that you must stay the course by standing up for what you believe to be just, and for what you believe to be the right thing to do to resolve the differences that you are experiencing.

Receiving criticism, and having colleagues differ with you are important factors in promoting personal and professional development in the workplace. Respond to the criticism you receive by presenting your own point of view in a professional manner. If you have been wrong, admit your mistake and try to solve the problem. Nothing can impact your credibility more in the eyes of your co-workers then being defensive or blaming toward them. Making excuses and blaming others only demonstrate that you are unwilling to accept responsibility for your own actions.

Self-confident employees handle criticism in a forthright manner and with a sense of calm and composure. Workers who are reasonably sure of themselves criticize more tactfully too. They do not try to put their colleagues down. They do not act superior when they challenge another employee's behavior. Instead, they thoughtfully offer another point of view for the co-worker to consider.

Employees who have confidence in themselves are not easily insulted either. They like themselves enough to take an insult with a grain of salt and perhaps even benefit from it. When a co-worker loses control and is unduly critical, self-confident employees do not take it as a personal offense. Instead, they remain calm and thoughtful as they consider the emotional episode to simply be a reflection of the critical colleague's perspective and functioning. Then, they try to find out what caused the upset and attempt to resolve the problem without making a big deal of it.

Be an "Actor" Instead of a "Reactor"

When employees are challenged by an oppressive or controlling official they typically become resistant and defensive. When criticized by manipulative work associates, the usual response of employees is to defend their positions by arguing against the criticism. Unfortunately, these responses usually lead to an impasse. The critic and the person being criticized become polarized, and seldom gain in their understanding of each other. When you are told by a critical employee that you didn't carry out an assignment properly, you might just say, "Thanks for letting me know. I will give it some thought and decide what to do." When you are told by a manipulative co-worker that that you have been accused of wrongdoing, you might respond with a remark like, "I guess you will have to decide whom you are going to believe." With these responses or with responses that are similar, you neither agree nor disagree. Instead, you leave yourself the option of checking to see if the critical employee has provided accurate information, or whether the individual was just trying to get a reaction from you. In either event, you will have handled yourself well.

Resist the need to defend yourself. Instead, be genuine in agreeing with the criticism you believe to be accurate. When appropriate, ask what the other person might believe to be the solution to the problem that is being presented. When you understand the issue, you have the choice of telling the person what you are prepared to do to resolve the problem. Or, you may choose not to respond to the person at all. Criticism can also help you to grow stronger. You learn to take the bad with the good. Remember too, that there is almost always a grain of truth in criticism, even if it sounds obnoxious and insulting. Face the truth and acknowledge it. If criticism is sincere and the source is reliable, it is worth considering.

The World's Foremost "Experts"

These oppressive supervisors and managers have opinions on everything. They believe themselves to be experts on just about any subject or issue. And, they present themselves to their employees as though they have answers to problems that nobody has even thought of yet. No matter what you say, the world's foremost "expert" is always one up on you. Even if they don't have a clear understanding of what the problem really is, they will present a complex, and typically unrealistic solution to any issue that is presented. Rarely will you hear them say, "How do you think you should approach the problem?" or, "What are your thoughts on how this should be handled?" When such questions are presented, they are almost always secondary to a litany of specific opinions and instructions that the "expert" has already provided. Then, when employees offer what they believe to be the solution to a particular problem, the oppressive official responds with a variety of reasons why the employee's ideas are not workable. The "expert" then reverts back to what he or she believes to be the way to solve the problem.

These oppressive and controlling supervisors will often resort to giving established and seasoned professionals detailed and specific instructions on how to handle even the most basic and routine of work assignments. In some circumstances, the official will describe in great detail, each and every step that the employee must follow in handling the matter. When a problem or conflict must be dealt with, the solution that the "expert" expects the employee to implement is almost always extremely elaborate, and not really workable or realistic from a practical standpoint. Then, when the approach fails, the "expert" simply ignores that fact, approaching yet another issue in the same manipulative and controlling fashion. Should the circumstances be such that the mishandled issue cannot be ignored, the "expert" typically attributes the failure to the shortcomings of others. In the extreme, these individuals will even claim that the approach was deliberately implemented as an "anticipated failure" to prove some obscure or unrealistic point.

These self-proclaimed "experts" are frequently bright, articulate, and ambitious. Although they have great intellectual capabilities, they almost always lack the ability to identify with the concerns of others when sensitivity or compassion is required. World's foremost "experts" are particularly fond of giving complex advice, but that advice is offered without true practical knowledge or experience. Their ideas are typically obtained from a book or from an article that they have read. They might also present a theory that has been made-up without foundation based on the "expert's" belief in how things should be handled. They love to demonstrate that their minds are quicker and better than anyone else's. But, their insights are often undermined by the condescending manner in which they offer them. Rarely are they able to sense other people's feelings, yet they insist that they must "make sure that things are done right."

Because of these dynamics, it is not at all unusual for employees to feel extremely hesitant to ask for guidance or advice from supervisors who present themselves as though they are the world's foremost experts. Employees who work under the supervision of these "experts" become painfully aware that any relatively simple or sensible approach that they might suggest to solve a problem or to complete a project will be promptly rejected and belittled. They also know that if they ask for guidance or advice from the "expert," they will then be compelled by the oppressive official to follow the elaborate advice or cumbersome directive to the letter. Employees who work under the supervision of this type of official realize that compliance with the directive will be required even though they are quite certain that the directive is ill conceived, and that it will most likely lead to failure, or to only make matters worse.

World's foremost "experts" often have natural organizational skills, and they are often genial and helpful to those who hold positions at the administrative levels of authority. But, they overdo and overreact to almost everything of significance as they interact with their colleagues and subordinates. As a result, they cause problems that are actually quite simple to resolve, to become extremely complex and difficult to manage. Preoccupied with the attainment of their goals, these driven men and women are involved in an intense struggle to achieve recognition and success. Although they may readily display humor in nonthreatening or social settings, they are almost always overly serious about anything of an official nature.

Dave Wondrous

Dave is a section chief in a major corporation in Georgia. He frequently caters to the wishes of company administrators and managers, but he is extremely controlling with his staff. Dave often schedules team meetings to inform his staff of current problems or concerns to be resolved. As ideas are presented, much to the annoyance of the team, Dave has an answer for everything. Dave becomes so absorbed in himself that he is oblivious to what his employees may wish to contribute. With almost every comment, Dave interjects his views, solicited or not. Once he has the floor, he expounds on and on, expressing idea after idea, whether they have substance or not.

When the "team" meeting is near an end, and when his employees are frustrated and defeated, Dave asks, in a rather patronizing tone, "Well gang, what do you think? Should we go ahead with it?" Then, should anyone offer a contrary opinion or alternate plan, Dave quickly responds with his own views of why the employee's suggestions or ideas will not work. His employees, tiring of Dave's controlling postures and repeated rejection of their idea's sometimes try subtle, direct, and even crude remarks in an attempt to redirect the course. Yet, the "beat goes on!" Dave is in love with himself and fascinated by what he will say next. When he hears the negative comments of his employees, they are ignored, or they are believed by Dave to be a reflection of the staff's regard for him, veiled under the cloak of "good humor." Over time, Dave's employees simply learn to comply with his unrealistic demands and expectations without objection. They offer no meaningful responses to his challenges, and they comply with his expectations under duress. They are defeated and they offer no true creativity or innovation as they carry out their assigned tasks in a mundane manner.

How to survive…The World's Foremost "Experts"

To be successful in your associations with these controlling individuals, it is essential to do the opposite of what you might be inclined to do. Do not impulsively confront them. That will only encourage them to further attempt to prove they are right and that you are wrong. Instead, sort any issue or concern into one of three categories. Those categories are:

"Wars Not Worth Fighting"

Should you realize that the issue or concern falls into the, "Wars Not Worth Fighting" category, simply let go and do the best you can to follow the oppressive supervisor's "expert" direction.

Negotiable Issues

Should you believe the issue or concern can be negotiated, approach the oppressive official only after you have carefully developed a well thought-out strategy, taking into account each objection that you believe that the "expert" might present. Then, present your case along with the message that your primary wish is to do the right thing. It is also important to indicate that you hope that the situation can be handled in the most professional manner possible.

Bottom-Line Postures

Should you strongly believe that the issue or concern involves a true bottom-line posture in which no negotiation is possible, again carefully plan your strategy and take into account, each objection that you believe that the "expert" might present. Then, get in charge of your emotions and prepare for an intense emotional battle and intellectual debate. If you show strength, determination, and resolve, it is possible that you will be able to persuade the "expert" that your ideas or solutions are sound.

As you encounter this type of oppressive supervisor, it is important to keep in mind that you will rarely, if ever, be able to convince these "experts" that they are wrong. Should they sense the accuracy of your words or posture, they will then offer a rather superficial and limited acknowledgment that you are right, but only partially so. They will be quick to point out, "after all, I had already considered the opinion you presented." However, the "experts" will make it clear that you have overlooked some minor point that they will then expound upon in great detail, regardless of whether they are accurate or realistically workable.

When dealing with a world's foremost "expert," don't attempt to be an expert in return. Instead, monitor your reactions when you associate with these controlling individuals. Or, if you do decide to assume the role of expert, make absolutely certain that you have done your research very thoroughly, and that you are as certain as you can possibly be that you have a strong and solid argument for presenting your case and position on the matter. Even then, be prepared for a tough battle that you may find very difficult to win.

World's foremost "experts" can be difficult to work with because their controlling postures and approaches create feelings of resentment and discontent. Should you feel offended, slow down and stay in charge of your emotions. When appropriate, offer them recognition by asking for their advice and make it clear that you value their valid opinions. Instead of telling them why their ideas won't work, ask questions to learn more about their perceptions and opinions. Remember that these "experts" have an intense need to be recognized for their knowledge and intelligence. As you work with them, you might discover that some ideas they present are useful and you will have established a more harmonious working relationship.

Challenging Your Colleagues

You are unlikely to accomplish anything of value if you challenge the self-respect of your work associates. Telling colleagues that you believe that they are "wrong," or that they "don't know what they are talking about," causes them to feel frustrated and embarrassed. This is particularly true when your remarks are made in the presence of co-workers or supervisors. They then become angry and resentful. Instead, show your willingness to listen and to respond in a professional manner. For instance, you might choose to offer a comment that conveys respect and understanding such as, "I believe you want to be fair about this." When appropriate, you might also say, "I know that you want to do the right thing."

As you continue your discussion, keep in mind that the purpose of challenging an employee's behavior is not to ease your anger, or to prove your colleague to be wrong. The purpose of the challenge should be to improve a troublesome situation by searching for viable solutions. While using a professional tone, tell the employee what the problem is as you see it. Do not make accusing statements or harsh remarks. They will only fuel the fire. Instead, remain calm and suggest a remedy without embarrassing or threatening the work associate that you are dealing with.

Responding to Unfair Challenges

Anxious and frustrated employees often give away their power by talking, defending, or explaining too much. Get to the point. Learn to say what you mean and then stop. The less you say, the more effective and powerful you will be. Here are a few examples:

- **To a statement you disagree with, but do not want to pursue or argue about:**
    "You could be right."
- **To agree with criticism:**
    "You are right, I did make a mistake," then stop talking.
- **To a public insult:**
    "Mark, that comment certainly deserves a response and I have one. Let's get together after the meeting to discuss it further."

- **To accusations that you are acting like a "know-it-all":**
  "I can be wrong about many things, but I am not wrong about this issue."

Deal With Anger Constructively

There is nothing wrong with displaying anger as long as the anger is expressed with sincerity and compassion, and not out of cruelty and vindictiveness. It is the way anger is expressed that can damage your credibility and offend workplace officials or other work associates. In fact, most of the things that we say when we are out-of-control only make matters worse. You do not have to shout to make yourself understood. Just present your concerns in a straightforward manner, but be thoughtful, fair, and respectful. Effective employees remain aware of their approaches, assessing along the way, when and how it might be best to express themselves, and when it might be better to remain silent and thoughtful, or more willing to listen and negotiate.

Do not react in the heat of the moment. When you are right, you have no need to lose your temper. When you are wrong, you cannot afford to. When you lose your temper, you may win the argument, but you may also lose the war! If you are not comfortable talking with the other person, get away for a while. An excellent way to stay in charge of the situation, and your behavior and emotions is to say, "You are making some interesting points. I will think about them before I give you a response. Perhaps we could get together tomorrow afternoon to discuss the matter further." The idea behind this strategy and posture is to give yourself time to examine the situation and your feelings more calmly. When you have calmed down, address the problem. Keep your cool and state your case calmly. Then, listen to the other person's response and concentrate on what might be done or said to resolve the situation.

"No-Holds-Barred"

Focused letter writing can be a remarkably helpful means of dealing with unresolved feelings and conflicts in the workplace. However, if the technique is going to provide maximum benefit, certain ingredients must be included. For example, before any words are written on paper, two decisions must be made. First, you must firmly establish in your mind that you will reserve the right to share or not share the contents of the letter with anyone, including the troublesome employee or oppressive supervisor to whom you have decided to write. Second, you must firmly resolve that the letter will truly be a "no-holds-barred" letter.

In other words, you must be determined to put in writing, each and every thought that comes to mind during the actual letter writing process. You see, by reserving the right to share or not share the letter, you stay totally in charge of the process. By becoming determined to say it all, you create an opportunity to free yourself from the unresolved feelings of anxiety and frustration through the process of writing out what is going on internally. Sigmund Freud spoke of such an approach as written or verbal "vomiting to cleanse," and that is exactly what can happen through the "No Holds Barred" letter writing process.

Now, once you start to write, use any form of "greeting" that you feel comfortable with. Then, if you "hate the person's guts," say that. Whatever comes to mind, no matter how hostile, silly, painful, or spiteful, just let it flow, editing nothing as you proceed. As you begin to write the letter, one of two things will be likely to occur. One is that the letter will "flow like wine." On the other hand, you might find shortly after you write the greeting, that you simply go "blank." Should you go blank, just, say that. What you write might sound like this, "You know right now, I'm going blank. In fact, I don't even know why I'm writing this letter. I just know that I read that idiot, Dick Werre's book, and he said this would help!" You see, whatever comes to mind should be written down, despite how inappropriate it might seem. If you approach the letter writing process in this manner, you will naturally evolve to saying just what you need to say.

Once the letter is completed, sign it off in any manner you wish. Then, seal the letter in an envelope and find an absolutely safe place to keep it. If you have to, keep it on your person at all times. If necessary, put it in a plastic "baggie" when you take it with you into the shower. ***This cannot be emphasized too much.*** The letter was written "for your eyes only." When the letter is safely placed, leave it there until the morning of the next working day. Then, privately open the letter and read it. As you read the letter, you may experience one of a number of responses.

Among them:

- You may discover that you just feel better about what has happened and about the person to whom you have written. At that point, you might simply decide that the issue is resolved for you and no further action is needed.

- As you read the letter, you might realize that what you have said in writing reflects the important issues that must be discussed and resolved. However, you must also bear in mind that the concerns presented in the letter were expressed in a "no holds barred" fashion to diffuse frustration and to bring clarity to your perceptions. Therefore, when you actually discuss those concerns with the other person, you must present your views in a thoughtful and professional manner to avoid unnecessary harshness, or an attacking posture.

Caution: Should you decide to mail the letter always remember, once the letter is sent to the other person, you have lost all control over what that person might do with it. ***Therefore, never release anything in writing that might later come back to haunt you.*** Instead, retain the letter. Then discuss the issues directly with the person. Having written and processed your thoughts through the "no holds barred" letter writing process, you will have gained in confidence. As such, you will be able to discuss them in a more capable and effective manner.

- Another possibility is that, as you read the letter after the incubation period, you may find yourself flooded with feelings. Should that occur, it is most often a sign that you have more inside that needs to be said. As promptly as possible, again write whatever comes to mind in a no-holds-barred fashion. When the second letter is written and signed, put it in an envelope with the first letter, seal it and protect it from discovery until at least the next day. After the incubation period, read both letters to determine your response and proceed accordingly.

"Bringing Closure"

When unresolved conflicts evolve between two people, there must always be an opportunity to bring closure to what has been said, and to what has occurred. This can come about in a number of ways. It can occur in part through the letter writing process, itself. It can occur through the incubation of thoughts, through reading and rereading, and through discussing the issues directly with the individual involved.

You may also choose to read the letter or letters aloud in the presence of a trusted friend. Having a trusted friend present as you read the letter(s) can bring, yet another level of clarity to the issue of concern. It can also assist in further easing the feelings of anxiety and frustration that you have been experiencing. This is particularly true if the person who has heard you read the letter(s), offers an objective response to what you have said about the circumstances that you are in.

Keep in mind that trustworthiness and honesty are the essential qualities that must be present in the other person if truly helpful results are to be achieved.

Once the letter has (or the letters have) been processed to the point where they have served their purpose, do not retain them longer than necessary. ***Due to the sensitive nature, you must be certain they are privately and permanently destroyed.***

The no-holds-barred, letter-writing process lets you get some of your anger out without offending the person or making things worse. It also helps you record the details of the problem while they are fresh in your mind. Finally, when you reread the letter(s) it may help you calm down and be better prepared to approach the other person in a more confident and effective manner.

Practice When it is Not so Vital to You

Face and challenge the troublesome people you encounter in daily life. Take risks to overcome fear of rejection in less threatening conditions. Speak up to waiters, salespeople, desk clerks, and others who are rude and inconsiderate. Practice saying "no" to people when it involves minimal risk, or when you know it is worth it. Especially when circumstances involve unfairness, the rudeness of other people, or excessive demands on your time and energy. I urge you, the next time such an incident occurs, do it! If you stand up for yourself, you will feel like a hero, and rightly so. You will have stood up for yourself in a positively assertive manner. And, when you practice being assertive in less threatening circumstances, you will gain new skills and self-confidence for challenging the more significant issues that you encounter in life, and in the workplace.

No, That's Not Acceptable…

A few years after we married, my wife, June, and I had put aside a portion of our limited salaries for several months so that we could buy a new thirteen-inch color television set. Since we were just starting out in marriage, we had endured a small black and white model for several years. Now with the chance to upgrade to color we were both elated and proud of our accomplishment. Having saved $287.32, we went to a local retail store one Saturday morning to take advantage of an announced sale. Making the purchase and hurrying home, we eagerly placed the new set and turned it on. Imagine our delight, and the delight of our children when the rich vibrant color appeared in our home for the first time. We were on our way with the most modern entertainment of the day.

Then, much to our dismay, the television set flickered momentarily and went into a total blackout. Feeling some disgust, but aware that the store would remain open for another couple of hours, we packed up the set to arrange an exchange. Arriving at the store a short time later, we reported our dilemma to the sales clerk who was quite apologetic. However, when we asked for a simple exchange, the clerk cited company policy stating that exchanges and refunds were not possible. She instead, offered assurance that a local service facility would have the set repaired and available for us to pick-up within a week. Although disappointed and somewhat angry, June and I reluctantly agreed to the plan. The set was returned several days and several phone calls later. Then, within an hour, the set again went into a blackout. Again the set was returned to the store. Remaining unassertive, June and I began a series of trips to and from the store during the next several weeks, growing increasingly angry and frustrated with each encounter and disappointment.

Finally, June and I had enough. We then developed firm intention to resolve the matter once and for all. First of all, giving consideration to timing, we decided to return to the store on Saturday afternoon during the busiest time of day. At that point, June and I wanted an audience to be available to create anxiety among staff and officials of the store. Arriving with television and sale receipt in hand, we went promptly to the television sales area where, as luck would have it, the very clerk we had been dealing with was again on duty.

Upon seeing us arrive, the clerk was immediately apologetic, saying "Oh, Mr. and Mrs. Werre, not again. I'm so sorry. I can assure you I'll have the service representative repair your set on a priority basis and you'll have it back within the week, this time for sure." Our response, "No, that's not acceptable. We want to return the set and we want our money back." The clerk responded, "But, folks, I explained that before. Company policy won't permit us to let you return the set. But, I'll tell you what. I will personally ask the service representative to fix your set Monday morning and you won't even need to pick it up. I'll ask that it be delivered right to your home." To which we responded…"No, that's not acceptable. We want to return the set and we want our money back."

The clerk repeated her explanation several times, with each exchange ending with our response…"No, that's not acceptable. We want to return the set and we what our money back." Finally, in exasperation the clerk said, "Well, Mr. and

Mrs. Werre, it's obvious that you are not going to be reasonable about this so you are going to force me to call the store manager." Ignoring the blaming message and tone, June and I responded with, "Yes, thank you. We would appreciate having a chance to talk with anyone who can permit us to return the set and refund our money." Following a few minutes of discussion on the telephone, the clerk announced that the manager would be joining us shortly.

By the way, in discussing what had occurred after the incident, June and I both acknowledged that we had been feeling somewhat sorry for the clerk. We realized that she was really caught in the middle, and that she was simply attempting to do her job in the manner mandated by company policy. Regardless, we stood our ground.

Upon arriving, and in a rather gruff and pompous manner, the manager turned to the clerk and asked, "What seems to be the problem here?" Upon hearing the clerk's explanation, the manager turned his attention to June and me. Then, in a rather critical and contemptuous tone, he said, "Well, you know folks, this young lady is right." The manager then cited company policy stating exchanges and refunds were not possible. Our response, "No, that's not acceptable. We want to return the set and we want our money back." With each effort to persuade us to reconsider our posture, and "listen to reason," we repeated our response. With each exchange, the manager became more demanding and furious. His complexion turned "beet red" and his veins protruded from his forehead and neck.

By then, a crowd had gathered behind us. With each exchange, the manager made quick glances in their direction. As I looked back at them, I noted several looks of amusement and apparent delight. The expressions conveyed the message, "Wow, I wish I had the courage to do that." Not only was that my impression, after the incident came to a close, two of the observers came to us with offers of congratulation for our willingness to stand up to the clerk and to the manager despite the pressures that they had placed upon us.

Finally, after several additional exchanges, the manager abruptly turned around. Filled with obvious rage, the manager smashed his hand down on the cash register with such resounding force that I doubted that it would ever work again. After a quick count, the manager turned to us and slammed $287.32 on the counter. At the same time, he grabbed the television set and threw it against the back counter. With those actions, a couple of people in the crowd that had gathered behind us gave a cheer and the manager abruptly departed. Our response as the manager initiated his departure…"Thank you both for your help." Justice had been served, and we left the store with a sense of true accomplishment. We also went to another store to purchase a thirteen-inch color television set that served us well for many years.

Never be a Quitter

The principles contained in the return of a defective product, in challenging the rudeness and unfairness of our associates in the workplace, or in standing up to defend those we love…are important events in the lives of people like you and me. We deserve to be treated with fairness and consideration when we address them. If you run your life according to the dictates of others, or if you do things you really would rather not do, you are not being positively assertive. You are allowing yourself to be manipulated by someone who wishes to control you. However, you can rarely be the victim of oppressive officials or other work associates unless you allow it to happen. How we react to criticism and unfairness depends on how we feel about ourselves. Employees who do not particularly like themselves do not deal well with criticism. Nor, are they willing to take the risks that are necessary to overcome the insensitivity of their work associates. Those who are filled with self-confidence, and those who have developed a thoughtful plan for doing it, can handle almost any challenge well.

Solutions to the difficulties we face among the oppressive and incompetent individuals in the workplace must come through emotional maturity, through taking appropriate risks, and through maintaining control of our lives. Having the strength to stick with whatever we are seeking to achieve can make the difference between success and failure. Often, it becomes our nature to give up on an effort when the going gets rough, threatening, or too difficult. What is the value of escape in the long haul? There will always come that decisive moment when we run out of excuses for our own inappropriateness or fear. In the final analysis, we all need to live with the decisions and choices that we make as we face the challenges that we encounter in oppressive work environments.

7

THE "PRESSURE COOKER" SYNDROME

Dealing With Crisis

Today's work environments are far more complicated than they were during earlier times. Restrictive policy and procedures manuals, production quotas, competitive markets, and state or federal regulations all cause evolving feelings of anxiety about compliance, and about meeting the demands placed upon the organization and its workers. Extreme deadlines, fear of disapproval, and concerns about oppressive workplace circumstances all have a significant impact on how employees feel about themselves and their jobs. These circumstances also have an impact on our ability to use sound judgment in times of stress and crisis. Conflicts with supervisors, co-workers, clients, customers, and potentially dangerous people are all very much a part of today's stress-laden workplace. The potential for loss of employment and the threat of litigation add to the intensity of the turmoil and anxiety that we experience.

"Burnout" is brought on by being involved in an intense situation in a troubled workplace for an extended period without realistic support, and without opportunities for employees to express their legitimate concerns. It is a result of feeling insecure and unappreciated. Extreme crisis evolves when employees discover that their jobs, and therefore, their means of a livelihood are in jeopardy. If the crises and pressures become so frequent and so intense that workers are constantly calling upon inner resources to respond, the stress and anxiety become overwhelming. Human beings simply cannot meet such demands for extended periods of time without opportunity for relief.

The "Pressure Cooker Syndrome" is a reflection of the levels and patterns of pressure and stress that we experience in the workplace. Properly handled, workplace pressure need not be a problem. But, unhealthy responses to pressure such as assuming an antagonistic attitude toward a supervisor, calling in and claiming to be sick when no illness exists, getting into arguments with co-workers, and a host of other unhealthy patterns may cause problems to fester for months on end. These patterns eventually cause a variety of physical and emotional problems. Employees become trapped in the cycle. They act and react to cope with pressure, and these actions only create more pressure and burnout. The more stress within a short time, the greater the effect. Being subtle in nature at times, employees are not always aware of what effect workplace pressures are having on them.

Symptoms of Workplace Pressure & Burnout

When especially stressful circumstances are a continuing part of experiences encountered in a troubled workplace, the frustration, and the emotional demands may become more than employees can handle. Decision-making becomes difficult. Otherwise capable workers are hesitant, indecisive, and they question their postures and perceptions. Employees become preoccupied, worrisome, and unwilling to admit mistakes. With too much pressure, employees blame others and they display negative postures toward co-workers and work assignments. Impaired ability to reason or function adequately becomes evident. Attitudes become suspicious and pessimistic. Mistrust of co-workers and management evolves.

As pressures build, workers become rigid, irritable, impatient, and belligerent. They become increasingly frustrated and they engage in behaviors that are irritating and annoying to their colleagues. They cannot concentrate, they experience confused thinking, and they display troublesome, and sometimes explosive reactions with little or no provocation. Employees become accident-prone. They begin to make mistakes due to distractions, and due to taking unnecessary risks in carrying out safety sensitive work assignments. Overall, employees who are under too much pressure develop a "who cares?" or "what's the use?" attitude and posture. These symptoms are most likely in employees who feel misunderstood and unappreciated. They become disappointed, angry, and cynical.

Dynamics of the Pressure Cooker

People are very much like pressure cookers used in the kitchen to quickly prepare meals for our enjoyment. As we are subjected to daily doses of tension, and anxiety, pressures build inside of us. The stresses we experience are like the flame that heats the standard household pressure cooker. However, when we think of ourselves as pressure cookers, the healthy person has a variety of valves with which to release the pressures. Creativity, spirituality, recreation, food, hobbies, friends, work, relaxation, family, intimacy, exercise, solitude, rest, and a host of other daily activities and interests can serve as valves for pressure reduction. But, when pressures become more intense, troubled employees begin to close off the valves that might otherwise serve to keep them functioning in a productive and healthful manner.

"Stressed out" and frustrated employees gradually close off these resources as they become increasingly preoccupied with the one, previously helpful valve that is now overwhelmed with an excessive amount of stress. Then, all of the built up pressures are concentrated for release through that single valve, and an explosion of inappropriate behavior occurs. This may happen when we have been through an intense period of trouble or exhausting work, are worn out, on edge, and cannot reason things through.

Patterns of Potentially Explosive Behavior

In recent years, we have seen an increasing trend toward violence in the workplace. When employees feel misunderstood and mistreated, the frustration and the loss of optimism that they experience may lead to retaliation and the wish for revenge. If these oppressive circumstances continue for an extended period of time, resentment and hostility begin to emerge. Should these troublesome conditions become more intense, the circumstances created by oppressive and incompetent officials, or by callous and insensitive co-workers may then cause the troubled employee to develop thoughts of suicide and the wish to "take them with me!" The overwhelming sense of injustice, combined with the evolving sense of despair can lead to such intense feelings of bitterness and rage that the only remaining solution seems to be through suicide or violence.

Most Common Causes of Workplace-Induced Pressures

- Workers believe they are not being recognized for their accomplishments.
- Employees believe their concerns are not being heard.
- Workers are exposed to conflicting demands and they are uncertain about what is expected of them.
- Employees are subjected to verbal abuse and harassment.
- Workers are required to do things against their better judgment.

- Employees believe (or have been informed) that their jobs are in jeopardy.

Most Common Causes of Self-Induced Pressures

- Employees do not believe in what they are doing.
- Workers fail to do the best they can.
- Employees do not do the right thing.
- Workers treat others unfairly.
- Employees try to be someone they are not.
- Workers engage in the excessive use of alcohol and other drugs.

Facing Potential Danger

In a volatile situation, the most common indication of potential for assault or violence is an ***intensely persistent preoccupation with one topic, situation, or theme***. This pattern is especially important to consider when, no matter what you say, and no matter what you do to try to reason with the disturbed person, the person repeatedly responds with a comment such as, ***"Yes but, you shouldn't have...!"***or, ***"Yea, I know, but he (or she) shouldn't have...!"*** This pattern, combined with an escalating display of ***agitation*** on the part of the troubled individual is the primary indication of potential for assault or violence. When you are dealing with an intensely preoccupied person who is displaying an agitated state, your wisest course is to approach that person with caution! Employees who are filled with frustration and rage often lose their ability to think clearly. They become so agitated that they have difficulty making sound decisions. It is the utter contempt and helplessness they feel, combined with their inability to accept or change their circumstances that make them especially vulnerable to move in the direction of self-destruction, or to commit a violent act.

Responding to the agitated behavior of a mentally disturbed person can be extremely challenging. You must attempt to assure your own safety and well-being. You must consider the safety and well-being of co-workers and others who are present. And, you must attempt to deal with the disturbed individual as best you can. When you respond to the potential for violence in the workplace, it is also important to understand that, if disturbed people claim that they are "crazy," most likely they are not. And, that could indicate that they are even more danger-ous. Acts of violence and cruelty in the workplace are most often committed by individuals who know exactly what they are doing. Those acts are almost always committed by people who just do not care about the lives, concerns, or feelings of workplace officials, or about the employees involved. The postures these individuals display may simply be a reflection of their callousness and indifference toward the needs of others. Or, the postures may be an indication of their frustration and rage due to the patterns of oppression and abuse that these troubled individuals have endured over time.

Should you be confronted with the possibility of explosive behavior or violence, thoughtful and effective responses are vital! If you are not thoughtful and effective, the encounter may lead to a life-threatening situation. A key point to remember in a hostage situation in the workplace is that there are no perfect answers. In fact, in those situations that erupt into violence and death without warning, there may be no answers at all beyond diving for cover with the hope that you will survive! However, there will be times when you do have an opportunity to diffuse the situation. If you are perceptive, and if you are aware of the evolving levels of agitation and frustration, you may then have an opportunity to save your own life, and to save the lives of others. You may be able to have a preventive impact before the movement toward violence evolves to such a destructive end.

Signs of Potential for Explosiveness or Violence

- Agitation, pacing and expressions of a wish for revenge.
- Harassing phone calls or direct verbal threats.
- Hostile letters or e-mail messages conveying hatred or desperation.
- Expressions of belief that problems cannot be resolved.
- Sudden outbursts of temper and irritability.
- Displays of anger and hostility out-of-proportion to the situation.
- Psychotic episodes, hearing voices or seeing things not there.
- Employees who are extremely defensive, frightened, blaming or suspicious with or without realistic cause.
- Workers who are despondent or agitated while under the influence of alcohol or other drugs.

Five Reasons for Explosive, Suicidal, or Violent Behavior

- An attempt to control others.
- An attempt to gain attention.
- An attempt to communicate needs.
- A desire for change in life or relationships.
- An intense wish to die and to take their perceived enemies with them.

Approaching a Volatile Situation

In potentially dangerous situations effective behavior requires self-knowledge, and an understanding of the disturbed person. If the agitated person makes comments that irritate you, remember that pressure and rage can cause people to say things they really do not mean. When you are in the midst of a volatile situation, maintain a neutral posture...and remain low key and non-confrontive. Do you remember the television program of the 1980's, "Hill Street Blues?" Two characters in the series illustrate the point beautifully. One character was known as Belcher. The other character was identified as Henry Goldblume. What was Belcher's approach to a dangerous situation? He would back up, take a run, and dive into the fray with fists flying. With a grunt and a growl, Belcher would take on three, four, or more opponents, teeth and weapons flying in all directions. Only once or twice in the series did Belcher end up hurt significantly enough to be hospitalized. Even then, he lived.

Now in real life, we might be able to "pull a Belcher" in a dangerous situation, but it is extremely unlikely that will be the case. In potentially violent situations we are best advised to assume that surviving like a Belcher only happens in the movies or on television. Our best course is not to try to handle the situation like Belcher, but instead, to try to function and respond like, "Henry Goldblume!" So, who was this character, Goldblume? Henry was the detective lieutenant and hostage negotiator that the officials called upon to negotiate dangerous and life threatening hostage situations. What was his style? Henry Goldblume was portrayed as an individual who knew people and their nature. He presented himself as calm, thoughtful, and self-assured, step-by-step moving toward diffusing the situation. The style of Henry Goldblume reflects the epitome of effective negotiation in a hostage situation.

What can you do when you are being threatened by a potentially dangerous person? How can you effectively manage the situation? And, how can you contain the feelings of anxiety and frustration that you will most likely experience? Making demands and engaging in angry outbursts often escalate feelings of anger and aggression. The most fundamental, and the most effective means of approach to a potentially violent person is to do so in a calm, non-accusing, and non-threatening manner. Your message should be one that attempts to align or contract with the individual. Never confront, threaten or challenge the person who may be evolving to a posture of explosiveness. The basic message you should attempt to send, "I'm just a person like you...and I want to be fair and to do what's right in this situation."

Overcome Your Fear

Explosive situations are frightening and difficult, but they can be managed by using sound judgment and reason. When emotionally distraught individuals threaten to harm or kill themselves, workplace officials, or other employees, they almost always have a sense of uncertainty about what they are thinking of doing. Most often what they really want is to somehow bring about a change in their workplace or life circumstances. However, due to the unresolved feelings that they harbor, and due to the levels of frustration that they are experiencing, they have lost sight of the alternatives that may be available to them. Once the potentially volatile situation has been contained, the primary concern of disturbed individuals is almost always that they will be treated fairly, and that they will now somehow have an opportunity to resolve the anxiety and conflict that they have been experiencing. The concept of fairness is universal. To illustrate this point, I once worked with the resident of a psychiatric ward who was confined to the facility due to engaging in the fierce assault of two innocent victims.

Just prior to an encounter that I had with the resident, Rueben had learned that I had advised his wife not to give in to his unreasonable demands and expectations. Although his wife needed food for the couple's children, Rueben, was demanding that Marie use a large portion of her limited financial resources to buy him a new color television. Rueben wished to have the set to enjoy in the privacy of his room so he would not have to watch his favorite programs in the day room with the other residents. Upon asking my advice, I encouraged Marie to stand firm and save the money to meet her needs and the needs of the children. When Rueben learned of my recommendation, he became extremely menacing, angrily demanding, "Werre, are you going to tell Marie to buy me that TV set or not?" As calmly as possible, I responded to Rueben's demand by saying, "No, I won't do that." When he heard my response, Rueben became livid with rage and screamed, "Werre...you're a dead man!" Upon seeing his condition and hearing his response, I simply remained firm and stood my ground.

Later, when Rueben had calmed down to some degree, I approached him with the most calm and self-assured tone that I could muster. During that encounter, I pointed out the facts of Marie's circumstances. I also reminded Rueben of his responsibility to consider the legitimate needs of his children. At the same time, I introduced the element of fairness, and asked him to give thought to what would be the fair and right thing to do. Within a few minutes Rueben, even in his mentally troubled state, indicated his awareness of what would be fair and what would be the selfish posture for him to take.

Stay Calm Under Fire!

One of the most challenging encounters that we can experience is to attempt to encourage reasonable behavior from a person who is creating a life-threatening situation. It is extremely difficult to try to assure safety in response to the threats and demands of an agitated person. Before allowing yourself to become anxious or irritated to the point where you may take unnecessary risks or cause further jeopardy, slow yourself down so you can stay in charge of your emotions. Instead of reacting impulsively, do the best you can to listen to the disturbed individual's concerns. By showing you are willing to listen, you are letting the troubled person know that you are concerned, and that you want him or her to be treated fairly, and with respect. Unless you see that the disturbed person is immediately dangerous, try to slow things down. Troubled people will typically calm down within a few minutes if they are not threatened or interrupted when attempting to present their concerns and complaints. Your willingness to listen, and your willingness to show interest in the disturbed person and the problem being experienced could show that you have the troubled individual's best interest at heart.

Remember to Breathe

An eastern philosophy suggests, "When we are in charge of our breathing...we are in charge of our lives." If you remain in control of your breathing, it will help you to overcome your fear and allow you to think more clearly. It also helps to remember that no negotiation is possible during an explosive episode. The situation must be contained first. If you remain patient, calm, and attentive, angry people will eventually defuse themselves.

Monitor Your Responses

People who are mentally disturbed are often remarkably perceptive. It is as though they have a human form of "radar" that permits them to scan the horizon in an attempt to detect any challenges, real or imagined, to their well-being or postures. They may quite readily sense any signs of weakness, fear or irritation that are experienced by those around them. Disturbed individuals may also quickly detect any attempts to deceive them. In retaliation, they may become highly manipulative or attacking as they call attention to displays of fearfulness, hostility, indecisiveness, and other points of vulnerability. If the disturbed person engages in a verbal attack on your integrity, reactions, or character, simply remain thoughtful and stay in control of your emotions. Try to keep in mind that the troubled individual is only using these tactics to overcome strong feelings of anxiety and frustration by attempting to belittle or threaten you.

While serving as an intern in social work practice, I was assigned to meet with a client in crisis. As I arrived at the scene, I found the young man in the midst of a highly emotional episode. The client vacillated between periods of menacing challenge directed toward anyone who might attempt to approach him, to displays of anguish and tearfulness. As he began to calm down, the young man told me of the many painful crises he had experienced in recent weeks. Upon hearing Mark's story, I placed my hand on his shoulder as he sat sobbing with his head resting in his hands. Then, abruptly, and in a menacing voice, Mark said, "Get your hands off of me. My mother doesn't care about me so why should you?" Upon hearing his words, and the tone in which they were expressed, I became immediately anxious. Yet, I felt compelled not to comply with the young man's demand. As such, I did not move, but neither did he. After what seemed like a very long time, the young man again began to cry profusely. As Mark's emotion flowed, I remained steadfast in my physical contact with him.

The incident with the young man happened more than twenty years ago. Today Mark is married, has two children, and he chose to return to school to pursue a degree in social work. He is now a successful and respected member of the profession. Mark openly admits that day changed his life, and provided him with the foundation for the productivity and contentment he now enjoys.

I believe this story illustrates that if we want to make a meaningful contribution there will always be a certain amount of risk involved. We must either take the risk to pursue what we believe in, or accept the less clear, but far more insidious risk of living a life without moments of achievement and success.

Keep your cool despite the high levels of anxiety, anger or fear that you may be experiencing. Do not get drawn into heated verbal exchanges because that could cause you to say or do something that could lead to disastrous consequences. Instead, try to recognize the sensitivity of the situation for you, for the disturbed person, and for others who may be present. By being in touch with your thoughts and feelings you will know you are about to lose your temper and have a better chance of remaining calm and thoughtful.

Avoid Deceptive Maneuvers

Do not make promises or agreements that you are not sure you can live up to. Employees who are being threatened by disturbed colleagues or other work associates sometimes resort to deception as an attempt to get the agitated individual under control. But, this should only be used when there is a real and immediate danger, and when there are no other choices available. Desperate employees and workplace officials sometimes trick hostage takers by telling them lies, or by making promises that they cannot or should not keep. The hostage takers believe the hostages and later find themselves to be in conflict with the law, or they are confined in a controlled setting contrary to what was promised. They may then feel so angry and betrayed that they will seek to retaliate at the first opportunity.

If you find that you cannot offer an honest or potentially satisfactory answer, you might respond with a comment like, "I am really overwhelmed about this, but I am still willing to try to work things out with you." That type of response lets the person know that you realize that you don't have all the answers either, but that you are willing to do what you can and not be dishonest or phony about it. Let the person know you will try to be of help in finding solutions to the concerns that are being presented. But, do not deceive the disturbed person unless you believe you absolutely have to. Instead, stay true to your word and do what you say you are going to do.

The Brubraker Principle

Several years ago, Robert Redford portrayed the central character in a fascinating movie called "Brubaker." The movie depicted an idealistic young warden named Henry Brubaker. Prior to assuming his role as the warden of Wakefield State Penitentiary, Brubaker entered the facility as an inmate resident. While living within the prison population, Brubaker became increasingly aware of oppressive policies and corrupt maneuvering by inmates, staff, and politicians alike. As such, he became determined to clean up the oppressive practices and widespread corruption. Within a short time, remarkable progress had been made in bringing improvement to the facility. However, Brubaker underestimated the truly corrupt nature of even the political regime in power.

In implementing his reforms, Brubaker became a threat to prominent state officials and to members of the prison board. His actions were also resented by some of the residents of the community located near the prison facility. And, he was frequently deceived by the corrupt members of the prison staff. These unscrupulous individuals were gaining enormous profits through engaging in the theft of prison property. The corruption even extended to the theft of prison food supplies leading to conditions of illness and near starvation of inmate residents. Although he received ominous warnings from administrative officials to curb his efforts toward reform, Brubaker remained firm in his resolve to do what he knew to be right.

Then one day the warden encountered an old and wise convict in a corridor of the prison. As the pair engaged in conversation, the convict told Brubaker, "You know, Warden, I really like the changes that you've brought to this place since you've been here. But, Warden, I'm worried about something. I'm worried that you may be offering these men hope where there is none." The convict's remark seemed to make an impression on Brubaker, yet he knew that what he was doing was right, and so he continued his reforms, one day to discover an even more horrible truth. He discovered that the corrupt political regime had been covering up the untimely deaths by foul play of a large number of inmate residents. The inmates, who had been tortured and killed, were secretly buried on prison property over the years. The warden aggressively took action in an attempt to learn the truth and to bring the guilty to justice. But again, Brubaker underestimated the corrupt nature of the political regime in power. He also underestimated to what extent they were willing to go to protect themselves, their cronies, and their ability to profit at the expense of others.

The last scenes in the movie complete the tale. In a scene as the movie is near an end, we have just learned that Brubaker has been fired by the corrupt administration. We see him arranging to leave the prison escorted by a trooper in a State Patrol vehicle. The scene then shifts to the prison yard. There we discover the new warden for the prison, chosen from the ranks of the corrupt administration's political cronies. As the movie closes, the new warden has assembled the convicts in the prison yard. He is standing on a platform extending from one of the prison towers as he addresses the inmates assembled in the yard. The new warden, speaking through a megaphone is announcing his new policies for the prison. The policies of course, provided a dark foreboding of what was to come. The new warden was announcing the very policies and political maneuvers that had led to, and escalated, the prison's corruption in the first place. The wise old convict's words rang true. "I'm worried that you may be offering these men hope where there is none."

This story clearly illustrates the power and importance of genuineness and credibility. The most powerful tools for building positive relationships are genuineness and credibility. To develop and retain these qualities we must demonstrate that we believe in what we are doing. But, if we wish to retain our credibility and reputation as genuine and effective persons, we must also never knowingly make promises we don't intend to keep…or cannot keep! In other words, we must never, "offer hope where there is none!"

Expect to be Tested

When you are threatened, frustrated, and anxious, be careful of impulsive responses to the demands of the hostage taker. Saying **"yes"** too quickly may give the impression that you are a "gullible fool." Being too abrupt when you find it necessary to say **"no"** may suggest that you are "cold and heartless." You may then convey the message that you are someone else who cannot be trusted or believed. Troubled people who are agitated to the point where they become menacing and take hostages are usually frustrated and angry. As a result, they may turn against you. They may attempt to insult you by calling you names, or by making belittling remarks about your comments, behavior or appearance. They may also express the belief that you really don't care about what is happening to them. They may even accuse you of wanting to harm them.

Keep in mind, agitated people are already angry, suspicious, and frustrated. Therefore, giving them orders, making demands, and directing threats toward them usually only make matters worse. If you present an antagonistic posture toward their attitude, behavior or remarks, they may then feel even more compelled to retaliate. They may also believe that they have greater need to become menacing and abusive as they attempt to defend themselves. When disturbed individuals are agitated and preoccupied, you may not be able to reason with them. But, if you remain thoughtful and attentive, they may begin to quiet down and then become more willing to join you in a search for solutions to their problems and concerns.

Never Argue in a Hostage Situation

Some professionals who work with dangerous people are frequently assaulted, while others are never physically hurt at all. Judgment is the key. When the troubled individual starts to show signs of losing control, avoid being forced into arguments. Even if the person is saying things in anger that are not true, do not become defensive or unnecessarily aggressive. People who lose control of their emotions in a volatile situation are at risk of placing themselves and others in jeopardy. Our most common sense of anger comes from the belief that we are trapped, and that we have no choices available to us. Keep in mind that you do have the choice of how you will approach and respond to the troubled individual if you remain calm and thoughtful. Don't take the attitude and posture of the disturbed person personally. And by all means, do not let the agitated individual cause you to lose your temper.

While working in a Penitentiary setting, I was asked to interview a new inmate resident who had been transferred to the facility from another State. The inmate was serving time for murder. As the interview began, I invited Gordon to have a seat next to my desk so that I could begin to gather background information. As the discussion evolved, Gordon developed a distant expression on his face. He then interrupted my questioning to ask, "Mr. Werre, is that your pen (referring to a ball point pin that was lying on my desk between us)?" My response was, "Yes, do you have need for one?" Gordon then said menacingly, "No, I just wanted to tell you that I was transferred here because I stabbed a guard with a pen just like that because he asked too many personal questions."

Of course, I became quite alarmed by his remark. As such, I continued briefly with the interview, thanked him for his time, and excused him from the area. In follow up, I was thinking, "Well, old Gordy was probably just pulling my leg to see how I would react." However, upon reviewing his criminal record, which was forwarded to my office the next day, I discovered that Gordon had been totally honest. He had actually stabbed an officer in the throat with the officer's own pen!

Since prison inmates must be dealt with despite the risks, I arranged for Gordon's long-term assignment to a male caseworker. In making the assignment, I provided the caseworker with a thorough briefing on the inmate's history of violence and potential for assault. I urged the worker to use sound judgment and caution when working with Gordon. I also gave him specific guidelines for creating a calm, self-assured, and non-threatening environment during any encounters with the potentially dangerous resident.

From that point, things appeared to evolve in a stable manner. Then one day, the caseworker scheduled a visit with Gordon in an office next to mine. As was my practice, I decided to remain nearby in the event that difficulty should surface. After about ten minutes into the visit, a voice could be heard from behind the closed door. Within seconds the voice had escalated in intensity, filled with expressions of out-of-control rage. Fearing the worst, I promptly called for reinforcements. However, before they arrived, the screaming and raging escalated to an even more intense level. Fearing for the life of the caseworker, I rushed to the door, opened it and stood in shocked surprise due to what I saw. Contrary to what I had anticipated, the caseworker was standing over the seated inmate, screaming and raging while pointing his finger at Gordon. Gordon sat cowering and motionless, with a look of anguish on his face. Directing my remarks to the caseworker, I said "I'm sorry to disturb you but you have an emergency in the cell house area. Perhaps you can follow-up with this discussion with Gordon later." With that, the inmate was excused and left without incident, escorted by the officers who had by then, arrived on the scene.

In the debriefing that followed, the caseworker acknowledged that he had become so enraged at what Gordon had said to him that he had lost all control. The inmate's remark had triggered a rush of unresolved feelings related to how the caseworker's father had approached him in childhood, causing him to explode like a volcano. Apparently, the rage of the caseworker was so intense that Gordon was momentarily in a state of shock and unable to retaliate. Information obtained later gave clear indication that Gordon was also enraged by what had happened. He made it known to fellow inmates and staff alike, that he would not hesitate to kill the caseworker at the first opportunity. We of course, took precautions to prevent that from happening.

Now, this is a classic example of how **not to approach** an explosive person. I am convinced that the abruptness of the caseworker's rage is the only thing that prevented his being subjected to serious bodily harm or even death. This is evidenced not only by Gordon's verbal threats, but also by the number of inmate residents and staff who were assaulted by Gordon during the time that he remained at the facility until his transfer could be arranged to a maximum security and more highly regimented institution.

Take Time to Think

Each encounter with a volatile person can lead to something unexpected. What works to resolve the crisis in one situation might not work under the circumstances that you face in the next. Resist the temptation to act impulsively, and before you understand the situation more thoroughly. Even in the most difficult circumstances, you will usually have a little time to think or to decide what to do before you need to respond. When you do get a chance to speak, it can be helpful to ask for more information so that you more clearly understand the concerns and messages being sent. However, while you are in the midst of an intense crisis, try to avoid discussion of the reason for the agitation because this could again arouse the anger and rage. Also, you must be careful not to compromise or embarrass the disturbed person in the presence of co-workers, or in the presence of anyone else who may be able to hear your remarks. As you decide what to say or do, consider how your actions might affect your own safety, and the safety of workplace colleagues or others who may be present.

There are no guarantees that any response that you give to a troubled individual will assure safety and prevent disaster. However, it is usually best to remain as thoughtful and accurate as you can when you respond to questions that the disturbed person may present. If you do not know the answer, say so, and offer to find out if you can. But, only do that if you are willing and able to follow through with the offer. You might also attempt to ease the tension by using phrases such as "Let me give this some thought. I don't want to do anything that would make things worse." Or, you might say, "This is obviously important to you. I want you to know it's important to me too! I want to make sure we handle it fairly!" If you act impulsively or take provocative comments personally, it becomes more likely that the disturbed person will be able to arouse your emotions and prevent you from managing yourself in a safe and productive manner.

Redirect the Course

An oriental saying suggests, "It is easier to ride a horse in the direction it is going." Always answer hostage takers on your terms. But, do not lock them in.

Do not convey aggression of any kind. Instead, divert attention to a neutral theme and when possible, keep focused on solutions. If something really damaging or troubling is said, respond to it only after the crisis is past. Do not answer anger with anger. When you are provoked or frustrated, you may be inclined to raise your voice in response to the angry person's negative comments or loud voice. Instead, speak as calmly as you can. This conveys a sense of self-assuredness, and causes the disturbed individual to listen more carefully.

Using a calm, self-assured approach will almost always increase the possibility that the angry person will then lower his or her own voice in response to your remarks. As the hostage taker quiets down, tensions should ease, and you will then be able to continue with your search for ways to solve the problem. When the person becomes calmer, send a clear message that you are going to do the best you can to be of help. Then, offer your thoughts on what might be the best way to resolve the disturbed person's concerns.

Let Them Ventilate

A cardinal rule in a volatile situation is *never match power with power unless you absolutely have to!* In responding to the power plays of the disturbed person, do not lose your temper. Remember the principle…"When you lose your temper…you lose!" It is usually not possible to solve a problem until disturbed individuals have a chance to say what is on their minds. As you interact with the troubled person, avoid phrases such as, "You have no choice" or, "You better calm down now." Such statements cause feelings of anger and resistance. Instead, it is usually most helpful to simply remain silent as troubled individuals talk, cry, scream, and otherwise express their feelings and opinions. By letting hostage takers ventilate, you are also helping them to "get it out of their systems" so that they will then be more likely to calm down.

Do not interrupt or attempt to stop the potentially explosive person from talking, even if the person is making threats or engaging in hostile verbal attacks. Having an opportunity to express anger and rage will often have a calming effect on an agitated person. As the individual calms down, begin to ask appropriate questions to increase your potential to engage in helpful discussion, and to help you to reason with the angry person. Thoughtful questions keep the other person talking so that concerns are revealed as the agitated person sees them. They also convey the message that you care and that you are interested in trying to solve the problem in a fair and respectful manner.

Seek Solutions & Alternatives

Attempt to align with the disturbed person as you seek acceptable solutions to the crisis. Letting disturbed individuals know that they are important, and that you are concerned about them causes them to feel better about themselves and about you. It also encourages more open discussion so that clearer perceptions and greater understanding can be reached. Once the most explosive anger has subsided, direct the conversation toward solving the underlying problems. As the agitated person calms down, provide guidance, and serve as an example for the person as you engage in a search for solutions by taking one thoughtful step at a time.

If the disturbed person is still too upset to look at things rationally, do what you can to slow things down. Hostage takers have problems because of their impulsivity and their inability to take satisfactory action on their own behalf. If you have an opportunity to do so, establish a course of action that allows the hostage taker to make positive choices. Then provide the support and encouragement that you believe is necessary to defuse the situation, and to bring closure to the difficult circumstances. As you assist the troubled individual to work through the crisis, do not put yourself down. The calm and sensitive person is often the most effective in hostage situations. Reassure the hostage taker that you value his or her opinion. Keep focused on solutions. Reach an agreement…then move on as you disarm the disturbed person through genuineness and sincerity.

Disturbed individuals often view life from extreme perspectives, and they tend to place themselves in situations where they believe they have no alternatives! In other words, "if not this…it must be that." "I see no way things can be better. Therefore, my only way out is to die and take my enemies with me!" Help hostage takers to see those alternatives! People who take hostages have a history of not getting their message across (or their needs met). They send an extremely powerful message when they act on their unresolved rage. Violence gets the hostage taker's message across without question!

"Don't Push the River"

Imagine yourself for a moment, standing in a river on a shallow riverbed. See the cold, clear water with its current flowing toward you. Now, in your thoughts, see yourself attempting to push that current back. As you attempt to do so, what do you imagine will happen? The current of course, will continue to flow in the direction that it was destined to go. Regardless of how hard you try, you will not be able to "push the river" in the direction you wish it to take. When you are in a volatile and intimidating situation with a disturbed person, you will be wise not to attempt to push the river. Instead, it will be best for you to remain centered in your thoughts, in your behavior, in your methods, and in your posture. Do not be the aggressor, but remain alert and at the ready. Then simply, "go with the flow!" When you are in doubt...remain silent and let the out-of-control person ventilate. Neutralize the situation when you can and be patient.

- Listen actively and with concern.
- Join the person in a search for solutions.
- Help the person explore new ways of coping with problems.
- Project confidence...presence, not physical size is the key.
- Convey messages of strength and compassion to the troubled person.

Do your best to remember the critical events that occurred during the intensity of the incident. But, do not write anything down while you are in the midst of the crisis. Your recollections may become valuable in terms of any investigative processes that may be initiated. They may also be of value in designing measures for the prevention of similar episodes in the future. Taking notes, however, could place you in great jeopardy if they are found in your possession or otherwise discovered.

Beware of Overconfidence

While working at the North Dakota State Penitentiary, I displayed a "professional presence" of a different sort. One day, Charlie, an inmate of the facility became enraged in the general inmate population. Being aware of his history of fierce assault, the officers quickly acted to restrain him. The officers then escorted Charlie to a holding area to assure safety and permit him to calm down. However, as the officers arrived at the secure area, Charlie suddenly broke free, lurching forward and locking himself inside the holding area. Once inside and barricaded, Charlie became menacing to the point where the officers were unable to regain access. Not wishing to use unnecessary force, the officers began a process of negotiation to talk him down.

After well over an hour without success, the officers contacted me to assist them. Coming upon the scene, I was at a loss as well, having no idea how to break the impasse. But, as luck would have it, approximately twenty minutes later, Charlie, apparently ran out of steam. He then calmed down to the point where he allowed access to the holding area. Being in an apparent conciliatory frame of mind, Charlie asked if he might visit with me in my office to explore why the incident occurred. Since no one had been hurt during the incident, the officers and I granted the request. We then escorted Charlie to my office where we began to discuss the matter. Since the incident had taken a significant amount of time, and being rather foolishly overconfident, I relieved the officers to permit them to catch-up on regularly assigned duties prior to change of shift.

Now, to illustrate how I really did not have any more influence with Charlie then the officers, as I began to comment on the incident, Charlie, without warning, again became enraged to the point of violence. In that state, Charlie lunged toward me, screaming and in a total state of rage. He stood with his face only inches from mine. Charlie jabbed his finger toward me as he shouted, "Dick, do you think you can hurt me? Nobody can hurt me! I am immune to pain and I will prove it to you." With those remarks, and with breath that could have scorched the barnacles off of a battleship, Charlie reached up, grabbed a huge clump of his own hair and ripped it out, scalp and all. He then threw the material on the floor, stomping on it with his boot and grinding it into the carpet saying, "Dick, do you think that hurt? It didn't hurt at all. Nothing can hurt me." Having said it, Charlie again reached up, ripping yet another clump of hair and scalp from his head and grinding it into the carpet.

And, what about my "professional presence?" Well, actually I believe I was in the midst of displaying it. I simply remained silent, and as motionless as I could, digging my fingers into the arms of my solid oak chair. In truth, I was so scared I do not really believe I was capable of doing anything else. Regardless, after what seemed like an eternity, with me maintaining total silence, Charlie paused momentarily from his raging to catch his breath. Then with each opportunity I quietly stated, "Charlie, I won't feel comfortable talking with you until you sit in that chair (As if I had a choice in the matter!)." After about fifteen minutes, Charlie's rage subsided and he walked over to his chair and sat down. Then, mustering my courage, I mentioned the time and the fact that Charlie had not yet had a chance to have his evening meal. Reaching that common ground, and with Charlie's agreement, I escorted him back to his cell in the holding area. By that time, I had no interest at all, in attempting to investigate the basis for his earlier states of rage.

Despite the fact that I did almost nothing to contain the situation, I believe that I displayed a professional presence throughout the ordeal. The clear evidence...I lived through it without being assaulted, and no one other than Charlie, by his own hand, was harmed. I do need to point out, however, my boxer shorts did need some special attention following the incident. Of course, after enduring Charlie's breath, their condition was a relatively small price to pay.

When Physical Restraint is Required

When you are in the midst of responding to a crisis with a disturbed person, you may realize that the individual is so agitated or violent that he or she must be restrained. When you see that is the case, do not try to handle the situation alone unless it is absolutely necessary. Do not hesitate to call for help if you have an opportunity to do so. Impulsive actions and unnecessary risk taking can lead to serious harm to you, to your colleagues, and to anyone else who may be present. The value of avoiding impulsive actions or unnecessary risk taking is clearly demonstrated by doctors, nurses, and other staff who work in mental hospitals or other potentially dangerous institutional settings. Even though they are regularly exposed to dangerous and volatile individuals, these professionals are seldom hurt. They have learned how to support each other's efforts as a team, and they know how to use quiet, firm authority with patients and residents. It is the aggressive, arrogant, and insensitive employee in the potentially dangerous circumstance that is more likely to be harmed.

A basic rule in a hostage situation is, if you must resort to a physical intervention, *never start strongly, and then quit.* When an individual is explosive, use restraint only as a last resort measure. Use self-defense measures only when needed...but, fight with all of your being until you have control of the situation if you are forced to resort to physical means. The reason is clear. If you begin defensive measures and then quit, your actions may have caused the disturbed person to become even more filled with rage. Even though, in the midst of the scuffle, the enraged person may convincingly promise to remain calm, once released, he or she may then retaliate with a vicious attack.

Establish an Escape Route if You Can

If the guidelines I have provided do not seem appropriate to the circumstances you are in, it may be wise to try to get away from the disturbed individual should the opportunity present it self. Or, if escape is not possible, simply remain as silent as the agitated person will permit. If you do decide to make an attempt to escape, carefully assess the situation before you proceed. Whether your escape attempt succeeds or fails, you can anticipate that your action may have a serious impact upon the welfare and safety of anyone else who may be present. It is also important to be aware, if your attempt fails, it could cost you your life. As soon as you are in a safe environment, provide prompt warnings to any potential hostages or victims, and alert appropriate officials and authorities to what is occurring.

If all else fails, making the comment, "Oh wow, I really have to go to the bathroom!" may provide a means of escape. The comment has been used by mental health professionals who report that it may have saved their lives. For example, a friend of mine who worked in a State hospital tells of being cornered one day by an enraged resident. The resident had broken the leg off of a solid oak chair and was threatening to use it as a club to do harm to Ray. Having exhausted all other resources to calm the resident, Ray recalled the phrase and abruptly expressed it to the resident. The need to go to the bathroom is a universally understandable condition. Apparently, it took the resident by such surprise that he quickly said, "Okay Ray, you go ahead and go, but get back here as soon as you're done. I'm not through with you yet." Of course, Ray seized the opportunity to escape the crisis, seeking reinforcements and resolving the situation. In fact, I won't say Ray was running as he left the room that day, but he certainly could have passed anyone that was!

Crisis Can Be a Good Thing

Prepare for the worst, as you hope for the best. Try to think ahead and plan a response for anything that could go wrong in the midst of a hostage situation. Envisioning worst-case scenarios will help you to respond more effectively should you encounter a violent circumstance. The mental exercises will help you even if the crisis that erupts is not one that you have anticipated. The most beneficial thing you can do in a hostage situation is to survive, and to offer support and protection to everyone that you can. It is also vital that you do what you can to provide an opportunity for the disturbed person to verbally express feelings and concerns. But remember, it is the disturbed person who must talk, not you! What you need to do is get them started, and then become a good listener!

You also must convey the message to an appropriate degree that you care about what has occurred, or about what might happen to the disturbed person. It helps to say, "Crisis can be a good thing," but when you say it…you must be prepared to say how. Be sure to look for the good things that may come about even though the crisis has occurred. It is important to let hostage takers know that as much as possible, you will allow and respect their right to choose, but not at the expense of your own rights and safety, or of the rights and safety of others. Send the message "Let's see if we can work this out together."

Recognize & Make Choices

When we think of the dangers of our times and the potential for us to one day encounter a life-threatening situation, it becomes increasingly tempting to consider a search for someplace to hide. Unfortunately, in today's world, the question is seriously presented whether such a place may even exist. With this dilemma in mind it might be helpful to consider the circumstance of Ted Kennedy after his second brother was struck down by the action of a coward.

Shortly after the death of Bobby, Ted, was asked by a member of the media, "Well Senator, what are you going to do now? Your brothers, John and Bobby are gone, and you are the only one remaining. Will you quit now and retire to private life?" Ted Kennedy's answer was superb. He said, "No, I am going to pick up the fallen standard like my brothers before me, because I know, there is no safety in hiding." I think we must remember those words as we face the pressures and risks that are an undeniable part of our world.

8

WEATHERING HARD TIMES

When Oppression is in the Wind

Successfully responding to oppression and crisis can be strengthening for employees, and for the workplace itself. Along with anxiety and stress, there are opportunities for achievement and a sense of true accomplishment as difficulties are faced and worked through. Those employees who learn how to accept workplace challenges and handle problems with colleagues are the ones who usually find employment a rich, full, and rewarding experience. They are able to weather hard times because they have a sense of perspective and they trust their ability to survive.

Now, it is true that we often have little choice about the conditions that oppressive officials and troublesome co-workers create for us. We also may not have much choice about many of the demands that they place upon us. But, we do have a choice in how we will respond to them. We can make the situation into a growing experience. How poorly (or how well) we handle oppression and callousness is determined by our attitude. Each time we face an oppressive posture or difficult circumstance, a fundamental decision must be made…"Do I give up, now?" or "Do I try one more time to make things better?" In times of challenge, choices must be made. Among fundamental choices are to quit and to move on, perhaps to even greater uncertainty and disappointment. Or, we may choose to stay, and to do what we can to make a meaningful contribution.

Meeting the Challenge

When we attempt to cope with stressful circumstances, we too often rely on routine approaches, and the ways in which we have grown comfortable in doing things. In oppressive situations, we may find it necessary to go beyond the ordinary even if it means going against what at an earlier time may have been so helpful to us. We also need to respond to our work-related circumstances as they really are, not as we wish them to be. Some levels of oppression and incompetence are inevitable in almost all realms of employment, as they are in life. When you manage to rise above these troubling and troublesome circumstances, the workplace can become an exciting and challenging place. By rising above the crisis, we experience growth, progress, and fulfillment. With crisis often comes fear of the future. But, meeting the challenge also brings hope! Employees who believe they are in control of their lives can experience an enormous amount of workplace pressure and even thrive on it. Workers who feel helpless can hardly cope at all.

Know the Value of Service

We can learn a great deal from Carl Sewell, a car dealer from Texas who is remarkably successful in the business world, and as a community leader. Mr. Sewell, who wrote the book, "Customers for Life" developed his business philosophy based on two simple concepts that he learned from his father. The concepts were, *"learn from those you serve"* and, *"do it right."* Carl applied these concepts when he started his first small business venture in the State of Texas. As he conducted informal surveys, Carl learned that his customers wanted loaner cars when they left their own automobiles at his shop for service. The customers often said, "You know Carl, we really like the car you sold us. It runs just fine. But, one of the things we don't like is that, when we leave our car at your shop for service, we don't have a car for the day. Now, it's nice that your staff gives us a ride to work, and we appreciate it when you pay for a cab. But, what we really want is a car available to us. That's why we bought the car in the first place."

Mr. Sewell then took his customer's concerns to heart, and he made five loaner cars available for that purpose. Five cars were all that he needed then, based on business he was doing. By the time his book was published ten years later, Carl Sewell had more than two hundred and fifty loaner cars available for that purpose! Carl also has his staff arrange to have the loaner vehicle fully serviced and ready for the customer with a full tank of gas, within one minute after the customer's business is concluded.

Doing It Right!

Don't forget Carl Sewell's second principle...*do it right!* Carl informs his staff at the time of hiring that if a car has been repaired or serviced, and is then returned due to dissatisfaction for whatever reason, they won't charge the customer. The employee involved is then required to redo the job without pay. It may not surprise you that Carl Sewell's organization has the lowest rate of return of cars to be re-serviced or repaired again due to customer dissatisfaction in the region. You may also believe that Carl Sewell would have difficulty with hiring and retaining mechanics because of the policy. But, that's not the case. Carl also has one of the lowest staff turnover rates of any business in the State of Texas. Why? Because Carl Sewell truly values the employees who work for him…and they know it. They know the policy up front, and of course, Carl is a fair man. He is there helping during those rare occasions when a service or repair job needs to be redone.

How can you follow Carl Sewell's example? For one thing, you can remember who you are…your good qualities. If you are anything like me, I am always less afraid and insecure when I believe I have something to offer. Also, there is a place in the world for anyone who says, "I will take care of it…and I will do it right!"

Take Care of Yourself First

Among the essential ingredients for the maintenance of personal strength and a self-confident personality is that we must satisfy our own needs first. It is not our job to please others first no matter who might have told us that. Whoever said that was wrong! Now, I'm not talking about being selfish when I talk about the importance of taking care of yourself first. No, I'm talking about taking care of yourself, physically, emotionally, and spiritually. In doing so, you will naturally have the ability to be "tough minded" in a positive sense when the difficult times and circumstances are upon you. Only when we have done our best to make the most of ourselves can we be of greatest service to our families, friends, and communities.

"Do You Know What They Are Going to Do to Us Now?"

Some employees just love to spread the bad news. They attain morbid satisfaction from being the first to know so they can spread it around. Or, they just enjoy seeing how other employees react when they have an opportunity to tell someone about circumstances they believe will lead to disaster. For example, some years ago an employee started a rumor in a local organization. The rumor was started with the classic phrase, ***"Do you know what they are going to do to us now?"*** The question was related to a restructuring process initiated by officials of the facility. The rumor, "Everybody in this place is going to have a 20 percent cut in salary!" Imagine the dissension and uproar. Within hours there were clusters of agitated employees throughout the facility. Some employees expressed anger and rage, while others began to display signs of depression and anxiety. One group began to form an employee action committee to issue a formal protest to the administration.

Of course, when the administration became aware of the evolving unrest, they acted promptly to dispel the rumor. As it turned out, there was not a shred of truth to the remarks that had caused all of the anxiety and discontent. In fact to this day, several years later, no one has been able to determine how the rumor got started in the first place. However, two things are certain. Not one person at the facility has been subjected to a decrease in salary. And, not a single employee has been let go due to budget shortfalls, or due to an administrative decision to implement a reduction in force. A lesson to be learned from this episode is to think, and to check things out before you react impulsively to inflammatory and unfounded comments in the workplace. I have found repeatedly, when I have had the presence of mind to do so, that the situation was not nearly as serious as I had been told or imagined it to be.

Become More Valuable at Work

Are you worried about losing your job? Do you feel frustrated by the manipulations of your co-workers? Are you being threatened by the controlling postures of oppressive workplace officials? Well, you are certainly not alone. But, that does not mean there is nothing you can do to prevent job loss if your personal and family responsibilities require you to remain in an oppressive circumstance. You can make it less likely that your employer will want to lay you off. How? Do your job to the best of your ability. You can also improve your job security if you display a positive attitude. You will enhance your value to any organization, oppressive or not, when you are willing to help out during difficult times, and when you demonstrate reliable work habits.

Be Part of the Solution

- Have you displayed self-initiative by establishing priorities and completing assignments in an organized and timely fashion?

- Have you asked your supervisor what you can do to improve your work performance?

- Have you taken the initiative to complete necessary tasks even though you have not been required to do so?

- Do you keep your supervisor informed of the status of projects you have been assigned to complete?

- Do you avoid involvement in "workplace politics" that promote a negative atmosphere in your organization?

- Have you volunteered to assist your co-workers when your own assignments are completed?

- Do you respect and follow "chain of command" structure when you have concerns related to supervision or other work-related issues?

Even oppressive workplace officials will respond more positively to employees who are willing to take on additional responsibility and who bring an enthusiastic attitude to the work environment. Give assignments the priority they deserve. Follow through on every work assignment in a professional, timely, and effective manner. The most successful workers are those who make a conscientious effort to provide quality service. They are organized and efficient. They make sure that what they do is done correctly, and they make sure that it is done well.

When You Realize that You Must Leave

Despite your best efforts, you may find it necessary to consider employment elsewhere if the pressures you experience in an oppressive work environment cannot be resolved. But, don't leave your position without having someplace better already established. One of the most painful experiences that employees can have is to walk out on their jobs and then discover that they have no place to go. If you have a family to support and decide to leave your job without an alternative source of income, you could then experience loss of self-respect and strong feelings of depression and anxiety. You could also experience deep concern about your financial circumstances and the welfare of those you love.

While you are looking for work, keep it quiet…

Do not announce your intention to leave until you have to:

- two to six weeks notice for a line position.

- six to twelve weeks notice for a supervisory position.

- twelve weeks to six months notice for a key management or administrative position.

While you are looking for work, do not make any negative statements about your current employer during job search interviews, or during conversations with colleagues or other work associates. Your remarks could just give oppressive officials and unscrupulous co-workers the excuse they are looking for to harass you even more. Also, do not make negative comments about the organization outside of the work environment. It could require several months for you to find an acceptable position. If you engage in undermining or seek to retaliate, such behavior may come back to haunt you. Instead, do the right thing and when it is time to for you to go, leave with integrity. Then, no matter what happens in the future, you will have a clear conscience, and you will know that you have done the right thing.

In closing out your employment, never under any conditions, "burn your bridges" through a negative or hostile resignation letter…no matter how bad it has been. If you cannot say anything positive related to your former employer or about the organization, then direct your comments to your own achievements. When you make negative and angry comments to an oppressive workplace official, either in person or in writing, you may do harm, and a far greater disservice to yourself. Of one thing you can be certain. When you put your thoughts and opinions in writing, and turn those statements over to someone else, that person then has total control over what you have said. Oppressive officials can do with your remarks, whatever they wish. It is extremely unlikely that the officials will accept responsibility for the harm that they have caused. Instead, the typical oppressive official will make disparaging remarks and jokes about your comments. Or the unscrupulous official will use the negative remarks you have made to further justify the oppressive actions. Either way, nothing of value will be gained.

How to survive in an oppressive organization when there is "no way out"…

- Develop a passionate interest in something outside of the work environment.

- Do your job to the very best of your ability.

- Implement creative approaches as you complete your daily work assignments to help you to feel fulfilled and productive.

- Do not express anger or resentment if you are given distasteful assignments to "teach you a lesson," or to "keep you in your place."

- Maintain close and supportive associations with family and friends.
- Quietly look for work.
- Do not announce your intention to leave until you have secured your future elsewhere unless you absolutely have to.
- Explore all of your resources and options.

When Your Future is Secure

- Leave after having provided fair notice.
- After you have departed from the oppressive work environment, don't waste your time by dwelling on the past negative circumstances.
- Instead, look to the future as you move in a positive direction.

Go to the "Bottom Line"

When you are struggling with difficult circumstances, it can be uplifting to realize that things could be worse. It can also be reassuring to know that you have a plan in mind in the event that disaster should occur. Go to the "bottom line" when you are struggling in an oppressive work environment, or when you are at risk of losing your job. Give serious thought to, "What is the worst that might happen...and what would I do then?" Having looked at the worst possibility, develop a realistic plan for how you will handle the crisis. As soon as you have a "bottom line" plan established in your mind, you will naturally shift from being a potential victim, to being a survivor. Should the worst scenario occur, you will know that you have a way to survive.

If you remain calm and thoughtful to the best of your ability, and if you develop a systematic and structured approach to oppressive workplace survival, you will be able to rise above the circumstances created in the troubling and dysfunctional work environment. If you remain steadfast in your efforts toward gaining employment elsewhere, opportunities for success in the workplace will return. As you look to the future, keep in mind that your situation is temporary, and life will not always be as it is in the "midst of the storm."

Coping When Disaster Strikes

Consider this circumstance. You have just been informed that you are being "let go," or that you have been fired. And so, you will no longer have a job. Now, what are you going to do? When employees are laid off, they experience a flood of emotions. Being fired can be one of the most traumatic experiences that you will ever be required to face. Employees who lose their jobs almost always experience feelings of powerlessness, frustration, and a sense of betrayal and alienation.

Patterns of Job Loss & Resolution

When employees lose their jobs, resolving the trauma may occur in "apple-pie" order, just as I will describe the process in this chapter. Or, the process may evolve in an extremely varied fashion. Each phase may come and go, momentarily, throughout the day, or a given phase may last for days, weeks, or months. The entire process may even last for years. The key point is that the phases are common to almost everyone who experiences unexpected or unwanted job loss. These patterns are also experienced by friends, relatives, and family members associated with the former employee. For healthy and effective functioning to return, the phases must eventually evolve to the point of closure. For instance, should a former employee or family member become "stuck" in the "protest" phase, the person may then present an unpredictable and unwarranted pattern of anger and belligerence. Former employees do not only direct those feelings toward the organization and officials who initiated the job loss. They also direct their unresolved feelings toward themselves, family members, and other close associates. In other words, the feelings may be displaced on innocent victims in a generalized way, and in a variety of directions.

For the most part, working through the impact of lost employment takes from as little as three months, and up to one year. Should resolution not be reached within that time frame, it is almost always an indication that the former employee is stuck, and might benefit from professional counseling to assist in bringing closure to the process. Factors that determine the length of time that a given individual will need to work through these feelings and conflicts include family circumstance, philosophical postures, problem solving ability, and the intactness of the support system available. Also of importance of course, is how quickly meaningful employment and levels of financial security can be restored.

Shock & Disbelief

When employees first learn of their job loss, their immediate response is almost always one of shock and disbelief. As shock sets in, employees become mechanical in carrying out any necessary activities during the balance of the day. Essentially, they are there, but in body only. Emotionally, they are overwhelmed with unresolved feelings and conflicts. Employees who have been informed that they are losing their jobs are simply too preoccupied to use sound judgment or to think clearly. They are overwhelmed with the awareness that they will now be out of work, and that they face an uncertain future. They find that they are unable to concentrate, or to focus effectively on their work assignments. They become emotionally isolated from the activities of their work associates, and from what is occurring around them.

When employees are in shock, their behavior is shallow, sober, and anxious. They are distracted by a deep sense of isolation and betrayal. The otherwise effective employee may now have difficulty making decisions, or the individual may simply shutdown and not be able to function at all. Employees who are in shock may impulsively resort to the abuse of alcohol or other drugs as a means of escape from the trauma that they are experiencing.

Protest

As the phase of protest evolves, the unemployed worker harbors strong feelings of anger and animosity. Former employees become angry because they believe they have been unfairly selected and mistreated. They may believe that they were betrayed by an oppressive workplace official or by a corrupt administration. They may also see themselves as the victims of the power plays and manipulations of an unscrupulous co-worker or other work associates. During the phase of protest, former employees may express the belief that no one really cares about what is happening to them. But then, when help is offered it may be abruptly rejected. The unemployed worker's circumstances lead to bitterness and resentment, both of which are usually combined with a deepening sense of isolation and frustration.

Resentment

As the reality of the lost employment becomes clear, strong feelings of resentment begin to surface. Former employees may enter a period of intense preoccupation with their frustrations and circumstances. They may spend a great deal of time focused on their belief that the termination should not have occurred. Feelings of irritation and indignation may be directed toward officials of the organization, the co-workers who have been selected to stay on the job, and even toward their friends and families. Unemployed workers may also have nagging feelings of resentment based both consciously and subconsciously on such postures as:

- "They have jobs and I don't."
- "The SOBs have shafted me."
- "They could have done something to prevent this if they had really tried."
- "I am being cheated."
- "Why wasn't that loser picked instead of me."

Fear & Anxiety

Unemployed workers and their family members experience increasing levels of fear and anxiety as unemployment continues. Their lives are often filled with unanswered questions and unresolved concerns. "What's going to happen to my family...to us? What's going to go wrong next? Will we lose our home? Will we have to use all of our retirement savings before I find work?" Unemployed workers and their families cannot live with fear for a long period of time. If they live with fear for too long there is an increasing risk that they will either give up or crack up. They give up as feelings of anxiety and depression take over. They may crack up through the excessive use of alcohol or other drugs. They may crack up through compulsive gambling, or through fights, arguments, and broken marriages. In the extreme, they may eventually come to believe that suicide is their only viable alternative.

Fear is the basic ingredient of all psychological warfare that human beings wage against each other. While living with the fear that comes with lost employment, former employees may become so desperate that they will say or do almost anything. Unreasonable fear, if not positively dealt with, can become so intense that unemployed workers may eventually find that they are unable to perform even simple tasks such as driving a car or answering the telephone.

Guilt & Shame

As unemployment continues, a deep sense of guilt may be experienced. Former employees may see themselves as failures, even though they were excellent employees. They may hold themselves responsible despite the fact that their loss of employment was initiated without their choice or awareness. No matter how hard they try to see things more clearly, unemployed workers tend to blame themselves. They start to think, and actually believe, "I must have caused this."

Along with guilt comes intense feelings of shame, and expressions of self-criticism. "How can I face the people who relied on me? Regardless of what they say, I just know that my parents, my spouse, my family and my friends believe that it was my fault. I should have seen it coming. I know that I have failed the people who trusted me. I should have been more prepared. I should have done something to prevent this." Feelings of shame related to lost employment affect people at the core of their being because they believe themselves to be inadequate, unacceptable, and worthless. As the sense of guilt and shame overcomes them, unemployed workers may withdraw from contacts and associations with their family, friends, and former co-workers.

Despair

The phase of despair reflects the phrase "It is always darkest before the dawn." As feelings of despair overwhelm the former employee, intense anxiety is experienced almost daily. "What will I do if I can't find another job?" Feelings of depression and hopelessness may evolve to expressions of "I just don't care anymore…so what!…or who cares?" In the midst of despair, the unemployed worker is disorganized, lacks a sense of purpose, and is often restless and agitated. Throughout the typical workday, they may engage in intense expressions of self-criticism because they know that others are at work, while they are not. Preoccupation with things increases, and there may be overemphasis on minor details or unimportant issues that lead to arguments and irritability directed toward family and friends for no apparent cause or reason. Inside, there is a deep longing for a return to productivity, contribution, and a sense of belonging.

Acceptance & Reconstruction

Going through these phases is an essential part of the return to self-confidence and productivity when employment is lost. Although financial resources may remain limited, and life's difficulties may continue, the crises and struggles of lost employment will eventually be resolved. Optimism and a sense of purpose will return as challenging opportunities are experienced in a new and more positive work environment. Resentment due to past circumstances and what might have been may linger, but will gradually fade. As the former employee begins to separate from the past and move toward a new and rewarding job, positive functioning, a sense of assuredness, and the courage to face the challenges of tomorrow will return. Former employees, having found new jobs, will find their lives to be back in order. As positive changes and opportunities for growth emerge, they will experience a renewal of hope for the future.

"Moving On"

The decisions and the attitudes of other people have very little effect on how we feel about ourselves unless we allow it to happen. It is how and what we decide that has the greatest impact. If you are out of work, doing something productive is bound to make you feel better. Engaging in self-criticism, and remaining bitter and resentful because you have lost your job will not be helpful or productive in the long run. In life, there are always choices to be made and circumstances to be faced that are beyond our control. In fact, it may be that all that a dynamic way of life really is…is a series of choices and decisions. Sometimes we make healthy choices, and sometimes we make mistakes, but decisions must be made. The only thing we have no choice about is making decisions. Sometimes we have to decide if what happened during a moment in time will defeat us. If we choose not to be defeated, we may then need to "swallow what is bitter from the cup and move on."

One of the most common mistakes of unemployed workers is to look at how things ought to be…rather than how they are. Instead of dwelling on past regrets and disappointments, focus on the facts of the present and develop realistic plans for the future. As you look ahead and start taking positive steps to find employment elsewhere, you may become stronger than you ever thought to be possible. Resolving the feelings and stress associated with loss of employment can be accomplished through maintaining thoughtful and productive patterns of lifestyle and adjustment:

1. Involvement with meaningful people

- Social interaction to provide diversion from the immediate struggle.
- A level of lightheartedness through retaining a sense of humor.
- Maintaining channels of communication with others.

2. Involvement with meaningful activities

- Maintaining a sound posture of physical fitness.
- Engaging in interesting or challenging activities to provide stimulation for the mind.
- Decisiveness and problem solving related to securing the future.

3. If one and two do not progressively evolve…

- Medication may then be an option through consultation with a physician.

The "Insider" Approach to Regaining Employment

In today's world, with a continuing difficult economy, patterns of downsizing in the workplace, and movements toward streamlining government and the armed forces, the search for employment can be both difficult and frightening. For example, when I first entered the job market more years ago than I care to remember, we lived in simpler times. The job market, in fact, was an employee's market. As such, it was not at all unusual for a job candidate to walk into an official's office and ask for a job. On the merits and tone of that meeting alone, the two individuals shook hands with the understanding that the newly established employee would be reporting to work on Monday morning at 8:00 a.m.

Today, for someone searching for a job that will offer a salary above minimum wage, the scene I just described is with rare exception, unheard of. In today's job market, elaborate screening and interviewing processes have been developed. In some cases psychological testing is conducted. Grid systems are established to assure "fair" employment practices, and to establish, "the best match for the job." Even then, thorough background checks are conducted before final decisions are made. The typical job applicant, if granted an opportunity to be considered at all, might be required to spend several hours completing a psychological test battery to provide an "employability" profile. The applicant may be required to spend a number of hours being interviewed by several levels of committee representation. Adding, "insult to injury," the applicant may be asked to leave each interview having received the message "Thank you for coming in, but…don't call us, we will call you." The standard phrase used by the committee chairperson or coordinator, "We will be making a final decision next week and will then get in touch with you." Once all of that has occurred, there is a good chance that several days later, the candidate will receive a brief letter from the official. The letter will say, "It was a difficult decision, and you were an excellent candidate, but we chose someone with more experience in…"

Don't Submit…Meet!

Now, how can you get an edge on the job market to insure at least a fair opportunity to be considered? Well, of course, there are many ways. Establish a systematic approach to employment search beginning with a written description of your work history. Develop a thoughtful and well-prepared professional resume. Actively explore the job market through screening of classified advertisements. Contact state and federal employment agencies. Consult with private job placement services. Make personal contacts with potential employers. However, the old model of just mailing a resume or job application, or the practice of just dropping one off at the personnel office has also diminished in potential. To counter the more complex trends toward gaining employment in today's job market, an *"insider approach"* might be far more successful.

To implement the insider approach to gaining employment, begin by developing your resume in the most professional manner possible. Then, give some thought to the organizations with which you might wish to gain employment, regardless of whether you are aware of openings that exist or not. Next, think about someone you know in the organization who has been successfully employed there for a significant period of time. If you do not know of anyone, discretely research the matter until you have someone identified. The type of person you should consider is someone who has a strong reputation for reliability, compassion and fairness. Keep in mind that you may not be able to identify a person who provides an ideal match for these qualities. Instead, simply use them as a standard for measurement of who might be of assistance to you.

With the person identified, give the individual a call and ask if you might be able to meet with him or her over lunch, or just to talk. When the meeting is underway, express gratitude for the opportunity to talk and the willingness of the person to take time from a busy schedule to meet with you. Then, after a brief period of social conversation, offer a comment such as, "You know, I am aware of how successful you have been in your employment over the years. And, I've been thinking...I would certainly be interested in what advice you might have for me about gaining a position at your facility or any similar organization." Now, do you see what you have accomplished? You have offered the individual an indication of your admiration and respect. You have asked the individual for advice as a recognized expert, and most important, you may just have established the individual as a potential employment advocate or resource.

For instance, you just might hear:

- "Hey, you know, I'm glad you contacted me. In fact, I've been giving thought to adding a position to my staff, and you would certainly qualify for the position. Why don't you leave me your resume and we can talk again next week."

Another possibility is:

- "Well, right now I don't have anything open. However, I know of another department that has an opening. Why don't you give the division manager a call and tell her I made the recommendation."

Or, you might hear:

- "Well, you know, I just don't know of anything right now, but, why don't you let me do some exploring. Give me a call next week and I will let you know what I come up with."

Now of course, you might also hear something like:

- "Oh gosh, you really don't want to work here. You know, the only reason I am putting up with this place is that my kids are still in school. They would be really upset if they had to move and give up their friends. But, as soon as the last one is on her (or his) own, I'm out of here!"

Now, even that response can be helpful to you. Here you have a respected individual strongly advising you to avoid getting caught in perhaps, yet another oppressive trap.

Despite the possibility of an occasional negative response, just remain persistent in your efforts. The insider approach to seeking gainful employment can be an excellent resource for establishing yourself as an active member of the workforce. When using the approach, obviously you would be wise to not use only one resource. Therefore, once you have contacted an individual, move on to the next individual that you believe may be a potential resource for you.

Continue the pattern by making contact with successful individuals until you have either exhausted your resources, or until you have secured satisfactory employment. It is also wise to touch base with each resource at reasonable intervals to assure continuity of interest on the part of the individual you have chosen, and to make sure that you demonstrate continued commitment to your job search efforts. But, be careful not to overdo the contacts. Perhaps one contact every other month with each resource would provide a reasonable balance.

The Measured Approach to Employment Search

When you are unemployed, it is important to attempt to determine how long you can reasonably survive without any further income at all. The answer will bring clarity to how quickly you must regain employment. It will also help you to understand how selective you can be in your job search efforts. When employees have lost their means of a livelihood, they often find themselves in a double bind that results in an evolving pattern of desperation. On one hand, they are desperate to regain some source of income for themselves and their families. On the other hand, they feel trapped and forced to accept whatever level of employment that is offered, just so they can be assured of a source of income. They are often painfully aware that, should they accept employment at a significantly lower level of compensation and potential, they may then also drastically limit their earning capacity and future quality of life. Should they not accept what is offered, they may miss the limited opportunity that has been presented, and there is no assurance that another opportunity will emerge in the foreseeable future. Those who are unemployed in this manner find themselves in circumstances in which they believe they cannot win, no matter which option they choose.

To counter this dilemma to the most reasonable degree possible, a thoughtful and measured employment search pattern is often helpful. In following this approach, the unemployed job seeker determines the level of salary and working conditions that will be acceptable, and on par with or improve upon, that which had been available prior to the loss of employment. The job search is then initiated and restricted to that level of what will be acceptable.

Should no opportunity for gainful employment present itself during the thoughtfully established time allotted, the standard for what will be considered acceptable is then reduced to a measured level of salary and working conditions. Then, should no opportunity for gainful employment present itself after an additional allotted period, the standard for what will be considered acceptable is again reduced in a thoughtful manner. Based on resources available, the measured approach to finding employment is continued until an acceptable job opportunity is established, or an entry level and possibly minimum wage circumstance must be accepted.

Remain Open to Potential

It sometimes happens that, within the first year or two after employees have lost or quit their jobs in an oppressive work environment, they one day, quite unexpectedly and without apparent reason, find themselves feeling a vague sense of uneasiness and guilt. This occurs even when employees are well established and accepted in new and far more rewarding employment circumstances. The employees feel guilty, but they just can't understand why. Then, with a period of reflection the answer is revealed.

Workers in a new and more humane working environment may discover that the guilt that they have been experiencing is associated with the belief that they really do not deserve to be treated as well as they are being treated in their new employment circumstances. This phenomenon is a reflection of the conditioning that had occurred due to the abuses that were experienced in the oppressive environment. Those abusive circumstances have caused the former employees to actually believe at either a conscious or sub-conscious level, that somehow, the abuse is what they really deserved.

Another common experience of former employees of an oppressive regime is that they become preoccupied with a sense of regret that they are no longer working in the oppressive work environment. These feelings are often accompanied by a sense of self-doubt, and the unrealistic belief that the previous job, "although a little difficult to handle," was really not that bad. This most often happens to an employee who was significantly and repeatedly abused in an oppressive work environment. The pattern is largely based on free floating, and most often unrealistic fears about whether the new employee can actually handle the assignments and responsibilities of the new position. It may also be based on concerns about whether the new employer will turn out to be as bad as the former oppressive employer, or even worse.

This phenomenon sometimes comes to the surface when a new supervisor offers even a slight amount of challenge or criticism related to the new employee's productivity or performance. The new employee almost instantly personalizes the criticism, projecting the characteristics of the former oppressive supervisor onto the new supervisor. The response is usually unrealistic, and it can occur regardless of how warm, sincere, and supportive that the new official might actually be.

Fortunately these patterns and responses are most often temporary, and will fade in direct proportion to evolving levels of positive performance, and through adaptation to a more trustworthy and sensitive work environment. These "flash-back" experiences can be overcome by employees if they simply do the best they can to learn from the past, let go, and move forward. Although it can be difficult, with many anxieties along the way, the trauma of lost employment and the controlling and unhealthy conditions experienced in an oppressive work environment can be overcome. It may take a while. Sometimes longer than you might have hoped. But, one day a sense of optimism and self-assuredness will return.

Survival and growth are possible, even during the most troubling of times. A basic ingredient for survival and success is the recognition that, although plans we have worked toward may be disrupted, and our beliefs and values disregarded, we alone determine our integrity. If we understand that our greatest gifts are our genuineness, our talents, and our ability to contribute, we will have what is needed to rise above any level of adversity we may encounter. Life's work can be lost, home and family disrupted, material wealth dissolved, friendship discarded. But, integrity is totally our own unless of course, it becomes our choice to give it away. We do that through our decision to behave in a manner contrary to our thoughtfulness, our judgment, our sensitivity to others, and our innermost personal values. Once an employee has endured the struggles created in an oppressive work environment, or the ordeal that comes with lost employment, that person must make a very personal decision! Does the former employee give up now, or does the person go on and live life the best way he or she knows how, and despite what has happened? Remember crisis can be a good thing. We become stronger and we learn new skills for survival.

A number of years ago I had the privilege of seeing a remarkable play, depicting conditions in a Siberian concentration camp. The story told of a camp located in one of the most desolate areas of the Soviet Union. Conditions at the camp were horrible. The weather and other elements were so severe that there was no need to surround the complex with a fence or walls. In its entire history, no one had ever escaped. Those who attempted to do so were soon found dead due to exposure.

The story focused on two men huddled around a small fire outside their dilapidated barracks. One captive, an older man about fifty years of age, had been a political prisoner of the camp for more than twenty years. The younger man, about age twenty-five, had been there for only a year. Years earlier, the older man had realized that food supplied by camp officials was not enough to sustain life. As a result, most of the residents died within three years of their arrival. The older man, for survival, had learned how to capture rats, dress them out, and then roast them over an open fire. Nourishment gained from this practice contributed to his longevity. Having befriended the younger man, the older resident had taught the younger one this, and several other methods of survival during the weeks and months they spent together.

In a powerful and moving scene, the two men were roasting their rats for the evening meal. During their conversation, the younger man, speaking in dismay, told the older man of his belief that he could no longer bear the atrocities of the camp. He was thinking of walking into the wilderness to die. It was then that the older man said, "You have no idea how often, during these past twenty years that I have considered the same thing. But, there have been three reasons why I have chosen to survive. One reason is that I know how the guards react when one of the residents does it. They send out the dogs to find the body. The body is then placed on public display and ridiculed in front of all of the residents of the camp. And so, I have decided I would never give them that type of sadistic satisfaction. But, the second reason I have chosen not to let myself die is the realization that, if somehow I can survive and one day escape, I will then know that no one can ever hurt me this much again. And, most important, if I can somehow survive, and one day escape, I will have an opportunity to tell the world of what has occurred here."

There is a rather sad, yet elegant closing to this story. The older man lived on, maintaining his dignity for another year or so. But then, he developed a severe health problem and died, never to have the chance to tell his story to the world. But, the younger man chose not to die. Instead, he continued to follow the older man's wise counsel and survived. Then one day, his moment came. He escaped to freedom where he fulfilled the older man's dream. He found the opportunity to tell the world of the camp, and even more important, he was able to share the older man's message that hope is eternal if we choose, despite circumstance, to live with compassion, fairness, and dignity. Failures or crises are not permanent. They are only temporary setbacks in a successful life. Failure and crisis can be transformed into creative achievement by assuming a posture of survival and weathering the storm, regardless of what the raging winds might bring in their wake.

9

RISING ABOVE THE STORMS OF THE WORKPLACE

A Journey of a Thousand Miles

A philosopher in ancient China once said, "A journey of a thousand miles begins with but a single step." Conscientious employees often experience feelings of frustration and discontent as they engage in their journey through the troubled work environments of today. Apprehension and discord assail them on every front. The selfishness and insensitivity of oppressive officials and troublesome co-workers rob them of many opportunities for achievement. Their own mistakes and feelings of inadequacy make for added anxiety and frustration. But, there is a way for all of us to travel through this world. There is a way that yields growth without harming others or placing important values in jeopardy. If we can adjust to the stress of everyday living, and if we maintain our fundamental beliefs and values, we will find moments of happiness and contentment. We will find life meaningful, with satisfactions, and with some accepted struggle and suffering along the way. We can make little progress in our own journey until we learn, accept, and apply fundamental facts about ourselves, about the nature of other people, and of life itself.

On the surface, many people appear to have strength and character. However, this is not always the case. The person who feels weak becomes a bully. The one who believes herself (or himself) to be inferior becomes the braggart. The abuse of power, tough talk, and callousness, are but symptoms of the anxiety within. We have all seen the hatred and wrath of one who gains secret pleasure through attacking the vulnerability of others. The paranoid Hitler's, the psychopathic Saddam Hussein's, and the treacherous Osama bin Laden's remain a part our world. Such brazenness is a reflection of those who are empty, pathetic, and despairing. Therefore, they seize on any opportunity to diminish others.

Accepting Who We Are

Some people will not respect you, no matter what you do, or how decently you live your life and treat others. Stop expecting other people to understand and accept you. You must decide for yourself if you like your behavior and who you are. If you don't, then make the changes you believe to be necessary without expecting anyone else to agree with you or understand. Accepting yourself and your actions permits you the privilege of being strong, and offers the opportunity to choose the course you will pursue in life.

Taking responsibility means never blaming anyone else for your shortcomings. Until you fully understand that, you will never be in control of your life. Taking responsibility also means not blaming yourself! Anything that takes away your power and strength makes you a victim. When we call people by high-sounding titles or credentials, it elevates them, but diminishes us. Granting others too much authority also grants them permission to victimize us. Do not permit yourself to be a victim of anyone, including yourself. Self-fulfilled persons see themselves as liked, wanted, able, and adaptable. They have postures and values capable of withstanding the storms, regardless of where their journey may lead them!

Our Creative Potential

Now, what is the secret of rising above the storms of the workplace? Well, I believe the answer is reflected in a picture I saw in an office many years ago. The picture depicted a flower growing through a crack in the sidewalk. Under the picture was the caption "Bloom Where You're Planted!" I believe that picture and caption illustrate what will be necessary to effectively meet the challenges of our rapidly changing world. We need to learn to bloom where we are planted! But, before we can "bloom," we need to overcome the patterns of resistance almost all of us experience when struggles and challenges come our way, or when change is in the wind.

People who are creatively alive keep their sense of adventure, and their sense of humor. They know how to laugh at themselves and with each other. It is these ingredients that are of such value in moving beyond the occasional failure that comes with being a creative human being. Creative people know that in life, the line between failure and success is often so fine that we scarcely realize when we pass it. How many people have quit at a time when with a little more patience…success would have been achieved? With a little more effort, a little more creativity, what seems hopeless can be turned into productivity, achievement, and success.

People who have no dreams to spur them on, who have no sense of creativity and adventure are already old. Age comes not in years, but in attitude. When hope and creativity fade, opportunities for creative growth are lost. People only grow disillusioned and old when they respond to new ideas with the attitude "We have always done it this way, so why do we need to change now?" But, some people stay permanently young, because of their positive attitude toward creativity and trying new ways to do things. Sometimes the most worthwhile things in life are accomplished by individuals who ask "I wonder what would happen if…" As long as you are enthusiastically beginning something new, you will remain creative in spirit.

Focus on "What is Right"…Not on "Who is Right"

Some workers have an intense need to be proven "right" in every situation. They are simply unwilling to admit that they have been wrong. But, employees who make meaningful contributions usually have a basic belief in service to others. They do not do it to look good, or to be proven right. They do not do it to be provided recognition and praise. They do it to serve. They recognize that demands and limitations are an integral part of every workplace. Because their commitment is strong, healthy workers accept reasonable demands, and they respond positively to the shortcomings of others. When a co-worker makes a mistake that could have been avoided, healthy workers resist the temptation to say, "I told you so." Instead, they offer each other acceptance and support. Together, they set specific, attainable goals for the workplace. In the midst of fulfilling their mission, they also include time to think, to talk, and to reward themselves and each other when landmarks of success have been reached.

The Ability to Say, "I Was Wrong"

Inordinate pride demands that oppressive officials and controlling employees must have approval and recognition from their work associates in everything that they do. They believe that they must never fail in any endeavor. They believe that they must cover up and deny even the most ordinary human weakness or mistakes. And so, the knowledge that they are not what they pretend to be causes feelings of inner turmoil and self doubt. But, you need not follow the troubled course that they have set. You can chose to admit your mistakes openly…whether an oversight or an unwise decision.

People are more likely to be accepting when you take responsibility for your actions, than they will be if you try to cover up or make excuses. Yet, healthy workers rarely, if ever say, "I'm sorry." In fact, "I'm sorry" may be the most over-used words that some employees express to each other. I believe this to be true because those words are so often said, yet rarely are they sincerely meant. Most often the feeling of being sorry centers around the fact that their indiscretions, or their acts of unkindness, have been challenged or detected. In other words, they are rarely sorry for what they have done. Instead, they are sorry that they have been caught. The truly healthy person has the ability to sincerely admit, "I was wrong. I had no right to treat you that way."

Do you remember the "Fonz" from the delightful television program of the 1960s called, "Happy Days?" The Fonz, also known as "Fonzie" was "cool." There were some things the Fonz just would not do. Certainly, the Fonz, being as macho as he was, found great difficulty in admitting that he may have had any shortcomings. And then of course, there was "Richie Cunningham." Richie was the idealistic dreamer, and almost every parent's idea of what a teenager should be. Occasionally, Fonzie, in his self-absorption would say or do something that hurt or offended a member of the "gang" with whom Richie and the Fonz associ-ated. Richie then, serving as a conscience for the Fonz, would call him aside and gingerly challenge him about what had happened. The Fonz, although initially quite defensive, would eventually see the error of his ways. With that in mind, Fonzie, encouraged by the urging of Richie, would become aware of the need to do what was necessary to, "make things right."

Do you remember what happened then? The Fonz, filled with the most sin-cere intentions would approach the offended person, with Richie overseeing the activity, of course. As Fonzie began to acknowledge his lack of consideration he would begin with "I was wro…, I was wrooo…, I was wron…," and finally, "I was wrong." In a somewhat touching, and yet humorous way, the Fonz conveyed his awareness that he had no right to treat the other person that way. Fonzie's dilemma also clearly illustrates how difficult it is for many of us to accept true responsibility for our lack of consideration for others.

As James Baldwin has said, *"Not everything that is faced can be changed, but nothing can be changed unless it is faced."* This powerful statement conveys the sentiment of someone who knows that the courage to face ourselves, and to face our struggles provides it's own reward. Baldwin's comment suggests that thoughtfulness, courage, and decency are inherently of value, in and of themselves. Because they are not ashamed of making mistakes, healthy employees accept their shortcomings. They know that no single mistake will pose a serious threat to their future unless it is of momentous importance and to some extent, deliberate. Yet, "I had no right to treat you that way. I was wrong." is too often left unsaid by too many.

Work With What You Have

The dissatisfactions that trouble most employees are not new. But, today they are more widespread and clearly visible than has been the case with any previous generation of workers. The modern workplace has its frustrations and tedium, its outrages and its troubling events. But, when it works, today's workplace provides moments of productivity, challenge, and achievement. And, employees who have known those moments know that the capacity for contribution among colleagues is what makes everything worthwhile in the work environment. In the end, it is inspiration, initiative, and hard work that make things happen.

Make the most of your strengths and limit your exposure to negative and pessimistic work associates as much as you can. Look for opportunities to engage in positive interactions with your colleagues, and do not burden them with your own pessimistic postures or negative outlook. Life is not always fair, at work or anywhere else. Somebody else may get the promotion you deserve, or more credit than you for a job well done. Don't whine about it. Accept the disappointment with grace. Come across as poised when others lose control. Projecting self-assurance and being in control will cause others to trust you more. They will realize that they can depend on you to come through day after day, as a member of the team.

Be Approachable

My first encounter with the value of approachability occurred many years ago when I was assigned to my first duty station as a Navy recruit just out of basic training. Arriving at the San Francisco airport, I contacted a cab driver who said he knew where I needed to go, and he agreed to take me to the Naval facility. Being a "green kid" from North Dakota, and away from home on my own for the first time, I grew increasingly anxious as we approached the base. None-the-less, the cab driver got me to my destination. Upon arrival, the cab driver said, "There you go, kid. Go in there and they'll take care of you." I paid the driver and thanked him for his help. He then drove off into the darkness.

It turned out that the driver was one of those characters that could easily recognize the new kid in town. Only later did I learn that he had not only given me a ride. He had taken me for a ride. The driver had taken me about twenty-five miles out-of-the-way. He then charged me about thirty-five dollars more for the ride than was actually necessary. Regardless, he did get me to my destination. Then, standing alone at the entrance to the administration building, I was overwhelmed with fear and anxiety. I felt compelled to just run away. But, I couldn't do that because I knew I would only be caught and thrown into the Navy brig. I was also aware that going AWOL would be a significant embarrassment to my parents and I certainly did not want to let them down. And so, I mustered my courage and entered the building.

As I reported in, the first and only person I encountered was a character who had no awareness of the importance and value of approachability, whatsoever. When he heard me enter the room, the guy didn't even bother to look up from the Playboy magazine that he had in his hands. Instead, he mumbled something derogatory about Navy recruits arriving during his shift. Then, he gruffly ordered me to "sit on the bench." The actual rating of this individual was "petty officer third class." And, I wholeheartedly agree. He was petty, and he was third class.

After several minutes of what seemed like an eternity, the telephone rang. At that point, a rather remarkable transformation took place. As the petty officer answered the phone, he spoke with the epitome of politeness and professionalism. "Yes, sir, I've already taken care of it sir. Yes, he has arrived, sir. Yes sir, right away sir!" The petty officer then hung up the phone and gruffly said something to me that I just did not need to hear. He said, "The Commander will see you now." When I heard his words, I became totally filled with panic. Now I really wanted to go AWOL, and yet, I knew I couldn't do it. You see, as a Navy recruit just out of "boot camp," I had heard about Commanders in the Navy, but had never actually seen one. Based on my perception at that time, as far as I was concerned, a Commander was ranked at about six levels above God…and now, I was going to have to talk to one.

The petty officer gruffly pointed toward a closed door about twenty feet away. As I walked toward the door I felt as though I was walking the last mile. Everything appeared to be happening in slow motion until I arrived at the door and knocked. A voice from behind the door said, "yes, come on in." By that time, I was so frightened that I could hardly stand, yet I knew that I had to do something. Being properly trained at the Great Lakes Naval Training Center, I entered the room and approached the Commander's desk. I then snapped to attention and saluted, shaking so badly that I thought I was going to fall apart. Still, I was able to utter the words, "Werre reporting for duty, sir."

The Commander, looking up from his desk, and seeing my anxious and troubled condition, turned out to be an approachable person. Unlike the petty officer out front, he not only understood the value of graciousness and approachability, the Commander also recognized the fear and anxiety of a "green kid" from North Dakota who was away from home and on his own for the very first time. Much to my amazement and relief, the Commander said, "Hey son, good to see you. Would you like some coffee? Here, have a chair and make yourself comfortable. Let me get you some coffee and a doughnut."

Before I could respond, the Commander was out the door. Within minutes, he was back with a carafe of coffee and a plate, piled high with doughnuts. He then said, "Here son, let me pour you a cup of coffee. Have a doughnut. I heard that you're from North Dakota. You know, about three years ago my family and I spent about two weeks in North Dakota and we just loved it. Boy, what great people...and what great fishing you've got up there. Let's see now, you've got that lake up there, don't you? Lake Sakakawegee, isn't it?" I then responded with, "No sir, it's called 'Lake Sacagawea'." He then said, "Oh yea, that's right, Lake Sacagawea. Here son, have a little more coffee. Do you want another doughnut? Relax son, let's talk about those great North Dakota people and the fantastic fishing that my family and I did at the lake."

The Commander and I spent about twenty minutes talking in his office that night. Then he told me where to go to get some sleep and where I needed to report in the morning. I never saw Commander Blasinski again, but I never forgot his name. Sometimes, though, I do momentarily forget how he treated me with such kindness and understanding. At times, when I am angry and frustrated with someone, I will approach that person with gruffness and insensitivity not unlike the way the petty officer had treated me. Then somehow, I hear a voice inside of me that says, "Hey, Dick…is that the way Commander Blasinski treated you?" Somewhat reluctantly, I will respond with, "Well, no it isn't." The voice will then say, "Well, Dick, what are you going to do about it?" At that point, I know I must offer an apology and change course. I also remember that the Commander knew the value of graciousness and approachability. He understood how to help a "green kid" from North Dakota to ease his fears and to feel all right with the world.

As I have encountered other people who have understood the value and power of approachability over the years, I have found that they share many common characteristics with Commander Blasinski. Persons who are approachable are energetic, dynamic, and fun to be with. Although they consistently accomplish as much, or even more than their counterparts, they also show a deep interest in others. When called upon, they convey a sense of unlimited time and attention to the concerns of those around them.

Employees are more effective when they know where they stand and what is expected of them. Speak and act as if everything you do is genuine. If co-workers don't feel comfortable with the way you respond to them, they will stop contributing their ideas and opinions. Be generous with praise and thoughtful of the opinions of others. And, be cautious with criticism. There is usually more than one side to a controversy. During disputes or challenges, remain calm and self-assured. Treat others as you would want to be treated. Remember the example of Commander Blasinski. Be an approachable person, and make it easy for your colleagues to come to you.

Serve as Your Own Conscience

As we associate with, and sincerely listen to our colleagues, it is not difficult to become aware of the things that we do to offend them. We see it in their reactions. We hear it in their responses to us, and to what we do. It is even easier for us to recognize our own sense of injustice and the belief that we have been treated unfairly. In life, the most valuable and enduring thing that we have to offer each other is our behavior. When you behave with fairness and decency toward me, I will feel better about our relationship. I will then learn to respect and trust you more. As a result, I will feel closer to you. The reverse is also true. When I behave with fairness and decency toward you, it then may cause you to feel better about our relationship as well. You may then learn to respect and trust me more. As a result, you will feel closer to me.

So, how then, can we enhance and improve our relationships with others? We can do it by serving as our own consciences. We can behave with decency and fairness toward all that we encounter. To truly do that, we must always keep in mind that, never in the history of civilization have, *"two wrongs ever made a right."* Others may not respond the way we wish. They may not do what we wish them to do. But, we can serve as our own consciences and do what is the fair and decent thing to do, regardless of how others may react or treat us.

Workplace relationships will be stronger, healthier and more enjoyable when they are based on mutual respect. Acknowledge your co-workers. Invite opinions, ideas, and viewpoints. Treat fellow employees honestly, fairly, with respect and with dignity. Respect your colleagues and do not attempt to change or manipulate them. Don't expect them to be like you, and don't try to become like somebody else. Never challenge the worth of your work associates or ridicule their ideas. Also be aware of age, limitations, and other special conditions that may merit additional sensitivity to some workers.

Standards for Decency

Throughout the past twenty-five years I have attempted to live my life based on the answers to four fundamental questions. When I have been troubled, when I have faced a crisis, when I have dealt with a troublesome person or troubling situation, the answers to these questions have never failed me. Whenever I have struggled with any crisis, whether created due to my own behavior, or due to the behavior of others, the answers have never failed to chart my course in a positive direction.

The first question I ask myself...
Do I believe in what I am doing?

- In everything that I do, I have found that when I fail to believe in what I am doing, somehow I always pay a price.

The second question...
Am I doing the best I can?

- Time and time again, I have discovered that I am just not designed to do less than my best. When I attempt to do anything less, I always experience a loss of worth and self-esteem.

The third question that I ask myself...
Am I doing what is right?

- It is vitally important for me to always do the right thing, rather than become overly concerned with the question of who is right during any area of struggle or disagreement.

And, the fourth question...
Am I being fair?

- For me fairness is essential to a positive outlook and way of life. If I do not remain fair in everything that I do, I discover that I then have difficulty living with myself, and with those around me.

Whenever I find that I can answer "yes" to all four of the questions, I then know that I am on the right track, and that I must stay the course. On the other hand, when I cannot honestly answer, "yes" to one or more of the questions, it is I who must change the course to get back onto the right track. When I have corrected my behavior in whatever manner necessary, I once again experience a sense of confidence and self-assuredness, regardless of how difficult the course has been, or is yet to be.

Roberta Treacherous

Several years ago, I was responsible for the supervision of a highly capable technician who performed the technical aspect of her job in an effective and efficient manner. Then, for some reason that I still do not fully understand, she did something of a highly treacherous nature. Roberta's actions in misrepresenting the facts related to a supervisory decision that I had made had a significant impact upon my employment circumstances until several weeks later. The conclusion of a formal investigation totally cleared me of any wrongdoing, whatsoever. However, in the midst of the investigative process, it came time for me to complete Roberta's annual performance appraisal.

Being aware that the appraisal provided a clear opportunity to seek revenge, I spent a brief period reflecting on the four standards for decency that I had adopted as a guideline for the kind of life I wished to live, and for the type of person I wished to be. As I thought of the treachery that the young woman had engaged in without foundation, and the opportunity for revenge that presented itself to me, I also asked myself the four questions. "If I seek revenge, will I believe in what I am doing?...Will I be doing the best I can?...Am I more concerned about who is right, or am I concerned about what is the right thing to do?…and finally, am I being fair?"

Based on the answers I gave myself to those four questions, I decided that the right thing to do was to rate the young woman on the basis of her technical abilities and performance alone. I so doing, I totally ignored the treacherous behavior that Roberta had directed toward me. As such, I rated her performance as excellent, and arranged for her to receive a ten percent salary increase.

Many years have passed since Roberta engaged in her treachery, and since the performance appraisal was completed. She has never apologized, nor has she thanked me for the salary increase. But, from time to time we see each other briefly in the community, or at a professional workshop. During those encounters, I notice that Roberta always seems so anxious and uncomfortable when she is around me. And, she always seems to have such difficulty looking me in the eye. On the other hand, I always feel quite comfortable when I am around Roberta. Not once, in all of the years that have passed, have I ever regretted my decision to follow those standards for decency in my association with her.

Dynamics of Integrity & Character

Employees with integrity and character have a positive orientation to life. They attempt to make a meaningful contribution in whatever they do, and they act in ways that warrant the respect and admiration of others. Aware that they cannot always win, people with integrity and character accept their limitations. Oppressive and incompetent individuals tend to make quick, headstrong decisions based on self-serving needs. The oppressive workplace is filled with employees who can't be counted on. They cannot be depended on during a crisis. They break promises and offer excuses for poor performance or unethical behavior. Strength requires courage, and courage requires integrity and character.

- Character is accepting responsibility for our mistakes and our behavior. It is being mature enough to say, "I was wrong." When right, the person with character has no need to seek the satisfaction of saying "I told you so."

- Integrity is the capacity to face unpleasantness, frustration, discomfort and defeat without complaint or collapse, and to be able to bear injustice without seeking revenge.

- Character is the ability to control anger and settle differences without making unreasonable demands or resorting to blackmail, and without engaging in violence or destruction.

- Integrity is the ability to make a decision and stand by it. It means dependability, keeping one's word, coming through in a crisis. Oppressive people are masters of the alibi. They leave a legacy of broken promises, unfinished business, and good intentions that somehow never seem to materialize.

Guiding Principles for Excellence

Move with strength. Focus on excellence. To become more of what we are, it is essential to begin with our strengths and use those strengths as often as possible. In my view, one of the most powerful moments in the history of the cinema was portrayed in one of the closing scenes from Steven Spielberg's movie, "Schindler's List." Do you recall the portrayal of Oskar Schindler, as he met with a small group of the more than one thousand people he had saved from Hitler's tyranny? Schindler of course, had done what he could do, risking his own life and family, and at an incredible cost to his personal fortune. His efforts were truly heroic considering the dangers and struggles he and others endured under the Nazi regime, and in the midst of the holocaust.

Yet, in the closing moments with those he had befriended, Oskar realized that he still had a medal given to him in recognition of support he pretended to direct toward the Nazi war effort. He also realized that he had retained his automobile. Then, flooded with emotion and the realization that he might have saved yet another life or two, had he sold the medal and vehicle, he said "I should have done more!" What power. What excellence by example. Here we have this magnificent humanitarian, chastising himself for not having done enough, although through his selfless efforts, and at unimaginable odds, more than one thousand lives were saved!

Healthy employees try to measure up to the values that they believe are important. They show their values in the way they act. Self-respect often comes from believing that you can effectively face the challenges of life, and that you are able to solve your own problems. It also comes from realizing that you are able to make your own decisions and meet your commitments. Do not let people down? If you do, then offer an apology along with a commitment to change, and a commitment to make things right. Without commitment, your promises will become a superficial game of which other people will quickly tire.

The Healing Power of Laughter

Everyone has ups and downs, good days and bad days. But, so many of us need to learn how to enjoy life more. A healthy dose of humor in the workplace can be good for everyone. When the work environment is pleasant, employees feel inspired and become more creative and productive. Laughter refreshes us by clearing our minds and by releasing bodily tension. Humor is an excellent resource for teaching new skills and abilities. People learn well when they are enjoying themselves. Laughter makes today better and raises hopes for tomorrow. If we cannot laugh at some of the absurd or difficult things that occur in our lives, we will never be truly happy. The next time you feel yourself getting tense over something you cannot control, step back, lighten up, and look for the humor in the situation.

There is a tremendous difference between being childlike, compared to being childish. If you behave in a childish manner, you pout, throw temper tantrums, and display other out-of-control behaviors to the point where family, friends, and work associates feel embarrassed, uncomfortable or angry. On the other hand, to behave in a childlike manner is a very refreshing quality. It promotes friendship, comfort, and camaraderie among people. The healthiest people are those who free themselves to be childlike at times. Laughter draws people together. Humor tends to diffuse anxiety, fade sadness, and diminish anger. It provides us with an emotional release so that we can more readily accept ourselves, and our comrades. One of the best measures of mental health is the ability to laugh at ourselves…and with each other in an accepting and understanding way.

A Philosophy for Living

Establishing a philosophy for living is vital for each of us. Your philosophy may be short or long, elaborate or simple, eloquent or practical. It may be yours alone, or it may be borrowed from the ideas and perceptions of someone you admire. The only essential is that regardless of the source, you truly believe in the concepts presented, and that you live your life according to those principles. When we have such a philosophy, we have a foundation for our lives in times of relative calm, and in times of stress and other forms of difficulty. Through the posture reflected in our philosophy, should we become caught up in the anxieties and turmoil of life, we can simply stop and remember..."This is who I am. This is what I believe!"

There will always be those who ask us to sacrifice ourselves beyond reason, if we allow it. There will always be those who take advantage of us, who persecute us, who rob us of our rightful place in this world. It is at times like these that we need more than ever, a philosophy for living. Having a personal philosophy serves as a source of strength when we are attempting to remain...or to become more caring, genuine, and responsible human beings. It is at those times that the basic principle of life most aptly applies. That principle, "It is not how we handle ourselves when things go well that makes the difference. It is how we handle ourselves when things do not go well that determines the quality of our lives, and the reputation that follows any action we take."

Lust for Money

I have found time and again that when I place money before service, I eventually become troubled. For example, from time to time, I have discovered significant inequities related to compensation I was receiving for my work. I learned that associates were being provided more compensation for doing work of less quality, and under less stressful levels of responsibility and circumstances. Upon making those discoveries, I have at times, allowed my feelings to simmer inside, thereby causing increasing frustration and resentment. When I continued with preoccupation about the inequities, nothing of value occurred. My own posture simply took its toll on me.

However, having experienced the futility of those preoccupations, I came to realize that if I put them aside, and go about my work in the best way I know how, the issue of money usually takes care of itself. Instead of placing my focus on money, I learned to focus on service. Then, almost every time, someone in authority has noticed the professionalism and quality of my work. As a result, from time to time, I have been called to the office of an official who commented on the positive contribution I was making. I was then offered increased compensation for my efforts.

The only exception to the pattern that I have just described involved a supervisor who was extremely self-centered. The supervisor made certain that he did not miss his own opportunities for advancement. At the same time, he took for granted the extra efforts I repeatedly demonstrated. He ignored those efforts despite his awareness that they contributed greatly to his own professional advancement. During our association, the supervisor advanced in salary by more than forty percent, while mine remained only three percent above the entry level. Although difficult to accept, I remain comfortable with my decision to not make an issue of it. If for no other reason, I have the satisfaction of knowing that I know, that he knows, that I know.

People who make satisfaction in their work a top priority are the ones who perform best. Those employees who make money their primary goal rarely achieve their desired economic status and often wind up chronically unhappy. If you are stuck in a job that you do not enjoy, you are unlikely to go very far in it even if you are paid well. If you enjoy your work, you will naturally do your best. Overindulgence and money are not needed for true wealth. When money is our primary interest, we almost always lose.

Dr. Albert Schweitzer once said, "To be truly happy, we must learn how to serve others." Many of the wealthy individuals in the world provide a true testament to Dr. Schweitzer's wisdom. Just consider the troubled lives of many of the rich and famous among us if you doubt the validity of that. Focus on money and power is the source of almost all of their unhappiness. The truism endures "True wealth is best measured by the absence of material things!" Never place money before service. Reduce your emphasis on material things as measurements for your success. If your self-esteem is based upon acquisitions, then you will always suffer from wanting more. Your esteem as a person is a matter of attitude, not accumulations, and until you really understand that, you will always lack self-esteem and contentment to some degree.

And, Who Remembers That?

Don't judge yourself so harshly. Judging yourself by extraordinary standards is another way of mistreating yourself. It can also become just another excuse for not trying, or for giving up when the "going gets rough." Wallowing in guilt and embarrassment is the greatest mistake of all. How many things do we experience that seem truly to reflect the end of our world…only to realize later that they really were not that important in the over all scheme of things? How important will what is happening now be a week, a month, or years from now? For example, throughout much of my childhood and early adult life I experienced overwhelming feelings of anxiety and fear in the presence of those I perceived to be powerful and authoritarian figures. In the presence of such individuals, I would remain anxious and silent. When unexpectedly called upon to speak, I would panic, becoming emotionally petrified to the point where I could not respond or otherwise function. Perhaps sensing my dilemma, and after a few seconds of what seemed to be an eternity, someone would shift the focus elsewhere.

Following such an incident, I would then spend days, and at times, even weeks, engaging in self-criticism and chastisement. Eventually the feelings would subside, only to have another episode occur at another time. In exploring these episodes in later life, it was not at all unusual for me to discover that what had been so painful was of no great significance to those around me. Noticed or not, those who had been present soon forgot about it. Yet, my own postures of self-recrimination continued because I knew that they knew, and "what must they think of me?"

Maintaining Belief in Our Journey

Life's difficulties are not easily faced, but we can overcome them, if we choose to do so. Most of our lives are about proving something, either to ourselves, or to someone else. Most often, the others do not really care. Perhaps it would be well for all of us to pause from time to time to remember, "a year from now, no one will really care." There are some things in life, and some decisions of other people that we just cannot control, nor should we try.

The self-reliant person can relate to others with compassion and understanding, while retaining confidence, objectivity, and poise. Those people who expect too much from themselves, experience repeated episodes of tension, anxiety, and frustration. They worry that they are not achieving as much as they should. They try for perfection in everything, and that becomes an open invitation to depression and failure. No one can be perfect in anything. Decide which things you do well, and then put your major effort into them. They will most often be the things that give you the greatest satisfaction, and a sense of positive achievement. And, what about the things you cannot do so well? Give them the best of your effort and ability, but do not take yourself to task if you cannot achieve the impossible. Our failures and mistakes teach us where we need to begin again, and they provide the most valuable lessons we will have the privilege to experience in life.

Rising Above Circumstance

Status and power do not satisfy our need to be accepted, or to have a sense of meaning and purpose. If we are compassionate human beings we search for the sense that our lives matter, that the world will be a little bit different because we have passed through it. It is acceptance of responsibility for our actions and the results of those actions that will make for long-lasting health and contentment. This does not mean conforming to the wishes of others. It means carefully weighing opposing postures and viewpoints. We may then discover that it is necessary to stand on principles that run counter to common practice because it is the right thing to do. As we accept that we can no longer justify our behavior on the basis of resentments from the past, or due to our fear of the postures or opinions of others, we may then come to realize that in the final analysis, we ourselves are responsible for what we do. We will then be increasingly free to function with decisiveness and integrity.

Menachen Begin

On the day Menachen Begin of Israel died, the television program, "20/20" also aired. As the program came to a close, Hugh Downs, co-host of the program turned to Barbara Walters and offered his condolences related to the former prime minister's passing. Hugh was aware of the closeness that had evolved between Barbara and the prime minister during the many news stories Barbara covered in Israel during Mr. Begin's term. In calling attention to the former prime minister's death, Hugh graciously invited Barbara to close the program by sharing any thoughts she might have about her association with Mr. Begin during those stormy years of his country's history.

Barbara responded, "No Hugh, I really don't want to say anything. Instead, I would like to show you and the audience a small portion of my last interview with Prime Minister Begin as he closed out his term in office." As the interview opened, Barbara asked one or two of the thought-provoking questions for which she has gained such admiration and respect. Barbara then asked, "Mr. Prime Minister, how would you like to be remembered as you leave your office to return to private life as a citizen of Israel?" Without a moment of hesitation, Prime Minister Begin responded, "I would like to be remembered as a decent person!"

Think of the power in that simple statement. We are hearing the sentiments of a man who held a pivotal position in the course of human history and world affairs. From his posture as his country's leader, Prime Minister Begin could have triggered a series of events that might have lead to catastrophic consequences. The initiation of yet another war, economic crises of immense proportion, and even the triggering of events that might have lead to a nuclear holocaust. Yet, despite the tremendous power and responsibility this man held, in his closing hours of public life, he offered this eloquent endorsement of what is really important. "To be remembered as a decent person." What a magnificent sentiment, and legacy for all of us to consider.

Keep Hope Alive

An action succeeds, a promise is honored, a commitment is met only at the moment of completion. When you have done what you said you would do. It is through such action that other employees know where you stand and they learn to count on you. In following through you gain self-assuredness, and a sense of power that is born of responsibility, and the satisfaction of a job well done. Then, no matter how things turn out, you will still know that you did the best you could. That makes all the difference as we continue our journey…and when it is completed! When terminally ill persons have been asked, "If you had only one hour to live, what would be so important that you would be thinking about it during your last hour on earth?" Not one of those people ever said, "With an hour left to live, I would think of my mutual fund." Nobody mentioned money or possessions of any kind. They talked about only two things. They talked about the people they loved, and wished they had loved more. And, they talked about their work, yet unfinished, that had an impact and made a difference.

Oppressive work environments are filled with supervisors who believe they can win by intimidating their employees. They do not win that way. Oppressive work environments are filled with employees who believe they can succeed by running roughshod over the needs and feelings of their colleagues. They do not succeed that way. Oppressive work environments are filled with employees who believe they can gain power through robbing other employees of their sense of worth and accomplishment. They do not gain power that way.

I believe, *"The meek shall inherit the earth"* really means we do not have to choose to be involved in the pettiness of the corrupt and oppressive people among us. We can rise above the storms of the oppressive workplace by not being like them! When we believe we can make no real difference, we give up wanting to do well. When we continually face conflicts we believe we are powerless to overcome, those experiences eventually lead to anxiety and despair. The result is surrender to destructive oppression. The one feeling we cannot live without for very long is hope. If we are forced to live without hope we will wither away and die...either literally, or emotionally due to a sense of chronic depression and hopelessness. Recognize the healing potential of hope...***there is little else.***

end

0-595-32914-4